Hindu Nationalists of Modern India

Hindu Nationalists of Modern India

A Critical Study of the Intellectual Genealogy of Hindutva

J. KURUVACHIRA

RAWAT PUBLICATIONS
Jaipur • New Delhi • Bangalore • Mumbai

ISBN 81-7033-995-2

Published by
Prem Rawat for **Rawat Publications**
Satyam Apts., Sector 3, Jawahar Nagar, Jaipur 302 004 (India)
Phone: 0141 265 1748 / 7006 Fax: 0141 265 1748
E-mail: info@rawatbooks.com
Website: www.rawatbooks.com

New Delhi Office
4858/24, Ansari Road, Daryaganj, New Delhi 110 002
Phone: 011-23263290

Also at Bangalore and Mumbai

Typeset by Rawat Computers, Jaipur
Printed at Chaman Enterprises, New Delhi

Contents

Preface

The contemporary religio-political scenario of India, with the emergence of Hindu cultural nationalism or Hindutva as a movement in the country, has its roots in the past and its core concepts are provided by certain Hindu nationalists of modern India. In the present study we critically examine a select group of six Hindu nationalists who in a certain sense are representatives of three centuries – the nineteenth, the twentieth and the twenty-first. They are: Swami Dayananda Saraswati (1824-1883), Swami Vivekananda (1863-1902), Bal Gangadhar Tilak (1856-1920), Vinayak Damodar Savarkar (1883-1966), Madhav Sadashiv Golwalkar (1906-1973) and Sita Ram Goel (1921-2003). This study is a 're-reading' of the writings of these personalities with a critical mind in order to trace the intellectual history of the present-day Hindu cultural nationalism and fundamentalism. While appreciating the good that the above persons have accomplished for the nation, we also wish to tell the citizens of India that as "all that glitters is not gold", some who are placed on high pedestals as patriots, freedom fighters, promoters of Indian culture, Hindu spirituality and so on, upon closer analysis, may not deserve all the honour they have been accorded. Behind each of these personalities there is a dark and hidden history of religious fundamentalism, fanaticism, narrow-minded nationalism, anti-minoritism, anti-secularism and intolerance. Unfortunately, these facts are not always known to the general public. Hence, it is these less known realities that we wish to highlight in this study.

I owe a debt of gratitude to several persons who have helped me in various ways in carrying out this study. In the first place, I am grateful to T. Mulayinkal for granting the permission to publish this book. I thank the staff and the students of Salesian College of Higher Education, Dimapur, especially V. Palathingal, the Director, and R.K. Guangdiat Nicholas, the Principal, for providing me the time necessary for pursuing this project. I gratefully acknowledge the help I have received from G. Plathottam in the various stages of this study through his critical observations. I thank the Jawaharlal Nehru University, New Delhi; Jnanadeepa Vidyapeeth, Pune; Salesian College, Dimapur; Sacred Heart College, Shillong, India Office Collections, British Library, London; National Archives of India (NAI), New Delhi; and Nehru Memorial Museum and Library (NMML), New Delhi, for making available to me their library facilities. I am grateful to J. Rudolf, T. Martinek and Mr. Fleischhauer, Germany, for helping me to find several important original writings on Adolf Hitler and Nazism which are now out of print. My gratitude is also due to J. Kallarackal, G. Plathottam, S. Aerimattathil and S. Pottenplackal who patiently went through the entire manuscript and gave their valuable observations for improvement in language, style, content and general outlay of the material. Finally, I thank Rawat Publications, Jaipur/New Delhi for undertaking the publication of this book.

Dr. J. Kuruvachira
Salesian College of Higher Education
Dimapur, India
e-mail: kurusdb@rediffmail.com

Abbreviations

ABVP	Akhil Bharatiya Vidyarthi Parishad
AIDWA	All India Democratic Women's Association
BJP	Bharatiya Janata Party
BJS	Bharatiya Jana Sangh
CBI	Central Bureau of Investigation
CBSE	Central Board of Secondary Education
EBC	Economically Backward Class
FISI	Friends of India Society International
Gitarahasya	*Srimad Bhagavadgita-Rahasya or Karma-Yoga-Sastra*
HMS	Hindu Maha Sabha
HRD	Human Resource Development
HSC	Hindu Student's Council
HSS	Hindu Swayamsevak Sangh
HSS-UK	Hindu Swayamsevak Sangh-UK
ICHR	Indian Council of Historical Research
ICSSR	Indian Council of Social Science Research
IGNCA	Indira Gandhi National Centre for the Arts
I.S.K.CON	International Society for Krishna Consciousness

L/P&J	Legal, Public and Juridical [documents]
MLA	Member of Legislative Assembly
MP	Member of Parliament
NCERT	National Council for Educational Research and Training
NGO	Non-Governmental Organisation
NHRC	National Human Rights Commission
NMML	Nehru Memorial Museum and Library
NRI	Non-Resident Indian
NSDAP	*Nationalsozialistische Deutsche Arbeiterpartei* (The National Socialist German Worker's Party)
OFBJP	Overseas Friends of the BJP
RSS	Rashtriya Swayamsevak Sangh
SA	*Sturmabteilungen* (Stormstroopers, the 'storming department' of Hitler's Nazi regime')
SC	Scheduled Caste
SIUK	Sewa International-UK
SPD	*Sozialdemokratische Partei Deutschlands* (The Socialist Party of Germany)
SS	*Schutzstaffel* (Security guard; the security service wing of Hitler's Nazi regime)
ST	Scheduled Tribe
UGC	University Grants Commission
VHP	Vishva Hindu Parishad
VHPA	Vishva Hindu Parishad of America

Introduction

India had reached the brink of totalitarianism and dictatorship with the BJP-led National Democratic Alliance (NDA) government coming to power in New Delhi headed by Atal Bihari Vajpayee, which was in reality the rule of the *Rashtriya Swayamsevak Sangh* (RSS) and its affiliated family called the *Sangh Parivar*. Until the eve of the general election results of April-May 2004 most people in India thought that the BJP-led alliance would win the election with an avalanche of votes in their favour and that with it the last nail in the coffin of secularism and democracy would be hammered. But, with the general elections of 2004, which routed the Hindu right-wing political party and its allies, India was once again saved from anarchy and from the dictatorship of Hindutva and its narrow-minded nationalism.[1] Thus, BJP's 'Mission 2004' remained unaccomplished. In other words, the unexpected election mandate saved India from the 'octopus grip' of Hindutva – at least for the time being.

Until the 1980s the main enemy of the Hindu nationalists were Indian Muslims. But, since the 1990s, they have openly declared war against the Indian Christians also. However, if we really go back to the history of Hindu nationalism, Christianity was always in its list of enemies, though it was spending more of its energy on the Muslims than on the Christians due to historical reasons.

Hindu nationalists of today wage a desperate battle in order to realise their goal of creating a Hindu *rashtra* (nation) in India with a monolithic Hindu culture. To this end they emulate the old icons of their ideology and borrow their time-tested tactics so that there is an unbroken continuity with the past. Their ultimate goal is to achieve, at least in this century, what they could not attain in the past. It was clearly stated by K.S. Sudarshan, the RSS chief, that the twenty-first century will be the century of Hindutva and that there will be an epic war between the Hindus and the non-Hindus of India.[2] Here, we are reminded of what Jawaharlal Nehru (1889-1964) said: "...a more insidious form of nationalism is the narrowness of mind that it develops within a country, when a majority thinks itself as the entire nation."[3]

Soon after the independence of India stringent measures were taken to prevent the spread of Hindu cultural nationalism by the uncompromising secularist, Jawaharlal Nehru.[4] He placed a number of Hindu nationalist organisations under censure for various reasons. Everyone thought that it was the end of Hindu fundamentalism and nationalism and that India would be secular for many years to come. But, unfortunately, it did not happen. After five decades of slumber it has once again emerged as a formidable movement in the country.[5]

Ashis Nandy says that often many things that die in colder climates in the course of a single winter survive in the tropics for years. Perhaps, the death of Hindu nationalism may not be as natural as that of some other ideologies.[6] We should learn from the past and be very cautious in dismissing the RSS, BJP, VHP, Bajrang Dal and the Sangh Parivar as defunct entities – just because they could not form a government in New Delhi after the general elections of 2004. If we think so, we are mistaken. The Hindu nationalists are planning their next strategy to come back to power with vengeance and to confront secularists and religious minorities of India, and if possible obliterate them from the face of the earth, for such is their hatred towards them. Most of the protagonists of Hindu nationalism are well disciplined persons with single minded purpose – but unfortunately for a vicious cause! Even now they have their ideologically trained persons in all possible departments to carry on their agenda. There are hardcore Hindu nationalists in disguise even in the Congress and other political parties.

Soon after the victory of the Congress-led alliance in the April-May 2004 general elections, some people sat back with the conviction that the era of the BJP is over. But can we be so certain about it? T.N. Seshan, former Election Commissioner of India, in his book *A Heart Full of Burden*, speaks about the survival ability of household kitchen cockroaches. He says that you can stamp on a cockroach. Five minutes later when you think it is totally dead, it suddenly turns itself upside down and runs away.[7] We may compare the Hindu nationalist ideology to such a cockroach. When everyone thought that Hindu nationalism was already history, it resurrected itself in the 1980s. It is now very much alive in the country as a national movement with formidable power and renewed enthusiasm to materialise its dangerous designs. In fact, hardcore Hindutva ideologues like Lal Krishna Advani, Murli Manohar Joshi and Narendra Modi are its Prime Ministers-in-waiting.

On 6 November 1932 the representation of Adolf Hitler's *Nationalsozialistische Deutsche Arbeiterpartei* (NSDAP: The National Socialist German Worker's Party) in the German *Reichstag* (German Parliament) was reduced from 230 to 196. The *Vorwärts* ('Forward') which is the central organ of the political party called *Sozialdemokratische Partei Deutschlands* (SPD, The Socialist Party of Germany) on 18 November 1932 'dismissed' Hitler as a non-entity and claimed that Hitler can never be the *Reichskanzler* (German Chancellor) because he had lost two million votes in just three months and that if the trend continued in fifteen months Hitler would be 'finished'. Again on 1 January 1933 the same newspaper published an article entitled "Hitlers Aufstieg und Untergang" ('The Rise and Fall/Decline of Hitler').[8] But, Hitler was not 'finished' nor was there an *Untergang* (decline). On 30 January 1933 Hitler became the *Reichskanzler* (German Chancellor) and the dictator of Germany.

The Hindu nationalists are die-hard fundamentalists who are schooled in militant tactics and intoxicated with the vicious idea of creating a Hindu nation out of India without any concern for ethics. In the past they have had recourse to militancy, extremism and terrorism to achieve their ends. They would not hesitate to repeat the same today and would go to any extent in order to capture political power once again.

The Hindu nationalists today project from history several personalities as their ideological mascots and use their methods as legitimate means to their end. But until the Hindu nationalists surrender their pet idea of Hindu *rashtra* and accept the fact that India is a secular and multi-cultural nation, the secularists must carry on the battle on all possible fronts. This study is meant as a reminder to every secular-minded Indian of the grave responsibility to fight communalism, religious fundamentalism, narrow-minded nationalism and anti-secularism epitomised by the concept of Hindutva.

As T.N. Seshan says: "Today, the world is crying for tolerance. The opposite to it is fundamentalism."[9] The present-day turbulence in India has not come from foreign invasion or conquest but from factors within, namely, Hindu fundamentalism and nationalism. As an ideology, Hindutva or Hindu cultural nationalism has a longer history than Hindutva organisations like the RSS, VHP, BJP, Bajrang Dal, Shiv Sena and the Sangh Parivar. It has been growing in the minds of many Indians for several centuries and some have been ardent protagonists of it in the course of history. The last decades of the nineteenth century, the first half and the last decades of the 20th century and the first decade of the present century are marked by many revolutionary convulsions in India due to the presence of Hindutva.

This study seeks to highlight the role played by six leading Hindu nationalists of modern India, whom I consider as 'hardliners', and who have nurtured and propagated the ideology of Hindu nationalism and the danger it poses to India's cultural pluralism and secularism. It is hoped that the study would help people to realise that some of the so-called patriots and freedom fighters of India had only a narrow vision of Indian culture which did not go beyond Hindu religion, Hindu culture and Hindu *rashtra.*

The methodology I have employed in this study ranges from the expository, descriptive, analytical and critical to the evaluative. I have tried to utilise the original writings of the personalities dealt with either by paraphrasing their views or making direct citations from them. I have abbreviated the titles of most of the books and articles which are long even when references are made to them for the first time in this study. However, the bibliography contains the full titles with the essential details of publication. Readers will also notice variant spellings for a number of Indian proper names and terms, and titles of certain classical works.[10]

Notes

1. Commenting on the election results Arundhati Roy said in California on 16 August 2004: "In India this year, we voted the Hindu nationalists out of office." A. Roy, "Public Power in the Age of Empire", 7. After the general elections of 2004, the BJP also lost its position as the largest party in the Lok Sabha.
2. See "RSS Boss K. Sudarshan said", 1077.
3. S. Gopal and U. Iyengar (eds.), *The Essential Writings*, vol. 1, 189.
4. This is precisely the reason why Nehru is one of the main targets of attack by the *Sangh Parivar*. For a typical anti-Nehru writing, see N.R. Waradpande, *The Nemesis of Nehru-Worship* (2001).

5. The rise of Hindutva in contemporary times is traceable especially since the early 1980s. See H.V. Seshadri, *Hindu Renaissance Under Way*, 139-206.
6. See A. Nandy, *Bonfire of Creeds*, 129.
7. See T.N. Seshan, *A Heart Full of Burden*, 37.
8. See H. Brüdigam, *Das Jahr 1933*, 11-12.
9. T.N. Seshan, *The Regeneration of India*, 131.
10. For example, Carvaca, Charvaka; Gita, Geeta; Jnana, gnana; Koran, Quoran, Qur'an; Kaladi, Kalady; Krishna, Krsna; Ksatriya, Kshatriya, Kyshtriya: Moslems, Muslims; Mohammed, Muhammad; Om, AUM; Sarasvati, Saraswati; shuddhi, suddhi; Siva, Shiva, Upanisad, Upanishad; Vande Mataram, Bande Mataram, etc.

• I •

Swami Dayananda Saraswati as a Hindu Fundamentalist and Nationalist

The aim of this chapter is to present the salient features of Swami Dayananda Saraswati's (1824-1883) religious philosophy, which is characterised by religious *fundamentalism*, *anti-'other' attitude* and *militancy*. In Dayananda we see the first stirrings of Hindu fundamentalism in modern India. Unfortunately, this aspect often goes camouflaged under the aura of his greatness as a champion of Hinduism and a social reformer.

Anyone familiar with the 'Indian Renaissance' of the 19th century will immediately be reminded of the 'luminous' figure of Swami Dayananda Saraswati – the Hindu social reformer and the founder of the Arya Samaj ('Noble Society'). He is considered as the 'first Hindu' in the 19th century to study and discuss other religions (i.e., non-Vedic faiths). In fact, some twenty years prior to the World Parliament of Religions in Chicago in 1893, in which Swami Vivekananda participated, Dayananda organised a conference in Delhi and invited representatives from all religions. In this, he was well ahead of the other thinkers of the time.[1]

Dayananda (originally known as Mulasankar) was born in a Brahmin family at Tankara, Gujarat, in 1824, and was raised up as an orthodox Saivite. He spent fifteen years as a wandering monk in search of personal salvation. In 1860 he met Swami Vrijananda of Mathura, a great Vedic scholar and grammarian, who later became his teacher and mentor. It was Swami Vrijananda who drew the attention of his pupil to the degenerated state of Hinduism. In addition, he implanted in him a great veneration for the ancient Vedas as the true source of pure Hinduism. For the rest of his life Dayananda taught in almost all parts of India the exclusive truth of the Vedas. He also founded the Arya Samaj in 1875, which loomed large on the intellectual and social scene of late 19th century Northern India.[2]

Dayananda authored numerous books, tracts and pamphlets.[3] However, it is above all in his *Satyartha Prakash* (The Light of Truth, 1875, 1884)[4] – considered as his *magnum opus* – that he expounds 'systematically' and with extraordinary clarity his fully developed philosophy of religion. Other important writings of Dayananda include, *Rigvedadi Bhasya Bhumika* (Introduction to the Commentary on the Vedas)[5] and *Rishi Dayananda Saraswati ke Patra aur Vijnapan* (A Collection of Letters and Notes Written by Dayananda).[6]

The ideological foundations of Dayananda Saraswati

In order to understand the attitude of Dayananda Saraswati towards other religions, it is necessary that we examine his ideological foundations. Dayananda emphatically affirmed that the Vedic religion is the only true faith revealed by God. This view is so central to his religious philosophy that one cannot understand his attitude towards other religions without it.

Satyartha Prakash first appeared in 1875 in Hindi. It consisted of eleven chapters and in the first ten a complete statement of his ideas on various subjects is presented. The eleventh chapter, which runs to a quarter of the book, is devoted to a critique of Hinduism, dealing with idol worship, miracles, pilgrimages, holy men, sects, *Puranas*, etc. Towards the end of his life he thoroughly revised this edition and added three more chapters dealing with Carvaka, Buddhism and Jainism which are religions of Indian origin, and Christianity and Islam which, according to him, are foreign faiths. This edition was published in 1884, though its proof reading was finished before Dayananda's death in 1883. A comparative study of the two editions reveals that Dayananda radically changed some of his earlier ideas during the last years of his life.[7] Thus, the revised edition contains more 'systematic' and fully developed ideas than the previous one with a criticism of all the major religions of India. This is also the work accepted by the Arya Samaj as the authorised edition.

Dayananda in his writings makes five outstanding claims that determine his attitude towards other religions: (i) the Vedic religion alone is true and infallible and it is revealed by God;[8] (ii) the Vedic religion alone existed in the whole world and all believed in it till 5,000 years ago;[9] (iii) all the extant religions of the world originated in India and are derived from the Vedas;[10] (iv) all knowledge including all sciences spread to other countries from India, first to Egypt, then to Greece, from there to Europe and finally to America and other countries;[11] and (v) the Aryans were the sovereign rulers of the whole earth till the *Mahabharata* war and they professed the Vedic religion.[12]

The exclusive truth of the Vedic religion

Dayananda starts from the premise that God is the eternal source of all knowledge and he reveals it to man through the Vedas and had he not revealed, there would have been no knowledge.[13] According to him, the Vedas give general teachings meant for *all* mankind.[14] This led him to maintain that in the Vedas alone and not in any other work has God revealed the truth. Hence, he claimed that what the Vedas expound are the truth and nothing but the truth.[15] Since the Vedas alone are the supreme authority in ascertaining true religion, whatever is enjoined by the Vedas is to be considered to be right, while whatever is condemned by them is to be wrong. He says: "...nothing should be accepted which is against the Vedas."[16] He also argues that the Vedic revelation is synchronous with man's first appearance on earth so that the Vedas becomes the first book of humanity.[17] The consequence was that he made *the Vedas the standard of reference for all truth,* both religious and otherwise. Thus, for Dayananda, the Vedas contain religious truth as well as every form of truth, *even scientific truths*.[18] Later, Aurobindo Ghose, commenting on this, not only agreed with Dayananda but also argued that the latter had rather understated than overstated the depth and range of the Vedic wisdom.[19]

Dayananda further argued that the Vedas are also infallible and that they are absolutely free from error.[20] Truth and knowledge, wherever they are found, are derived from the Vedas. He says: "It is to be borne in mind that wherever and whatever truth is to be found it has proceeded from the Vedas and all untruth has its origin outside them and has not proceeded from God."[21] He also stated that the Vedas are eternal just as God is eternal.[22] This amounts to maintaining that there can be *only one true religion*, and that religion is the one that is based on and derived from the Vedas. In other words, Dayananda was affirming the *exclusive truth* of the Vedic religion.

Dayananda then set out to provide proofs for the truth of the Vedic faith. *First*, the Vedas consistently proclaim pure *monotheism*, which alone can rationally be sustained. In the Vedas there are not many gods but one God. The multitude of names signify not different Divine beings, but different aspects of one Supreme Being.[23] *Second*, the truth of the Vedic faith is that, it is the most *rational* religion because in it there is nothing that offends reason. In a letter to Colonel Olcott, Dayananda affirms that the true religion is expounded in that eternal Vedas practised by the wise in conformity with reason.[24] *Third*, the Vedic religion is the true religion because *morality* lies at the very basis of it. According to Dayananda, there is nothing in the Vedas that offends morality. In reality, righteous conduct consists in rejecting all that is opposed to the Vedas, and in practising whatever has been enjoined by them.[25] *Fourth*, the Vedic religion is the true religion because it is *universal*. It is meant for all time – past, present and future – for all places, and for all people.[26] H. Coward notes: "Dayananda made Hinduism a religion of the book by adopting the Protestant principle of *sola scriptura* [only scripture] and applying it to the Vedas."[27] Dayananda also maintained that Sanskrit is the language in which the Vedas are revealed. Sanskrit belongs to no country but is the source of all languages and all peoples.[28]

Plurality of religions is unnecessary

Dayananda was one of the Hindu thinkers of the 19th century who paid serious attention to the problem of the relationship between different religions. He maintained that in essence, there are only four main non-Vedic or 'other' religions, namely, Pauranikas, Christians, Jains and Muslims. These cover all sects.[29] According to J.T.F. Jordens, Dayananda began to think of Hinduism in relation to other religions only after his visit to Calcutta in 1873 where he met the leaders of the Brahma Samaj who were much influenced by the teachings of Christianity and Islam, and this led him to consider Hinduism in a wider context of these religions.[30]

Dayananda bewailed the plurality of religions because of their mutual hatred and strife. According to him, often, one who is prejudiced tries to prove that his untruth is truth while the truth of his opponent is untruth.[31] He believed that in the midst of conflicting truth-claims of religions, it is the duty of everyone to discover and to embrace what is true and reject what is false.[32] Hence, he dedicated much energy to the study of other religions both through discussion with their teachers and by studying them from the original sources.

It has been argued by many that it is necessary to have a plurality of religions because people differ in their nature, temperament, character and level of spirituality. Therefore, there is need for a diversity of religions, because there can never be one religion that suits the needs of all mankind. But Dayananda was not convinced of this argument. He also rejected another popular view that all religions are good and therefore, it is not proper to criticise any one of them.[33] According to him, they contain untruth and falsity.[34] Hence, for Dayananda, there was no need for a plurality of religions because only one among the many religions can be true, and for him, the one true faith is the Vedic religion.[35] Therefore, diversity of religions is unnecessary as they are *products of ignorance and false beliefs*.[36]

Religions other than the Vedic faith are false

In maintaining that the Vedic religion alone is true, Dayananda is emphatically asserting that all other religions are false. In his *Satyartha Prakash* he often refers to them as 'false beliefs'.[37] When the Aryans gave up the Vedic literature which alone could help people to distinguish between truth and untruth, ignorance prevailed and many anti-Vedic religions, cults and sects sprang up.[38] He argued that the founders and teachers of them, even if they knew the truth, did not teach it, because they feared that they would lose their followers and their means of livelihood. The religious teachers who do not advocate the Vedic faith are hypocrites, defrauders and tricksters. He says: "All these cults are an outcome of ignorance and antagonistic to learning. They mislead the foolish, low and uncivilised people into their net to serve their own ends."[39] Thus, Dayananda considered all religions, except the Vedic faith, as false. He observes: "...there ought to be only one right religion [....] We have been all along emphasising this point."[40]

Dayananda claims that there was a time in the ancient past since the beginning of the world when only one religion prevailed in the world, and that was the Vedic religion. This religion was taught everywhere in the world and all firmly believed in it. As a result, peace and happiness reigned everywhere. But this state of perfect harmony was disrupted 5,000 years ago when the Great War of the Mahabharata broke out in which most of the learned men, sages and seers were killed. As a consequence, the study of the Vedas and other true sciences disappeared, the light of knowledge grew dim, and with it the dissemination of Vedic religion also came to an end.[41] Thus, in the place of the true religion of the Vedas, many *false religions* came into being.

Other religions may contain elements of truth

If all non-Vedic religions are false and products of ignorance, there arises the question whether there is any truth at all in them. Dayananda admitted that some religions contain *elements of truth*. In fact, on certain occasions, he says that he accepts whatever is true in all religions.[42] In the introduction to the *Satyartha Prakash* he admits that there are undoubtedly many learned men among the followers of every religion.[43] There are also certain universal truths found in all religions. These truths are those in which they all agree with each other, and in whatever they differ with each other is false and therefore they are to be *rejected*.[44]

However, a reading of the *Satyartha Prakash* as a whole gives us a different picture. Even though there may be elements of truth in other religions, it does not make them worthy of acceptance, for two reasons: first, whatever truth is found in them is derived from the Vedas. Dayananda says: "Wherever and whatever truth is to be found has proceeded from the Vedas."[45] It follows then that, since there is the totality of truth in the Vedas, there is no need to follow any other religion which may have only elements of truth. Therefore, whoever sincerely seeks the truth, must embrace the Vedic religion.[46] Secondly, the truth that is found in other religions is mixed with untruths, like the best food mixed with poison. Hence, they are to be *rejected*.[47]

Criticism of popular Hinduism

One of the major concerns of Dayananda was to regenerate Hinduism by purifying it from such corrupted beliefs and practices as polytheism, idolatry, animal sacrifices, priestly privilege of the Brahmins, worship of popular deities, long pilgrimages, ritual ablutions, etc. He argued that the *Puranas* and the *Tantras* and other new scriptures which supported and encouraged such beliefs are to be abandoned.[48] So he rejected these texts as concocted by hypocritical and selfish priests to deceive the ignorant masses. Chapter XI of the *Satyartha Prakash* is particularly dedicated to a critical analysis of the sects and cults of Hinduism.[49]

Dayananda insisted that the study of the Vedas should be open to all, including *Shudras*, and not just to the Brahmins alone.[50] He argued that nobody becomes a Brahmin simply because he is born of Brahmin parents.[51] If God revealed the Vedas only for them, then He is to be regarded as partial and prejudiced and this would imperil God's justice.[52] Therefore, he advocated that God has revealed the Vedas for all and that all men and women, i.e., the whole mankind, have a right to study them.[53]

P.S. Daniel opines that Dayananda's harsh condemnation of Hinduism was aimed at its regeneration for which he urged the Hindus to "go back to the Vedas".[54]

Jainism is the most dreadful religion

In Chapter XII of *Satyartha Prakash* Dayananda treats Carvacas, Buddhism and Jainism as typical anti-Vedic religions[55] and the atheistic cults of India.[56] However, it is against Jainism that he directed much of his criticism. According to Dayananda, the Jains were prejudiced against and hostile towards the non-Jains. He argued that there is no religion which enjoins so much hostility towards people belonging to other faiths as Jainism.[57] He also called Jainism the most dreadful religion, the founders and followers of which are in dense ignorance. Even their

Tirthankaras were ignorant and their teachers were devoid of knowledge. He says: "Your *Tirthankaras* had no conception of truth, otherwise they would not have written such nonsense. As are your teachers so are your disciples."[58] Further, the Jaina scriptures are full of stories that delude people.[59]

In this way, Dayananda presented the Jains as biased, perverse, ignorant and enemies of truth and upright living. He says: "...all Jaina saints, family men and *Tirthankaras* including [... are] given to prostitution, adultery, theft and other evils [....] He who will associate with them will get same sort of evils in his heart also."[60] "Therefore, we say that the Jains are drowned in the hell of condemnative [sic] and religious bigotry."[61]

Islam is the religion of the uncivilised and the ignorant

Dayananda conceived Islam as a real threat to the existence of Hinduism and dedicated much space in discussing it.[62] He considered Islam as the religion of the uncivilised and the ignorant and wondered how the ancient people of Arabia accepted a religion of the kind.[63] According to Dayananda, the *Quoran* (*Koran*) is the product of a mind destitute of all knowledge of God. He says: "Quoran is not made by God. It might have been written by some deceitful and fraudulent person."[64] He further argued that the *Quoran* causes rebellion and destroys peace.[65] It is full of errors, distortions and contains all untruth, and even the little truth it contains is distorted[66] and therefore it is to be considered as a great hoax.[67] He also held that Mohammed was not a pious man[68] but a quarrelsome,[69] immoral and self-indulgent person.[70] Further, the God of Islam incites the prophet and the Muslims to fight against non-Muslims.[71]

Therefore, Dayananda concluded that he who believes that the *Quoran* is revealed, that Mohammad is a prophet, and that Mohammadan God to be omniscient, just and merciful would be a perfect idiot. He says: "...this book [*Quoran*] is neither God's revelation nor the work of any learned man, nor a book of knowledge;"[72] "...the Quoran, the Quoranic God and the

Moselms are full of bigotry and ignorance;"[73] "...the noble qualities of justice, mercy, etc. remain at a distance from the God of Moslems."[74] Therefore, it is not true that the believers of the *Quoran* are on the right path.[75] In addition, all through its history, Islam has been intolerant of followers of other religions.[76] Thus, Dayananda maintained that Islam is a *false religion* which does harm to mankind, and therefore, it is to be *rejected* and the Vedic faith is to be accepted by all.[77]

Christianity is a religion of the book

Sumit Sarkar says that the polemics with the most far-reaching and long-lasting consequences against non-Vedic religions was undoubtedly launched by Dayananda in Chapter XIII of *Satyartha Prakash* where he deals with Christianity.[78]

Dayananda treated Christianity as a religion of the book – the 'religion of the Bible'.[79] Hence, his study of the Christian religion was confined exclusively to the Bible. His conviction was that the claims of Christianity stand or fall with the Bible because the Christians believe that it is the revealed Word of God. If it is proved that the Bible is not the Word of God, then the whole foundation of Christianity as a religion collapses. Therefore, the main concern of Dayananda was to show that the Bible is *not* the Word of God but a human composition and that it combines many things that need to be condemned.

Christianity is a degraded religion

Since 1880s Dayananda was seriously engaged in combating Christianity. He used methods like street debates, re-conversion ceremony (*shuddhi*), publication of tracts and pamphlets. He sent members of his Arya Samaj (Samajists) to organise fairs against the preaching of the Christian missionaries. Thus, a battle of words went on between both sides, especially through their publications in the form of tracts and pamphlets, the contents of which often sunk to the level of insults, calumny and maligning the other. For example, Dayananda writes: "It appears that Mary conceived through some man, and either he or somebody else gave it out that the conception was through God."[80] "Hullo Jesus! What science told you that stars will fall.[...] Had Jesus a little education he would have known that the stars are worlds and cannot fall down."[81] "Marriages are performed in the paradise of the Christians. It was there that God celebrated the marriage of Jesus Christ. Let us ask who were his father-in-law, mother-in-law, brother-in-law etc?"[82] Dayananda wrote that the appellation 'Pope' means those persons who are hypocrites and accomplish their selfish ends by cheating others[83] and that the Popes get themselves and their feet worshipped.[84]

Dayananda also attacked Christianity by identifying it with the West, by attempting to refute its claims of religious, moral and cultural superiority, and by asserting the religious and the cultural degradation of Christianity and the superiority of the Vedas.

The God of the Bible is wicked

Dayananda argued that the God of the Bible is unjust,[85] cruel,[86] jealous,[87] a flesh-eater,[88] destitute of mercy,[89] malicious[90] and an ignorant savage.[91] He is temperamental, emotional and subject to passions. He is jealous, immoral and limited by space and time. He is also responsible for innumerable evil deeds. He says: "The God of Christians behaves exactly like a man."[92] Therefore, Dayananda concludes that such a being can never be considered as God and he is not even equal to a learned yogin.[93] Commenting on Gen. 30, 22-23 which says that God 'opened' the womb of Rachel who was barren he says cynically: "Well done! O God of Christians! What a great surgeon you are! What instruments or medicines did you use in opening the wombs of women?."[94]

Dayananda further stated that the God of the Bible is not omniscient, for had he been so, he would not have created Satan because he would have known that Satan would tempt man to commit sin.[95] Again, had he been an all-knowing being, he would have known Abel's death without inquiring from Cain,

"Where is thy brother?"[96] Further, if he had been omniscient, he would have been able to find out all about the firmness of Abraham's faith without tempting him to sacrifice his son Isaac.[97]

The Bible contains statements that offend reason

Dayananda claimed that the Bible contains statements that offend reason, logic, science and laws of nature. He rejected such beliefs as the birth of Jesus from a virgin, his resurrection from the dead, etc., as impossible and opposed to the laws of nature.[98] He also condemned all miracles of Jesus as superstitious, irrational, impossible and a hoax.[99]

According to Dayananda, the Bible displays a crude ignorance of scientific knowledge.[100] He argued that self-contradictory statements abound in the Bible. For example, while it is said in many places in the Bible that sins will be forgiven, it also says that each one will be rewarded or punished according to one's deeds.[101] He contested that sin can never be forgiven because it will imperil God's justice, and His justice demands that each person should receive the reward or punishment according to his or her deeds. Again, the belief that a person will be punished or rewarded eternally cannot be logically sustained because the finite action of finite souls cannot produce infinite results.[102]

The Bible contains immoral and cruel stories

Dayananda argued that the Bible contains many stories and precepts that are immoral and cruel. Some of the stories that are morally repulsive and give licence to immorality and cruelty are the visit of God to Sarah making her to conceive,[103] Mary's conception by the Holy Spirit,[104] the killing of the first born in Egypt,[105] accounts of animal sacrifice and beef-eating[106] and the like. The doctrine of the remission of sin through repentance, which besides being irrational, is also unjust as it encourages people to commit sin, because if repentance absolves one from sin, nobody would be afraid of committing sin and thus there would be an increase in sinfulness in the world.[107] Belief in immaculate conception could lead to loss of control over women, and any virgin who happened to conceive can claim that she conceived through God.

Dayananda alleged that Christianity taught not only sacrifice in the Old Testament but also cannibalism in the New Testament. For example, the Christians eat and drink the body and blood of Christ imagining all the time that their bread and their drink are the flesh and the blood of Christ, respectively, and they call it the 'Lord's supper'.[108]

The Bible can never be the Word of God

The conclusion that Dayananda arrived at after his so-called study of the Bible was that, it cannot be the Word of God because it is full of absurdities, and its authors are ignorant savages. He says: "Therefore, your Bible is not God-revealed."[109] "The Bible is a human composition and not a revelation of God."[110] "Their Bible has many things which are condemnable. [...] With the exception of a few things all else is untrue. As the contact of falsehood makes the truth also impure, similarly the Bible is also not acceptable."[111]

It is evident that Dayananda misinterprets Christianity and the Christian teachings. He does not really enter into the spirit of the Bible. He makes a literal reading of it and is prejudiced by his *a priori* assumptions. He also resorts to the study of Christianity exclusively from the Bible since he judges Bible alone to be the source of the Christian faith,[112] and is convinced that Christianity stands or falls with the Bible.[113] Thus, Dayananda carefully chose biblical passages in order to present a demonic Christianity.

Jesus Christ was a savage and a hoax

According to Dayananda, Jesus Christ was one who talked nonsense like a wild savage,[114] destitute of knowledge and understanding. P.S. Daniel observes: "The term 'barbarous' or 'savage' is repeatedly used over twenty-five times applying them to Christians, their God and their scriptures (the Bible)."[115] Dayananda spoke of the ignorance and foolishness of Jesus Christ and argued that Jesus was not a seer, that he was not even an enlightened person. He says: "Had Jesus got even a little education, he should not have said such nonsense. [...] The presence of Jesus was a great thing in a country of uneducated savages."[116] He then claimed that Mary – the mother of Jesus was not a chaste woman[117] and that the Bible abounded in absurdities and therefore could be the work of an enlightened man. All Christian missionaries say that Jesus was a very calm and peace loving person. But, in reality, he was a hot-tempered persons destitute of knowledge and who behaved like a wild savage.[118] This shows that Jesus was neither the son of God, nor had he any miraculous powers.[119] He did not possess the power to forgive sins.[120] The righteous people do not stand in need of any mediator like Jesus.[121] Jesus came to spread discord which is going on everywhere in the world.[122] Therefore, it is evident that the hoax of Christ's being the son of God, the knower of the past and the future, the forgiver of sin, has been set up falsely by his disciples. In reality, he was a very ordinary ignorant man, neither learned nor a yogi.[123] He was merely a carpenter's son, living in a wild and poor country.

Christianity is a religion of fools and barbarians

Dayananda's so-called study of Christianity lead him to condemn Christianity as a shallow, barbarous, false and foreign religion, believed only by fools and barbarians. He presented all the prophets of the Christians from Moses onwards as uncivilised and devoid of culture.[124] He spoke of the 'trap' and 'mesh' of the Christian religion and the 'net' of the Christian missionaries, and asked everybody to escape it.[125] He then went on to claim that only wild savages believed in Jesus and his only achievements are dissensions and discords.[126]

The Christians are educated to a great extent. But political considerations and obstinacy do not allow them to forsake their *hollow religion* and be open to the Vedic faith.[127]

Dayananda states: "...the Bible is not God-revealed, nor its God good, nor its followers religious."[128] Therefore, he exhorts the Christians: "Hear, O Christians, it is high time that you should leave this *wild religion* and accept the Vedic faith."[129]

Benjamin Walker remarks that, in spite of Dayananda's vigorous denunciation of Christianity, he borrowed many ideas from it. The foundation of such organisations as the Arya Tract Society, Women's Arya Samaj, Young Men's Arya Samaj, Vedic Salvation Army, and his schools, colleges, orphanages, widows' homes and relief centres were all due to direct Christian inspiration. Besides, the Arya Samaj rites include Sunday worship, the reading, preaching and teaching of the Vedas.[130]

Dayananda's militant attitude towards other religions

Dayananda was a militant Hindu who could not tolerate any religion other than the Vedic. With him tolerance gave way to militancy. In 1877-78 he visited Punjab and there he discovered for himself the threat Hinduism was facing from the proselytising activities of the Christian missionaries and Muslim teachers, and this made him denounce these religions.[131] G.S. Saxena says: "The views of Swami Dayananda were radical and militant."[132] P.S. Daniel observes that if Dayananda was militant, it was, to certain extent, because he had two militant religions to counteract, namely, Christianity and Islam.[133]

Lala Lajpat Rai acknowledged the militant nature of the Arya Samaj which Dayananda founded. He says: "The Arya Samaj is militant, not only externally - i.e., in its attitude towards other religions - but it is equally militant internally."[134] M.G. Chitkara says: "Dayananda carried war into the opponents camp and was the first, after centuries of abject passivity, to take offensive against the Christian missionaries and others."[135] The aggressive attitude of Dayananda gave a new self-confidence to the Hindus and acted as a bulwark against the proselytising activities of the Christian missionaries and the Muslims.[136]

Dayananda's militant response to non-Vedic religions had already produced a most dangerous effect in India. It had increased the hostility between the Hindus (Arya Samajists) and other religious communities ever since its foundation. Dayananda's method of attacking other religions through polemic literature, public lectures, educational institutions, proselytisation through re-conversion (*shuddhi*) became strong weapons in the hands of Arya Samajists. This was one of the important factors which led to the outbreak, especially of Hindu-Muslim communal riots that continued to recur in many parts of India.[137]

Polemical style of writing

Dayananda wrote extensively in the form of books, pamphlets, tracts and letters but most of them were polemic in nature. In fact, a part of his *Satyartha Prakash* was banned for a time in some parts of India because of its fundamentalist and militant nature. Romain Rolland says that Dayananda "thundered against all forms of thought other than his own, the only true one."[138] A.L. Basham says that Hinduism took offensive for the first time for centuries in Dayananda. He was also a mighty fighter in the cause of the 'Church' he founded and made fierce polemic speeches against its opponents.[139]

Commenting on the writings of Dayananda, H. Coward notes that his reading of the texts of other religions was always more polemic than scholarly in style. Passages would be selected for criticism where points of logical inconsistency or moral weakness could be shown. Much of this was motivated towards the winning of public debates or private theological discussions, rather than the ideal of dispassionate search for truth.[140] P.S. Daniel corroborates Coward's viewpoint when he affirms that Dayananda's sole aim seems to have been to vanquish the opponents in arguments, and the means he adopted to achieve this end, whether fair or foul, were of a matter of no concern to him.[141]

In spite of this, Dayananda had the audacity to state that the aim of his writings on religions was not to hurt the susceptibilities of others or to condemn falsely anyone, but to further the cause of truth and eradicate error and thus contribute to the elevation of human race and enable all human beings to sift truth from falsehood. He also claimed that he accepted whatever is true and good in every religion.[142] However, his attitude towards other religions betrayed the denial of these noble sentiments. In fact, as J.T.F. Jordens has rightly remarked, Dayananda's views are strongly condemnatory, predominantly negative and positively intolerant and aggressive. He says that there is quite a lot of sarcastic bitterness in his criticism of other religions.[143]

All non-Vedic religions should disappear

Dayananda maintained that all non-Vedic religions that are found in the world are products of muddled intellects.[144] But the Vedic religion is the only true religion and therefore all other religions are 'false beliefs' which should be *refuted* and *rejected.*[145] Thus, he speaks of the *snares* of the Jains, Christians and Moslems.[146] Besides, the existence of diversity of religions only leads to hostilities and strife which greatly increases sufferings in the world.[147] Humanity can expect no progress unless everybody followed the same Vedic religion because it is the religion of light, culture and righteousness, which will give true happiness to the entire humanity. Therefore, the salvation of the world consists in rejecting all the false religions and accepting the one true religion as revealed in the Vedas, and consequently all the false faiths must disappear. In a letter to Colonel Olcott, he wrote: "We pray the Lord that by his grace and the effort of men one day all these religions may *disappear*, and that in the midst of all people may be established the one true religion which throughout the tradition has been preserved by the Aryans."[148]

Therefore, Dayananda considered it his mission to replace all the religions, including certain forms of Hinduism, with the pure Vedic religion. In fact, he looked forward to a future in which all the existing religions will vanish from the world and the Vedic religion alone will reign supreme.

Misrepresentation of other religions

In the introduction to *Satyartha Prakash*, Dayananda presented four concrete principles that are to be taken into account in interpreting other religions. They are: (a) *akanksa,* which demands the interpreter to enter into the spirit of the speaker or author; (b) *yogyata,* which means fitness or compatibility of a word and the meaning it signifies so that it gives rationality to the text; (c) *asatti*, which demands that a text be taken in its total context; and (d) *tatparya*, which insists in giving the same meaning to the words which was intended by the user or speaker.[149] P.S. Daniel notes that when Dayananda interpreted other religions and their sacred texts, he totally ignored these rules, which he himself had recommended. He took the scriptures in their most literal sense, ignoring the context and the spirit in which they are written.[150] Benjamin Walker, commenting on Dayananda's Vedic religion also, notes that his interpretation of the Vedas was largely fanciful and often forcibly adapted to suit his preconceptions, and as he knew no English his inspiration was derived mainly from indigenous sources.[151]

It is an accepted fact that religious ideas are expressed in symbols and myths. Hence, in interpreting religious texts or ideas, one needs to go beyond the words, symbols and myths and seek their deeper meaning, through proper hermeneutics. But Dayananda took the mythical and symbolic expressions found in the scriptures of other religions in their literal sense, making no effort to grasp their hidden meanings. Jordens says: "Dayananda was hampered in his theological thinking by his complete inability to grasp the value and meaning of myth and symbols in the elucidation of the sacred. To him only pure rationality was acceptable in the realm of theology."[152]

P.S. Daniel says that more often in Dayananda's criticism of other religions and the interpretation of their scriptures, it was not rationality that guided him, but malice and spite.[153] Coward observes that although Dayananda possessed a laudable desire to study other religions, and though he commendably went to great lengths to work on primary texts, his *a priori* assumptions frequently prevented him from understanding them.[154] F.K. Khan Durrani says that Dayananda's arguments degenerated into wholesale abuse.[155] He further notes that for Dayananda a thing is right if it is found in the Vedas. But, if it is discovered in the *Quoran* or in the religious scriptures of some other religions, it is objectionable and false. Hence, what Dayananda really seeks is victory and not truth.[156] J.N. Farquhar characterises much of Dayananda's writings on other religions as 'stinging taunts'.[157]

Satyartha Prakash as the most disappointing book

Perhaps, the most virulent criticism against Dayananda's fundamentalist ideology came from Mahatma Gandhi. The latter, after reading the Dayananda's *Satyartha Prakash* in 1942 in Yerwada Prison, wrote in *Young India*: "I have read *Satyartha Prakash*, the Arya Samaj Bible. Friends sent me three copies of it whilst I was resting in the Yarwada Jail. I have not read a more *disappointing book* from a reformer so great. He has claimed to stand for truth and nothing else. But he has *unconsciously misrepresented Jainism, Islam, Christianity, and Hinduism itself*. One having even a cursory acquaintance with these faiths could easily discover the errors into which the great reformer was betrayed."[158] Gandhi then pointed out that one's respect for Dayananda would have been greater if he had not written such a book as *Satyartha Prakash*, especially the chapters on other religions. The comments of Gandhi invited strong protests from the Arya Samajists to which Gandhi responded saying that there was not a single word in his comments that was written without deep consideration and that his writings are therefore deliberate.[159]

It is also to be recalled that the Sindh government banned Chapter XIV of *Satyartha Prakash* which deals with Islam because it promotes feelings of enmity and hatred between people. The government order particularly specified that the author of *Satyartha Prakash* ridiculed some of the religious beliefs of Muslims, misrepresented and reviled the teachings of the *Quoran*, attacked and belittled the authority of the Prophet Mohammad and that the book contained matters calculated to hurt the susceptibilities of Muslims.[160]

Practice of *shuddhi* (re-conversion) as a weapon against Christianity and Islam

Dayananda was greatly threatened by the activities of proselytisation by Christian missionaries and Muslim teachers. He said: "Do you not see that before your very eyes fraudulent cults are increasing and many men are embracing Christianity and Islam."[161] In order to counteract it, besides employing the usual methods of public lectures and writings condemning these religions, he also introduced a new weapon called *shuddhi* or the re-conversion ceremony. K.W. Jones says: "...*shuddhi*, [is] a ceremony of purification which was employed to return those who had been lost to Hinduism through Christian or Islamic conversion."[162]

Shuddhi was an ancient Hindu concept referring to the quality of purity necessary for the proper performance of religious rites and social duties. By extension, the term signified the rite by which pollution is removed and ritual purity is restored for performing religious rituals. Traditionally, it was also used for the re-admittance of Hindus who had fallen from caste fellowship, consciously or unconsciously. Initially, orthodox Hindu rituals were used in *shuddhi* ceremony.[163]

However, the credit goes to Dayananda for extending the ancient practice of *shuddhi* to re-convert to the Vedic faith those Hindus who embraced other religions, especially Islam and Christianity. Later, he also used it to *convert* non-Hindus to Vedic faith, thus making Hinduism both a *propagating religion* and a *converting religion.*[164] Dayananda found in *shuddhi* something appropriate for the specific Christian challenge to Hinduism which he started in Punjab and which in the course of time became a considerable movement in the entire Gangetic plains.[165]

Thus *shuddhi* became a forceful response to the so-called converting activity of Christianity and Islam, for the recovery of lapsed Hindus, converting people to Hinduism, and raising the status of low castes including the untouchables. He also used it as a powerful technique to reform Hinduism from within.

Dayananda himself took the lead to re-convert Christians and Muslims to Hinduism. In 1877, during his visit to Punjab, at Ludhiana he gave a lecture on *shuddhi* and prevented the conversion of a Brahmin called Ramsharan, who was a teacher at the Christian mission school. In Amritsar, about forty students who were strongly attracted to Christianity were persuaded by Dayananda to abandon the idea. At Jullandhar, he himself performed the re-conversion of a Christian. He was also actively involved in the re-conversion to Hinduism of several other Christians.[166] Dayananda's denunciation of Christianity and Islam was in full swing during and after his visit to Punjab (1877-78), where Hindus felt the threat of Christianity and Islam most acutely.[167]

Arya Samaj as an organised proselytising religion

The founding of the Arya Samaj in 1875 was the concrete response of Dayananda to the problem of religious pluralism. Jordens notes that, it was the most important and far-reaching decision taken by Dayananda because it planted his message and his reform firmly in the soil of North India.[168] It was to become a movement on the vanguard of the Hindu response to the challenges of other religions in the 20th century. Sir Herbert Risley observes that the Arya Samaj was bitterly opposed to Christianity and laid itself out not merely to counteract the efforts of missionaries but to reconvert to Hinduism persons of high castes who had become Christians.[169]

Dayananda stated at the end of the *Satyartha Prakash* that the sole aim of his life is to help to put an end to this mutual wrangling of different religions and to bring all men into the fold of one religion, namely, the Vedic.[170] It was with this goal that he founded the Arya Samaj, the duty of which was to recall India to the forsaken Vedic path.[171] Dayananda, in his will, left his property to a society called *Paropakarani Sabha* to be used for the preaching and teaching of the Vedic Dharma by initiating a body of preachers to be sent across India and outside so that truth may be accepted and falsehood may be rejected.[172] In this way, he made the Vedic religion a *preaching religion* (*pracaraka dharma*) and a *propagating religion*. Dayananda says: "christianity [sic], Islam and Jainism are on the increase while Vedic people are deteriorating. But they do not open their eyes. [...] You cannot protect your homes and *convert people* from other religions."[173] Thus, as P.S. Daniel says, what he advocated was not co-existence of different religions on the basis of mutual respect but the acceptance of one religion by all.[174] In this way, the Arya Samaj became an organised proselytising religion, like Islam and Christianity, and it also aspired to convert the whole world to its faith through constructive propaganda. Jones notes: "Proselytisation then became a major activity of the Arya Samaj."[175]

Fearing that the Christian missionaries would convert Hindus through their schools, Dayananda also established schools operated by the Arya Samaj. The raising of the status of the low castes through *shuddhi* ceremony was another method he employed against the challenges of Christianity. Dayananda also preached cow protection and founded the famous Cow Protection Association.

Dayananda as a Hindu nationalist

Dayananda was not only a religious leader and social reformer, but also a political thinker. He derived his nationalist ideas from the originality of his own understanding of Indian culture and without any direct influence of Western thought. He noted that a nation is a people that is conscious of its historical identity, cultural uniqueness, common language, common territory and claim to self-rule. Dayananda's concept of nationalism met all these requirements and he arrived at it about 1875, a decade before even the Indian National Congress was founded. Though the Arya Samaj is not a political organisation, in the strict sense, it has a political philosophy of its own. It is a national movement in the Indian context because it has a definite approach in all matters affecting the lives of the people and the country – religious, social, educational, cultural and political. Among the aims of Arya Samaj we read: "Its [Arya Samaj's] prosperity and future depends upon the reconciliation of Hinduism with that greater *ism* – Indian Nationalism."[176] C. Jaffrelot notes that although the Arya Samaj was not a proponent of Hindu nationalism, it was a militant organisation from which Hindu nationalism would emerge.[177] He affirms: "Its (Arya Samaj's) ideological characteristics were such that it became one of the first crucibles of Hindu nationalism."[178] "The Arya Samaj represents the militant strand from which, in particular, Hindu nationalism would spring forth."[179] Jordens observes that Dayananda developed an aggressive nationalism, especially in his later years.[180]

Dayananda's ideology and Hindutva

An ideology can be considered to have succeeded when new generations of people begin to talk that language. Though more than a century has passed since Dayananda's death, his religious philosophy continues to inspire a great portion of the Hindu intelligentsia in India. The unprecedented rise of militant Hindutva since the late 1980s is a proof of it.

The link between Dayananda's philosophy and Hindutva

There is an ideological link between Dayananda's religious fundamentalism and the present-day Hindutva. Dayananda was perhaps the first in modern times to politicise Hindu religion. Through the interpretation of the Vedas he politicised Hinduism in a subtle way and to a degree no other Indian thinker had done before him. He attempted to justify that Hindu culture was to be the natural and the necessary basis of the nationalism. Dayananda considered the Vedic Dharma as the exclusively and absolutely true faith and therefore superior to all others. Hence, he gave a clarion call to all the Hindus to "return to the Vedas". He says: "The prosperity of a country depends upon the fulfillment [sic] of certain conditions, such as the study of the Vedas and the Vedic literature, due observance of the rules of the four *Ashramas*, *Brahmacharya* etc."[181] He also spoke of a Golden Age in which the Aryans of the Vedic era are presented as the chosen people to whom God revealed perfect knowledge of the Veda.[182] Again, Dayananda also considered India as the land of Aryans and that Indians were Aryans. We read in *Satyartha Prakash*: "Now, we shall examine the merits and demerits of the religion professed by the *Aryas* or people of the country of the *Aryavartta* [India]. In the whole world there is no country like India. [...] For this reason did the Aryas come to this land and settle here in the beginning of the universe."[183] He also used the term *Aryavartta* for India,[184] *Indraprashta* for modern Delhi,[185] *Prayaga* for Allahabad[186] and *Avantikak* for Ujjain.[187] Here it may be noted that one of the agendas of the Hindutva ideologues of today is to restore some of these ancient names.

Dayananda proposed Sanskrit as the common language of India and made attempts to revive it, though later abandoned it for Hindi. He projected Christianity and Islam as 'alien faiths'[188] or 'faiths of other countries'[189] and Carvacas, Buddhism and Jainism as 'cults of India'.[190]

Attempts to impose Vedic culture

Among the hardline Hindutva ideologues of India, we perceive a systematic attempt to resurrect the Vedic culture under the name of the 'study of the Vedic culture' and Vedic sciences and assert the superiority of the Aryan race by imposing on the nation the ideology of Hindutva. For instance, there is a strong tendency among the Hindutva ideologues to prest the Vedic civilisation as the foundation not only of Indian civilisation but also of the world civilisation. Serious efforts are also being made to impose Vedic studies in school and university education. We can recall here the systematic efforts in this direction by the National Council of Educational Research and Training (NCERT) and the University Grants Commission (UGC) when the former BJP-led NDA government was in power in New Delhi. In the name of bringing the so-called 'real history' to people, distortion of Indian history is being done by Hindutva historians. For example, they present the Aryans as the indigenous people of India, declare that the Aryan invasion is a myth, argue that the Vedic people and the Harappans were identical and that the authors of the *Vedas* were the builders of the Harappan civilisation.[191]

Symbolic gestures can have not only local but also global significance. Dayananda's call of "back to the Vedas" is heard overseas as well. The American-born David Frawley (who became Vamadeva Shastri) may be considered as a 'personification' itself of "return to the Vedas". Frawley claims that he became a Hindu by studying the Vedas: He notes: "In my case I simply didn't build bridge to the East, I crossed over them and left them far behind. I immersed my being in the soul of the East so completely that I almost ceased to be a Westerner, not only in my thoughts but also in my instincts. I moved from a Western intellectual rationality to a deeper cosmic rationality born of the *Vedic insight*."[192] Frawley has also written many articles and books which can be considered as a continuation of the mission of Dayananda to bring people to the Vedic faith. Another example of a Westerner who responded to the call to "return to the Vedas" is Ishwar Sharan – originally a Canadian Christian – who took his *Vedic initiation* at Prayaga in 1977. Today, through his writings, he wages an ideological battle against Christianity – his former religion.

Attempt to impose Vedic model of education

In October 1998, in a conference of the Education Ministers and Education Secretaries of states organised by the former Union Human Resource Development Ministry, the 'experts' from the All India Conference of the Vidya Bharati recommended, among other things, that Vedas and Upanisads should be incorporated into the basic curricula of education and that Sanskrit learning should be made obligatory for students from Standard II to X.[193] Similarly, in a seminar conducted in 2003 on 'Indianisation of Education: Reforms and Restructuring', it was observed that the Vedic model of education was the *only solution* to elevate the level of standard of Indian education. The seminar also dealt at length with Vedic civilisation. Those who participated in the seminar included well-known personalities like the former HRD Minister, Murli Manohar Joshi, the RSS leader K.S. Sudarshan and the former NCERT director J.S. Rajput[194] – all of them acknowledged Hindutva hardliners of contemporary India. Thus, once again, what we find is people responding to the 'call' of Dayananda to "return to the Vedas".

Intolerance towards religious minorities

Again, the 'war' which Dayananda declared against the Muslims and Christians continues to be waged without any respite even today. Even after a century, the main targets of attack continue to be practically the same, and the reverberations of the 'war drums' are heard not only in the media and in the streets but also in the Indian parliament. The only difference is that the bulk of the 'artillery' and 'ammunition' for the war are carried to the battlefield, not by Arya Samajists but by the Hindutva brigade of the RSS, VHP, BJP, Bajrang Dal, Shiv Sena, and other affiliates of the Sangh Parivar, and the Hindutva stalwarts.

Revival of the practice of re-conversion

Dayananda engaged in polemics against all the religions extant in the India of his time, and his *Satyartha Prakash* continues to remain as a notorious monument to religious intolerance.

Many practical methods employed by the Hindutva ideologues today to combat the religious minorities of India find their inspiration in Dayananda. For example, the practice of re-conversion (*shuddhi*) ceremonies, cow protection movement, proselytisation by Hindu volunteers, introduction of the so-called 'Freedom of Religion Bill' to prevent conversion, the view that India is the fountainhead of all cultures, concept of India as a Hindu nation from time immemorial, publication of polemical and provocative writings in the form of tracts and pamphlets, gross misinterpretation of the dogmas and beliefs of other religions, superficial study of their scriptures and citing them out of context in order to spite and to malign, ridiculing their divinities and saints, the projection of Hindutva as the 'one religion for all' Indians, and so on, have their ideological as well as methodological inspiration in Dayananda and in the Arya Samaj he founded.

The campaign of maligning by 'Voice of India'

The *Voice of India*, New Delhi, which is one of the principal mouthpieces of the Hindutva today, seems to imitate the method adopted by Dayananda a century ago in his *Satyartha Prakash*. In fact, the *Voice of India* regularly publishes books, pamphlets and monographs of highly inflammatory nature against other religions, especially Islam, Christianity and the secular ideologies of India. Although the scholarship of many of these publications is questionable, they have a wide circulation both in India and abroad. Judging from the nature of their literature, the ultimate purpose of *Voice of India* seems to be – just as it was in the case of Dayananda – to impress, indoctrinate, misrepresent, malign, fabricate stories, politicise religion and play on the emotions of the masses against the minority religions and secularists of India, in order to win the battle against their opponents, using any means, fair or foul.

Dayananda's style of engaging in polemics and hurling insults against religious minorities is being imitated by several contemporary Hindutva ideologues. Authors like Arun Shourie (see his *Missionaries in India*, 1994; *Worshipping False God's*, 1994; *Harvesting Our Souls*, 2000), Sita Ram Goel (see his *Jesus Christ: An Artifice for Aggression*, 1994; *Catholic Ashrams: Sanyasins or Swindlers*, 1994; *History of Hindu Christian Encounters*, 1996; *Genesis and Growth of Nehruism*, 1993; *The Story of Islamic Imperialism in India*, 1994), Ram Swarup (see his *Hindu View of Christianity and Islam*, 1992; *On Hinduism Reviews and Reflections*, 2000), Ishwar Sharan (see his *The Myth of Saint Thomas and the Mylapore Shiva Temple*, 1995), David Frawley (see his *Arise Arjuna: Hinduism in the Modern World*, 1995), Koenraad Elst (see his *Psychology of Prophetism: A Secular Look at the Bible*, 1993; *Negationism in India. Concealing the Record of Islam*, 1993) are among the outstanding disciples of Dayananda in this field. A critical reading of their writings reveals that, in essence, their discourses are hardly different from that of Dayananda in his *Satyartha Prakash*. In other words, all these are subtle ways of responding to the call of Dayananda to "return to the Vedas", to assert the Vedic faith and the superiority of the Aryan race. Therefore, we may rightly maintain that much of the inspiration for the present-day Hindutva writers is derived from Dayananda, either directly or indirectly. In this way, Dayananda continues to aliment Hindutva.

However, it is paradoxical that the same Hindutva ideologues, who are so strongly under the ideological spell of Dayananda, have conveniently avoided being influenced by the social reforms initiated by him, such as, repudiation of traditional caste system, untouchability, Brahmanic domination of Indian culture, discrimination against women and low castes and attempts to reform the Hindu religion from such evils as polytheism, idolatry, superstitious rituals, exploitation of the ignorant masses, etc.

Dayananda as the 'father' of modern Hindu fundamentalism

As we have already seen, Dayananda upholds the view that the Vedic religion alone is the absolute truth and that it is superior to all other faiths. As the *Sanatana Dharma* (Eternal Religion), it is for all time and all peoples. He says: "The *Sanatan Dharma* or Eternal Religion is that set of universal doctrines which belong to all countries and all men, which were accepted in the past, are being accepted in the present, and shall be accepted in future by everybody and which it is impossible for anybody to go against."[195] He affirms again: "All men, should, therefore, accept this firmly established doctrine [of the Vedic revelation]. They should accept none else."[196] What is implied is that all religions other than the Vedic are false and products of ignorance, worthy to be obliterated from the face of the earth. He says: "One who disrespects the Vedas or the scriptures written by master-minds in agreement with the Vedas, is an anti-Vedic heretic and *should be turned out of the nation, society and country*."[197] Dayananda's religious intolerance of other faiths is evident in this statement. Here, we may quote the words of Meera Nanda who says: "Hinduism refuses to grant other faiths their distinctiveness and difference, even as it proclaims its great 'tolerance'. Hinduism's tolerance is a mere disguise for its narcissistic obsession with its own greatness."[198]

Arya Samaj began as a defensive organisation of the Hindus. But soon it became an offensive one against people of other faiths. The Samaj also launched programmes to convert followers of other religions to the Hindu faith.[199] To counter the proselytising activities of Christian missionaries, it borrowed many organisational techniques from them. It sponsored missionary activities to convert Muslims and Christians and performed ceremonies to raise outcast Hindus to the twice-born status.[200] The *shuddhi* (re-conversion) programme of the Arya Samaj is now being pursued as an aggressive agenda of the Sangh Parivar.

D.D. Pattanaik says that history of modern Hindu nationalist thought begins with Swami Dayananda Saraswati. He advocated rejuvenation of Hinduism as India's national religion on the doctrine of Vedic infallibility, as the foundation of Hindu society and Hindu nation. Thus, Dayananda spoke of nationalism in religious terms, and laid down the foundations for neo-Hindu nationalism.[201] Pattanaik even places him next to Adi Sankara. He says: "Next to Adi Sankaracharya, Dayananda was the greatest and foremost to check onslaught on Hinduism and its genuine scriptures."[202]

In the saffronised NCERT school textbook of Social Sciences for Class IX, Dayananda is presented as a great patriot because his slogan was "back to the Vedas" and he instilled in people a pride in the ideals of *swadeshi*.[203] However, it may be more correct to call him a patriot of Hindu *rashtra* and a champion of Vedic religion than a true patriot. It has been said that many terrorists and extremists were inspired by the Arya Samaj he founded.[204] His ideas have also influenced the militant Hindu Mahasabha[205] and the Jana Sangh.[206]

Thus, ultimately, what Dayananda propounds is a *single culture*, *single religion* and a *single identity* – namely, the Vedic. The glorification of the Vedic culture amounts to the glorification of Hinduism and the ethnic pride of Aryans. For example, he says: "Just as there is one God there should be *one religion* of all people [the Vedic]."[207] "From the dawn of creation up to a little before five thousand years ago, the *Aryas were the sole overlords* of the whole world."[208] "It is very difficult to make any progress without *common faith*, *common interests* [...] and *common feeling*."[209]

From the above, it is not difficult to infer that Dayananda advocated for India the theory of one religion, one race and one culture. Here, we are reminded of Adolf Hitler's concept of *ein Reich, ein Volk, ein Führer* (one nation, one people, one leader!). Such an ideology demonstrates Dayananda's callous insensitivity towards people of other faiths, his religious intolerance and his intention to crusade against religious freedom. Because of his inability to accept religious pluralism, what he advocates in reality is a *clash of religions*, and consequently, *religious fundamentalism* and *militancy*. Subash Anand says: "Dayananda's weakness was a fundamentalist reading of his religious tradition."[210]

Thus, Dayananda's religious philosophy hardly contributes anything to inter-religious dialogue or understanding of civilisations or peaceful co-existence of people of different faiths. His exclusive religion of the Vedas is a danger for the secularist and the pluralistic framework of India. Therefore, we may rightly claim that his anti-'other' philosophy qualifies him to be the 'father' of the modern Hindu fundamentalism, not only because of the nature of his views but also due to the extent of their influence on contemporary India. In fact, after an analysis of Dayananda's religious thought, Ninian Smart affirms that Dayananda was in a stronger sense than Ram Mohan Roy a fundamentalist, and an early nationalist, and the Arya Samaj he founded had some influence on the militant Hindu Mahasabha movement.[211]

Conclusion

In order to understand the present, one needs to know the past. The seeds of religious fundamentalism which Dayananda sowed more than a century ago are bearing abundant fruit in contemporary India in the form of aggressive Hindutva against the religious minorities of India, especially the Muslims and Christians, as evident by the innumerable acts of atrocities committed against them in recent years. Thus, the true face of Dayananda, which has so far been hidden beneath the mask of his being a frontline Hindu social reformer, now emerges as that of a Hindu fundamentalist and nationalist.

The ability of Dayananda's philosophy of religion to aliment Hindu chauvinism, even after a century, once again tells us most eloquently that ideologies rule the world, and that an ideological aggression, if not resisted in time, can lead to lasting tragic consequences. Therefore, the popular conception of Dayananda as a benign Hindu social reformer is only a half truth. The other half is that the roots of contemporary Hindu fundamentalism and militancy against the minority religions, to a great extent, lie deep in the 19th century, especially in the religious philosophy of persons like Dayananda Saraswati. Therefore, the ideological link between Dayananda and the contemporary Hindutva is too evident to go unnoticed.

Notes

1. See A. Sharma, *Swami Dayananda Saraswati and Vedic Authority*, 188.
2. See D. Saraswati, *Autobiography*, 11-45, 67-83.
3. For a list of his works, see D. Saraswati, *Autobiography*, 84-89. See also J.T.F. Jordens, *Dayananda Sarasvati*, 345-347.
4. The first edition of *Satyartha Prakash* was published in 1875 followed by an enlarged second edition in 1884. We refer to the English translation of the latter edition by Ganga Prasad Upadhyaya entitled *The Light of Truth*, Allahabad, 1956.
5. We refer to the edition by Ghasi Ram (1925).
6. We refer to the edition by Y. Mimamshak (1955).
7. See J.T.F. Jordens, *Dayananda Sarasvati*, 92-126, 249-269.
8. See D. Saraswati, *Satyartha Prakash*, 283-284, 288, 849.
9. Ibid., 385.
10. Ibid., 385, 387-388.
11. Ibid., 284, 391.
12. Ibid., 385, 387-389.
13. Ibid., 281, 288.
14. Ibid., 508.
15. Ibid., 551-552.
16. D. Saraswati, *Satyartha Prakash*, 446.
17. See D. Saraswati, *Satyartha Prakash*, 283. See also his, *The Ten Commandments,* 41-42.
18. See D. Saraswati, *Satyartha Prakash*, 292. See also his, *Rigvedadi Bhasya Bhumika*, 46, 47, 136.
19. See Aurobindo, *India's Rebirth*, 117-118.

20. See D. Saraswati, *Satyartha Prakash*, 849.
21. D. Saraswati, *Rigvedadi Bhasya Bhumika*, 76.
22. See D. Saraswati, *Rigvedadi Bhasya Bhumika*, 49. See also his, *Satyartha Prakash*, 287.
23. See D. Saraswati, *Satyartha Prakash*, 12.
24. The letter is reproduced in J.T.F. Jordens, *Dayananda Sarasvati*, 209.
25. See D. Saraswati, *Satyartha Prakash*, 446.
26. Ibid., 846.
27. H. Coward, "Dayananda's Approach to Other Religions", 267.
28. See D. Saraswati, *Satyartha Prakash*, 283, 285.
29. Ibid., 385, 556.
30. See J.T.F. Jordens, *Dayananda Sarasvati*, 78-98; D. Saraswati, *Autobiography*, 74-75.
31. See D. Saraswati, *Satyartha Prakash*, 2-3.
32. Ibid., 3.
33. Ibid., 555-556.
34. Ibid., 2-5, 7-9.
35. Ibid., 385, 555, 581.
36. Ibid., 5.
37. Ibid., 5, 8, 385.
38. Ibid., 581.
39. D. Saraswati, *Satyartha Prakash*, 559.
40. Ibid., 555.
41. See D. Saraswati, *Satyartha Prakash*, 385.
42. Ibid., 9, 848.
43. Ibid., 3.
44. Ibid., 3, 4.
45. D. Saraswati, *Rigvedadi Bhasya Bhumika*, 76.
46. See D. Saraswati, *Satyartha Prakash*, 846.
47. Ibid., 551.
48. Ibid., 5.
49. Ibid., 387-580.
50. Ibid., 80.
51. Ibid., 394.
52. Ibid., 80.
53. Ibid., 846.

54. See P.S. Daniel, *Hindu Response*, 100.
55. See D. Saraswati, *Satyartha Prakash*, 385, 581.
56. Ibid., 583.
57. Ibid., 638, 639, 640.
58. D. Saraswati, *Satyartha Prakash*, 622-623.
59. See D. Saraswati, *Satyartha Prakash*, 674.
60. D. Saraswati, *Satyartha Prakash*, 656.
61. Ibid., 648.
62. See D. Saraswati, *Satyartha Prakash*, 761-845.
63. Ibid., 822.
64. D. Saraswati, *Satyartha Prakash*, 797.
65. See D. Saraswati, *Satyartha Prakash*, 814, 843.
66. Ibid., 828, 843.
67. Ibid., 800.
68. Ibid., 785.
69. Ibid., 787.
70. Ibid., 822, 835.
71. Ibid., 836.
72. D. Saraswati, *Satyartha Prakash*, 843.
73. Ibid., 785.
74. Ibid., 798.
75. See D. Saraswati, *Satyartha Prakash*, 824.
76. Ibid., 780.
77. Ibid., 789.
78. S. Sarkar, *Beyond Nationalist Frames*, 229.
79. See D. Saraswati, *Satyartha Prakash*, 683.
80. D. Saraswati, *Satyartha Prakash*, 723.
81. Ibid., 734.
82. Ibid., 756.
83. See D. Saraswati, *Satyartha Prakash*, 395.
84. Ibid., 397.
85. Ibid., 694, 755.
86. Ibid., 712.
87. Ibid., 694.
88. Ibid., 695, 702.
89. Ibid., 699, 712.

90. Ibid., 700.
91. Ibid., 715.
92. D. Saraswati, *Satyartha Prakash*, 695.
93. See D. Saraswati, *Satyartha Prakash*, 697.
94. D. Saraswati, *Satyartha Prakash*, 708.
95. See D. Saraswati, *Satyartha Prakash*, 693.
96. Ibid., 696.
97. Ibid., 705.
98. Ibid., 722, 726, 742.
99. Ibid., 723, 729, 735, 738.
100. Ibid., 692, 734.
101. Ibid., 729-730.
102. Ibid., 553.
103. Ibid., 704.
104. Ibid., 722-723.
105. Ibid., 712, 720.
106. Ibid., 715-717.
107. Ibid., 552-553.
108. Ibid., 736, 751.
109. D. Saraswati, *Satyartha Prakash*, 688.
110. Ibid., 695.
111. Ibid., 769.
112. See D. Saraswati, *Satyartha Prakash*, 682, 760.
113. See J.T.F. Jordens, *Dayananda Sarasvati*, 267.
114. See D. Saraswati, *Satyartha Prakash*, 731, 734, 736.
115. P.S. Daniel, *Hindu Response*, 93.
116. D. Saraswati, *Satyartha Prakash*, 731.
117. See D. Saraswati, *Satyartha Prakash*, 722-723.
118. Ibid., 734.
119. Ibid., 723.
120. Ibid., 730.
121. Ibid., 728.
122. Ibid., 728-729.
123. Ibid., 736-737.
124. Ibid., 700, 711.
125. Ibid., 724.

126. Ibid., 742.
127. Ibid., 734.
128. Ibid., 718.
129. Ibid., 717.
130. See B. Walker, *Hindu World*, vol. 1, 271.
131. See *Rishi Dayananda Saraswati*, 438, 446.
132. G.S. Saxena, *Arya Samaj Movement in India 1875-1947*, 27.
133. See P.S. Daniel, *Hindu Response*, 103.
134. L.L. Rai, *The Arya Samaj*, 172.
135. M.G. Chitkara, *Hindutva*, 75.
136. See N.K. Devaraja, *Hinduism and Modern Age*, 104; Chamupati, "The Arya Samaja, 636.
137. For details of such religious conflicts see K.W. Jones, *Arya Dharma: Hindu Consciousness in the 19th Century*, 19-20, 39-47, 120-153, 186-223, ID., "The Arya Samaj in British India", 33-52.
138. R. Rolland, *The Prophets of the New India*, 100.
139. A.L. Basham, "Hinduism", 249.
140. See H. Coward, Dayananda's Approach to Other Religions, 273.
141. See P.S. Daniel, *Hindu Response*, 96.
142. See D. Saraswati, *Satyartha Prakash*, 3, 4, 846-847.
143. See J.T.F. Jordens, *Dayananda Sarasvati*, 267.
144. See D. Saraswati, *Satyartha Prakash*, 385.
145. Ibid., 8, 385.
146. Ibid., 395.
147. Ibid., 386.
148. The letter as reproduced in J.T.F. Jordens, *Dayananda Sarasvati*, 209 (Emphasis added).
149. See D. Saraswati, *Satyartha Prakash*, 8-9.
150. See P.S. Daniel, *Hindu Response*, 94.
151. See B. Walker, *Hindu World*, vol. 1, 270.
152. J.T.F. Jordens, *Dayananda Sarasvati*, 277.
153. See P.S. Daniel, *Hindu Response*, 96.
154. See H. Coward, "Dayananda's Approach to Other Religions", 265, 267, 272, 273.
155. See F.K.K. Durrani, *Swami Dayananda*, 160-167.
156. See F.K.K. Durrani, *Swami Dayananda*, 142-144.

157. See J.N. Farquhar, *Modern Religious Movements in India*, 122.
158. *The Collected Works of Mahatma Gandhi*, vol. 24, 145 (emphasis added).
159. See, *The Collected Works of Mahatma Gandhi*, vol. 24, 180-181, 228-229.
160. See P.S. Daniel, *Hindu Response*, 116 note 186.
161. D. Saraswati, *Satyartha Prakash*, 565.
162. K.W. Jones, "Swami Dayananda Saraswati's Vision", 283.
163. See P.S. Daniel, *Hindu Response*, 103-104.
164. Ibid., 88, 104.
165. See J.T.F. Jordens, *Dayananda Sarasvati*. 170-171.
166. Ibid., 170.
167. See K.W. Jones, *Arya Dharma*, 8-20.
168. See J.T.F. Jordens, *Dayananda Sarasvati*, 127.
169. See H. Risley, *The Peoples of Indian*, 244-245 as cited in L.L. Rai, *The Arya Samaj*, 162.
170. See D. Saraswati, *Satyartha Prakash*, 846.
171. See H.D. Griswold, "*Arya Samaja*", 59.
172. See Dayananda, *Autobiography*, 90-95.
173. D. Saraswati, *Satyartha Prakash*, 565 (emphasis added).
174. See P.S. Daniel, *Hindu Response*, 88.
175. K.W. Jones, "Swami Dayananda Saraswati's Vision", 282
176. L.L. Rai, *The Arya Samaj*, 183.
177. See C. Jaffrelot, *The Hindu Nationalist Movement*, 14, 17.
178. C. Jaffrelot, *The Hindu Nationalist Movement*, 17.
179. Ibid., 14.
180. See J.T.F. Jordens, *Dayananda Sarasvati*. 268.
181. D. Saraswati, *Satyartha Prakash*, 566.
182. See D. Saraswati, *Satyartha Prakash*, 385, 387-391.
183. D. Saraswati, *Satyartha Prakash*, 387.
184. See D. Saraswati, *Satyartha Prakash*, 386, 387, 548, 569, 581, 846,
185. Ibid., 570, 572, 573, 576, 577, 579, 580.
186. Ibid., 574, 580.
187. Ibid., 575.
188. Ibid., 548.
189. Ibid., 4.

190. Ibid., 2, 583.
191. See M. Pingle, "Bring Real History of the Country before People", 14.
192. D. Frawley, *How I became a Hindu*, 7 (emphasis added).
193. See A. Pupshparajan, "A Secular Critique of Hindutva", 241.
194. See *Organiser*, 5 January, 2003, 17.
195. D. Saraswati, *Satyartha Prakash*, 846.
196. D. Saraswati, *Rigvedadi Bhasya Bhumika*, 31.
197. D. Saraswati, *Satyartha Prakash*, 79 (emphasis added).
198. M. Nanda, "Postmodernism, Hindu Nationalism", Part I, 81.
199. D.D. Pattanaik, *Hindu Nationalism*, vol. 2, 12.
200. W.K. Andersen and S.D. Damle, *The Brotherhood in Saffron*, 18.
201. D.D. Pattanaik, *Hindu Nationalism*, vol. 2, 8.
202. Ibid., 12. It may be recalled here that E.M.S. Namboodiripad had described Adi Sankara as the symbol of degradation of India. See S. Chandrasekhar, "Sanskrit Varsity in Kerala", 4.
203. B.S. Parakh (ed.), *Contemporary India*, 22.
204. D.D. Pattanaik, *Hindu Nationalism*, vol. 2, 13.
205. See N. Smart, *World Philosophies*, 316.
206. P.C. Swain, *Bharatiya Janata Party*, 61.
207. From the letter to Colonel Olcott reproduced in J.T.F. Jordens, *Dayananda Sarasvati*, 209 (emphasis added).
208. D. Saraswati, *Satyartha Prakash*, 387 (emphasis added).
209. Ibid., 375 (emphasis added).
210. S. Anand "The Emergence of Hindutva", 197.
211. See N. Smart, *World Philosophies*, 315-316.

• II •

Ambivalence, Contradictions and Religious Intolerance in Swami Vivekananda

Narendranath Datta (1863-1902), who later became Swami Vivekananda, was born in Calcutta on 12 January 1863. Being a child of well-to-do parents he received a good liberal education in school from 1871 and in college from 1875.[1] While in college he passed through a period of rationalism[2] and agnosticism which eventually led him to search for God. Looking for a man of God he met Ramakrishna Paramahamsa (1836-1886) in 1881.[3] Soon, he became a member of the small group of young disciples who gathered around Ramakrishna. After the death of Ramakrishna in 1886, Narendra became the leader of the disciples. In 1888 he undertook a pilgrimage to holy places after which he continued his life as an itinerant monk.[4] Then on, his only aim in life was to preach and teach the message of the Vedanta to all. In 1893 he went to Chicago to participate in the World Parliament of Religions.[5] He took the occasion to preach Vedanta in the West, especially in the USA and England. He formed the organisation of the Ramakrishna Math and Mission, a monastic and missionary institution, which would carry on the teachings of Ramakrishna. He died on 4 July 1902.

Swami Vivekananda was perhaps the first Hindu in modern times to champion the cause of Hinduism outside India, especially in the West. He is also considered by many as the first Indian to recognise the fact of religious pluralism and to respond to its challenges. Our present is built on our past. In order to understand the reasons for the contemporary Hindu fundamentalism, we need to look into the past, and in this endeavour, Vivekananda is a personality to be studied closely.

A certain type of Hindu religious thinking prevalent in the late 19th and early 20th centuries was a factor that inspired the rise of Hindu militancy and fundamentalism in India. Here, we would like to examine some elements of Vivekananda's religious thought which seem to have played an important role in setting in motion the Hindu fundamentalist movement in modern times – an aspect which is rarely discussed in scholarly circles, probably due to the great esteem and respect with which people hold Vivekananda. Consequently, Vivekananda continues to be treated solely as a champion of universalism, unity, harmony and tolerance of religions – which no doubt he was, on numerous occasions – neglecting in the process certain controversial aspects of his religious thought. However, objectivity demands that we examine also the 'dark side' of his religious philosophy.

Ambivalence and contradictions in Swami Vivekananda

Vivekananda's response to religious pluralism has not been without ambivalence, inconsistencies and contradictions. P.S. Daniel traces three basic positions in Vivekananda's religious thought.[6]

First, Vivekananda held the view that all religions are one in essentials,[7] that they all have the same goal[8] and that they all have truth.[9] He said: "We believe not only in universal tolerance but we accept all religions as true."[10] This led him to reject both exclusive truth claims and the superiority of any religion over the others, and to uphold the unity and harmony of all religions.[11]

There is a second view, more dominant than the first in Vivekananda's speeches and writings, which is incompatible with the above position of the equality of all religions. According to this, all religions are not to be considered equally true. He gives them a subordinate position and admits their value as preparation for Advaita, which is the fulfilment of all of them. Therefore, other religions are seen as partial, incomplete and imperfect. Vivekananda calls Advaita the essence and kernel of all religions.[12] According to him, there is a religious growth of humanity from lower to higher forms, and any religion can be included in it. He identified dualism (*Dvaita*), qualified monism (*Visistadvaita*) and non-dualism (*Advaita*) as the three main, progressive stages in the evolution of religion.[13] He places Christianity and Islam in the stage of *Dvaita.*[14] Thus, for Vivekananda, Advaita Vedanta is not just one religion among many but religion itself in its most universal, absolute, final and complete form. It is the final goal of all religions.[15]

The third position of Vivekananda does not regard religions other than Advaita as having any use, and deny that they are fulfilled or included in Advaita. He asserts the exclusive truth of Advaita as the only True Eternal Religion[16] and totally rejects other religions as false, unnecessary, useless and therefore to be discarded.[17] This last position naturally leads to the conclusion that all religions other than Advaita are false.

P.S. Daniel observes that it is not that Vivekananda moved from one position to the other successively, rejecting the previous ones. All these different views are often found in the same speech or writing.[18]

Thus, we see that Vivekananda's response to religious pluralism was ambivalent and contradictory. Though he often exhibited a spirit of universalism, tolerance and respect for other religions, he also lapsed into a sort of dogmatic exclusiveness, religious fundamentalism and fanaticism, rejecting outright any real value in religions, except in Advaita.

Elements of 'fundamentalism' in Vivekananda

There is obviously an element of religious 'fundamentalism' and 'fanaticism' in some of the writings and speeches of Vivekananda. Not to pay attention to this aspect is to miss a significant aspect of his religious philosophy. It is important to examine these elements from a historical and existential perspective, because, the exclusive Advaitic Hindu ideology of Vivekananda seems to have provided inspiration for the rise of Hindu militancy in the last century. It is also reasonable to consider that his views continue to provide nourishment and direction to the contemporary Hindu fundamentalism, represented especially by the Hindutva ideologues and organisations.

Advaita Vedanta as the absolute and the exclusively true religion

Vivekananda, in several of his writings and speeches, upheld Advaita Vedanta as the absolute and the exclusively true religion. It is a view which is more dominant in his writings than his doctrine of the equality of all religions. He argues that even if all religions are true, they are not to be considered as equally true. Some are better or truer than the others. But, at the highest rung of the ladder of religions, Vivekananda places Advaita Vedanta, not as one among the many religions, but as the most universal, final and the absolute religion. He says: "Let me consider the question a while and lay before you my reasons why I think that the *Vedanta*, and the *Vedanta* alone that can become the universal religion of man, and that none else is fitted for the role."[19] "Advaitism, the last and, what we think, the fairest flower of philosophy and religion that any country in any age has produced, where human thought attains its highest expression."[20] He even suggests that it would be better if Hindus call themselves Vedantists.[21]

However, it is to be noted that though Vivekananda maintained the absoluteness of Advaita, he did not reject other religions as totally false or unnecessary – at least in some of his writings – but gave them a subordinate position and considered them as preparations for Advaita, which is the fullness of all of them. He says: "Ours, as I have said, [Vedanta] is the universal religion. It is inclusive enough, it is broad enough to include all the ideals."[22] Thus, Advaita is the one eternal religion in which the goal of all particular religions is expressed and manifested. It is the essence of all religions. Vivekananda notes: "...the truth is that Advaitism is the last word of religion and thought and the only position from which one can look upon all religions and sects with love."[23] Thus, no religion can claim the perfection which Advaita possesses.

Vivekananda also frequently taught that Advaita Vedanta is the only true religion. He says: "Ours is the true religion, because above all it teaches renunciation, and stands up with the wisdom of ages to tell and to declare to the nations who are mere children of yesterday in comparison with the hoary antiquity of the wisdom that our ancestors have discovered for us in India [...]. Therefore, ours is the *only true religion*."[24] What follows from the above is that no religion can claim the finality and absoluteness of Vedanta because Advaita is the only universal religion – a religion for all people in all places and at all times.[25]

P.S. Daniel remarks that one cannot expect such words from one who believes that all religions are true, and therefore, all religions should be equally respected. What is implied is that all the doctrines and practices of any religion that do not agree with Vedantic Hinduism are to be rejected. In other words, if there is any truth in other religions, it is the truth of, and derived from, the Vedanta which is the essence of all religions.[26] Further, when Vivekananda claims that all religions are equal, he means that all religions are equal among themselves *except* the Advatia, which is the goal of all religions.[27] This is so because Advaita is the crest jewel of all spiritual thought.[28] Thus, Advaita for Vivekananda is not merely superior to other religions but it is the culmination of all religions. Consequently, no religion can claim the finality and absoluteness of

Advaita. According to P.S. Daniel, it is nothing but religious imperialism and a 'big brother' attitude. It makes all religions subordinate and inferior to Advatia. They are simply tolerated as a concession shown to the weak and the ignorant, to those who are not mature enough spiritually.[29]

Religions other than Advaita are false and useless

As a consequence of his religious exclusivism, Vivekananda did not consider religions other than Advaita as having any use. He totally rejected other religions as false, unnecessary and useless. They are considered as positive obstacles in the path of man to realise the truth. P.S. Daniel maintains that there is a clear break from and a negation of lower truths when the highest truth is realised. Without such a break from and negation of the 'lesser truth' one cannot have a perfect vision of the absolute truth. By calling other religions as 'lower or lesser truth' Vivekananda is simply changing the label. So, to say that other religions are 'lower or lesser truth' is actually nothing but to say that they are not true in the ordinary sense.[30]

These considerations naturally lead to the conclusion that other religions are neither included nor fulfilled in Advaita. Besides, there are also repeated statements in the writings of Vivekananda to the effect that all religions other than Advaita are false. P.S. Daniel argues that in asserting the exclusive truth of Advaita, Vivekananda often lapses into intolerance and acts like a religious fanatic in the sense that he shows the least generosity towards other religions. Vivekananda thus condemns all religions other than Advaita as false, wrong, lie and darkness. He does not see any value in them. They are useless and degrading. But, in condemning other religions, he contradicts his own teaching about the harmony of all religions. He also departs from his own position that Advaita includes and fulfils all religions.[31]

The superiority of Hinduism

Vivekananda always maintained the superiority of Hinduism and the Indian thought over all other religions and philosophies. Even when he says that Advaita alone is absolutely true, it is his contention that Hinduism as a whole is superior to and truer than all other religions. It is the mother and source of all religions which contains all ideas in their perfections.[32] Thus, he claimed that Hinduism based on the Vedas is the only true religion.[33] He further contented that Hinduism is the oldest and the purest of the world's religions. He said that he was proud to belong to a religion which has taught the world both tolerance and universal acceptance.[34] All that is best in the religions of the world has come from Hindu India. He says: "You hear of claims made by every one of the different religions as being the universal religion of the world. Let me tell you in the first place that perhaps there never will be such a thing, but if there is a religion which can lay that claim, it is only ours [Hinduism] and none else."[35] For Vivekananda, there is no religious idea preached anywhere in the world, which is not found in the Vedas. Whatever the great teachers like the Buddha, Jesus Christ and others have taught, they took it from the Vedas.[36]

Hinduism as the national religion of India

Vivekananda also propounded Hinduism as the national religion of India. He was of the opinion that religion was the bedrock upon which the whole edifice of the Indian nation was built.[37] In March 1901, in Dacca, he claimed: "...in search of religion, I had travelled among various sects, [...] I had begged at the door of others, not knowing then that in the religion of my country, in our *national religion*, there was so much beauty and grandeur. It is now many years since I have found Hinduism to be the most perfectly satisfying religion in the world."[38] He identified love for Hinduism with patriotism, which also reveals his nationalist spirit. He reprimanded the Hindus for their indifference and lack of patriotism in not defending their religion and called them cowards cowed down by the missionaries. He said: "I am the one man who dared to defend his country, and I have given them such ideas as they never expected from a Hindu."[39] He also argued that Hinduism should have a hold on the spiritual as well as the secular education of the nation.[40] D.V. Athalye remarks that Vivekananda's patriotism was but another name for his love for Hinduism. Religious zeal and patriotic fervour were interdependent in him so that in his dictionary both were synonymous terms.[41]

Conquest of the world by Hindu spirituality

Although Vivekananda considered that a person's hereditary religion is the best for him, he did begin a crusade to conquer the world by Hindu spirituality. He believed that Advaita should be taught to all people everywhere, not only in India but also outside. He maintained that the tragedy of the world is that Advaita was never allowed to reach all people. So, he demanded that it should be taught to the whole world with the voice of thunder, to every man that is born, to saints and sinners, men, women and children, to the man on the throne and to the man sweeping the streets so that they may drink 'the streams of life', instead of 'the ditch water'.[42] In a speech he delivered in Madras, Vivekananda said: "...the world must be conquered by India. This is the dream of my life, and I wish that each one of you who hears me today, will have the same dream in your minds, and stop not till you have realised the dream. [...]This is the great ideal before us, and every one must be ready for it, the conquest of the whole world by India is noting less than that, and we must all get ready for it, strain every nerve for it. [...] Up, India, conquer the world with your spirituality. [...] heroic workers are wanted to go abroad and help to disseminate the great truths of the Vedanta."[43]

Thus, with the spirit of a crusader, Vivekananda spoke of a conquest of the world by the Hindu race and Hindu religion, and invited all his fellow religionists to get ready for it and to sacrifice everything for it. He said: "Now is the time to work for India's spiritual ideas penetrating deep into the West. [...] We must go out, we must conquer the world through our spirituality and philosophy. There is no other alternative; we must do it or die."[44] "Therefore, preach the Advaita to every one so that religion may withstand the shock of modern science. Not only so, you will have to help others: your thought will help out Europe and America."[45]

In making Advaita a propagating religion, Vivekananda also made it a *converting* religion. He wanted all people to accept the only true religion of Advaita, which certainly implied giving up one's ancestral religion.

Crusade against religious conversion

In Vivekananda there was a hidden element of *intolerance* towards Christianity, Islam and other so-called proselytising religions. D.V. Athalye notes that nothing pained Vivekananda so much as the reckless conversion of the people by Muslims and the Christian missionaries.[46] Vivekananda claimed that when the Muslims first came to India there was a great number of Hindus in this country. But, today, their number has dwindled considerably, and everyday they are becoming less, and some day they will disappear completely and with it also Advaita – the jewel of all spirituality.[47] Hence, he made a clarion call to all the Hindus saying: "Therefore, arise, awake, with your hands stretched out to protect the spirituality of the world."[48] He accused Christianity of being intolerant. He presented Hinduism as the most tolerant of all religions, which has never persecuted, never conquered and never shed blood.[49] Athalye says that Vivekananda was of the opinion that the Hindu society should not allow their sons and daughters, brothers and sisters to be taken away by foreigners because they are the children of the Vedic sages and, therefore, they should not become toys in the hands of scheming missionaries of rival religions – be it that of Buddhism, Islam or Christianity.[50]

Proselytisation by Swami Vivekananda

Vivekananda often held the view that a religion in which one is born is the best religion suited to one's nature. Hence, a

Christian is not to become a Hindu or Buddhist, nor a Hindu or Buddhist to become a Christian. But, each must assimilate the spirit of others and yet preserve his individuality and grow according to his own law of growth.[51] This means that religious conversion in the sense of changing religion for another is ruled out. Vivekananda said: "Do I wish that the Christian should become a Hindu? God forbid. Do I wish that the Hindu or the Buddhist should become a Christian? God forbid."[52] But, in his practical life, he often deviated from this doctrine and engaged in proselytisation. D.V. Athalye notes that it was the considered opinion of Vivekananda that Hinduism must not only begin to reconstruct people but also proselytise.[53] Vivekananda once declared: "Take Madras. We must start a temple, must have a temple, for, with Hindus religion must come first. [...] along with this temple there should be an institution to train teachers and preachers. These teachers must go about preaching both religion and secular knowledge to our people; they must carry both as we have been already carrying religion from door to door. [...] gradually we shall have similar temples in other centres, [...] we will go to every country under the sun [...]. We must enter into the life of every race inside India and outside India."[54]

There are instances in the life of Vivekananda in which he actually converted non-Hindus to Vedantic Hinduism. When Vivekananda opposed conversion, he opposed conversion of Hindus to other religions, not conversion of others to Hinduism. A.L. Basham notes that from the first visit of Vivekananda to America, neo-Hinduism has been slowly making converts outside India.[55] Among the converts in the USA were Madam Marie Louise and Herr Leon Londsberg who came to be called Swami Abhayananda and Swami Kripananda respectively.[56] Similarly, in England, J.J. Goodwin, Margaret Noble and Mr. and Mrs. Sevier became his disciples. Margaret Noble later became Sister Nivedita.[57]

In 1895, at Thousand Island Park, Vivekananda initiated Christina Greenstidel together with three others into

Hinduism, and all of them took the vow of *brahmacharya* (celibacy).[58] In 1896, he gave to some of his students formal *diksha* (initiation) into Hindu way of life; to some others he gave *brahmacharya* (celibacy) and to a select few he gave *sanyasa*. One Dr. Street took *sanyasa* and Vivekananda named him Swami Yogananda. He was the third *sanyasin* he made in America.[59] Again, in one of the letters of Swami Kripananda, we read: "Swamiji made several young men and women his disciples, giving them a mantra [.... he] gave vows of brahmacharya to at least three people – Miss Waldo, Mr. Goodwin and young Mr. Van Haagen."[60]

About Margaret Noble's conversion to Hinduism, Romain Rolland writes that she was twenty-eight when she made up her mind to place her fate in Swami's hand. He made her come to India, forced her to become a Hindu, to Hinduise her thoughts, her conceptions, her habits and to forget even the memory of her own past. She took the vow of *brahmacharya* (celibacy).[61] About the efforts of Swami Vivekananda to make Margaret Noble change her faith, we read: "Patiently, though not always gently, for the time was short, the Swami unearthed, unmasked, demolished all that stood in the path of her potential greatness and usefulness."[62] "Swamiji steeped her mind in his; he imbued her with a profound understanding of India [....] he initiated her more and more deeply into the realms of spirituality."[63] "Giving Margaret Noble the first monastic vows – the vows of brahmacharya – shortly after her arrival in Calcutta, the Swami bestowed upon her the name Nivedita – 'the dedicated'."[64] Later Vivekananda wrote to Swami Ramakrishnananda: "Miss Noble is really an acquisition."[65]

Thus, Vivekananda, in making Advaita a propagating religion, made it a *converting religion*. He wanted all people to accept the only true religion of Advaita which certainly implied the giving up of one's ancestral religion. This is nothing but conversion in the sense of change from one religion to another, which he often opposed. Besides, one of the aims of establishing the Ramakrishna Mission was to preach Advaita. He set up Ramakrishna Mission centres in the USA and Europe.[66]

Advocate of re-conversion to Hinduism

Vivekananda not only converted non-Hindus to Hinduism but also strongly advocated re-conversion of those Hindus who accepted other religions. He disparagingly called those who have been converted to Islam and Christianity 'Hindu perverts'.[67] When asked whether it was legitimate to receive back into Hinduism those who have been converted, Vivekananda said that "they can and ought to be taken [back to Hinduism]".[68] If re-conversion is not done, he argued, the numerical strength of the Hindu would go on weakening the Hindu society. He even insisted to give Hindu names to those 'aliens' or non-Hindus who are converted and those who are re-converted to Hinduism, because he says that there is a great deal in a name.[69] Only a person with an extreme sense of fanaticism can say the words that were uttered by Vivekananda: "...every man going out of the Hindu pale is not only a man less, but an enemy the more."[70]

P.S. Daniel observes that when Vivekananda opposed conversion, what he opposed was conversion of Hindus to other religions. But, for him, the conversion of others to Vedantic Hinduism was an imperative. Such a narrow view from a much respected person like Vivekananda, who claimed to have dedicated his whole life for the propagation of the idea of religious tolerance on the basis of the harmony and unity of all religions, hardly differs from the aggressive and militant attitude of Swami Dayananda Saraswati.[71]

Attack on Buddhism

Vivekananda was at times aggressive and militant in his attitude towards other religions. In fact, he was a vocal critic of all religions other than his own. For example, he considered Buddhism as the rebel child of Hinduism.[72] He argued that as a religion Buddhism was extremely iconoclastic, superstitious and negative in outlook, which explains the reasons for its disappearance from the land of its birth.[73] According to him, the Buddhists have degraded India. He says: "To-day [sic] it is the fashion to talk of Buddhism, and Buddhistic agnosticism [...]. Little do they dream that this degradation which we have in our hands to-day [sic] has been left by Buddhism."[74] Then, he adds: "Perhaps my Buddha brothers will be offended at this remark, and fret and fume; but there's no help for it; the truth ought to be told, and I do not care for the result."[75]

According to Vivekananda, the essence of Buddhism and even the great ethical principles of the Buddha were borrowed from some Upanishads.[76] Concerning the philosophical battle that went on between the Hindus and the Buddhists for centuries, he says: "On the philosophic side the disciples of the great Master [the Buddha] dashed themselves against the eternal rocks of the *Vedas* and could not crush them, and on the other side they took away from the nation that eternal God to which every man and woman clings so fondly. And the result was that it had to die its natural death in India."[77]

While in India Vivekananda seldom had a good word for Buddhism and maintained that the most hideous ceremonies, the most horrible, the most obscene books that human hands ever wrote or the human brain ever conceived, the most bestial forms that ever passed under the name of religion, have all been the creation of degraded Buddhism.[78] But, contrary to this, as occasion demanded, especially during his travels abroad, the same Vivekananda played a different tune. For example, while in America, he said: "Buddhism is the most important religion of history, representing the most tremendous religious movement the world ever saw."[79] "We cannot live without you [Buddhists], nor you without us [....] you cannot stand without the brain and philosophy of the Brahman, nor we without your heart. This separation between the Buddhist and the Brahman is the cause of the downfall of India."[80]

Attack on Christianity

Vivekananda made statements about Christianity which were also equally aggressive. He considered Christianity as nothing but "a collection of little bits of Indian thought" and 'a very patchy imitation' or 'an offshoot' of Hinduism. According to him, Christianity is always propagated by the sword.[81] He said: "...the christian [sic] nations have filled the world with bloodshed and tyranny. [....] You drink the idea in your mother's milk that you are angels and we are devils."[82]. "With all your brag and boastings, where has your Christianity succeeded without the sword? [...] I know your forefathers were converted. They had to be converted or killed, that was all."[83] About Western Christianity he said that the influence of Roman and Greek religions is all there in Christianity. In it one sees old gods coming in a new fashion with changed names. Thus, the goddesses became Marys and the gods became saints.[84] He adds: "What did I learn in the West, and what did I see behind those talks of frothy nonsense of the Christian religious sects saying that man was a fallen and hopelessly fallen sinner?"[85] "These 'churchwomen' are awful fanatics. They are under the thumb of the priests there [America]. Between them and the priests they make hell of earth and make a mess of religion."[86] "Therein lies the difference between the scriptures of the Christians or the Buddhists and ours [Hindus]; theirs are all Puranas and not scriptures [...] So far as the Bible and the scriptures of other nations agree with the Vedas, they are perfectly good, but when they do not agree, they are no more to be accepted. so with the Koran."[87] "In Europe, there is My Lord the Cardinal who is struggling hard and spending thousands of pounds to prove the nobility of his ancestors, and he will not be satisfied until he has traced his ancestry to some dreadful tyrant."[88] He also criticised some of the basic beliefs of Christianity, such as the doctrine of the Body and Blood of Christ, sense of sin, role of history, etc. Speaking about the care of the poor and the downtrodden by Christians, he said:

"Christian missionaries come and offer life but only on condition that the Hindoos [sic] become Christians."[89] Once in Madras, he publicly stated: "...one fifth and – one half – of your Madras people will become Christians if you do not take care."[90]

Attack on Islam

Vivekananda was also highly critical and pessimistic about Islam. He remarked: "Mark, when the Mahomedans first came into India, there were 60 millions of Hindus here: to-day there are less than 20 millions. Everyday they will become less and less till the whole disappear. [...] And with them will disappear this marvellous Advaita, the created jewel of all spiritual thought. Therefore, arise, awake, and with all your hands stretch out to protect the spirituality of the world."[91]

Influence of Swami Vivekananda on Hindutva ideology

Swami Vivekananda interpreted the *Bhagavadgita* along the line of Bal Gangadhar Tilak, insisting on action or *karma-yoga*.[92] Tilak wrote in the *Mahratta* that Swami Vivekananda is the real father of modern nationalism.[93] He founded the Ramakrishna Mission in order to teach *karma-yoga* and *shakti* (power, energy). His *karma-yoga* influenced Tilak and Aurobindo. *Shakti* is the feminine aspect of the divinity which symbolises power and energy. Vivekananda believed that national rejuvenation would come only when Indians tapped this potential source of power. He advocated the *Shakti* cult, which was later taken up by Aurobindo Ghose and his brother Barindra Ghose.

The RSS has found Vivekananda's message of Hindu revivalism quite compatible with its own belief system. In fact, he has become an important symbol within the RSS and an inspiration for a Hindu lay-order dedicated to strengthening Hindu identity among groups vulnerable to other creeds. M.S. Golwalkar translated into Marathi the speeches of Vivekananda.[94] Vivekananda's picture hangs on the walls of many swayamsevaks' homes. Books about him serve as primers on nationalism. His message of self-esteem and national revitalisation are the subject of innumerable RSS *baudhik* (intellectual discourses) sessions.[95]

To commemorate the Swami Vivekananda's birth centenary in 1963 the RSS leadership decided to bring out a collection of Vivekananda's writings. Eknath Ranade was commissioned to edit the volume. After completing the book Ranade became intrigued by the idea of further popularising the views of Vivekananda and in time decided to establish a secular lay-order to do so.[96] Vivekananda's thoughts have also influenced Jan Sangh.[97] On 22 February 2004, when the BJP-led NDA government was in power, foundation was laid for the Vivekananda Kendra International in New Delhi.[98]

The double face of Vivekananda

Vivekananda was a staunch defender of Hinduism. Through his militant speeches and writings, polemic statements and hypercritical remarks he kindled among many Hindus a spirit of religious fanaticism, militancy, dislike for other religions, and became a symbol of Hindu arrogance and superiority. Unfortunately, this was in addition to projecting himself as a champion of Hindu tolerance and unity of all religions. Therefore, we may rightly maintain that Vivekananda had *two faces* as far as his religious philosophy was concerned: one of religious *tolerance and universalism*, and the other of Hindu *fundamentalism and fanaticism*. The two contradictory faces were quite in keeping with his concept of religion, for he said: "The intensest [sic] love that humanity has ever known has come from religion, and the most diabolical hatred that humanity has known has come from religion. The noblest words of peace that the world has ever heard have come from men on this plane, and the bitterest denunciation that the world has ever known has sprung from religious men. [...] Nothing is as cruel as religion, nothing makes us so tender as religion."[99] Again, it was Vivekananda who declared that fanaticism is a peculiar disease of the humankind and the most dangerous of all diseases, and he did not hesitate to call them lunatics.[100] He knew well that religious exclusiveness was the root cause of religious hostility and intolerance. Yet, on occasions, *Vivekananda himself was a victim of that terrible 'disease' called fanaticism,* as is clear from the above analysis of his religious thought. He not only defended Hinduism with the spirit of a crusader, but was also actively engaged in an aggressive, offensive and militant polemic against other religions, and advocated Hindu proselytisation and re-conversion of those Hindus who accepted other religions. Athalye observes that to make Hinduism aggressive and dynamic was the mission of the Swami.[101] Some even consider Swami Vivekananda as a freemason.[102]

Conclusion

The seeds of religious fundamentalism, fanaticism and militancy, which Vivekananda so subtly sowed a century ago, are still bearing abundant fruit in post-modern India in the form of the revival of Hindu fundamentalism, nationwide network of Hindu militant organisations, aggressive propagation of the Hindutva ideology and politicisation of the Hindu religion, re-conversion (*shuddhi*) and proselytisation activities. We may rightly sum up our analysis of the religious thought of Vivekananda in the words of P.S. Daniel: "Hidden in the Hindu tolerance is a sort of acute intolerance which can be noted not only in Vivekananda but also in many modern Hindu thinkers."[103]

Notes

1. Professor William Hastie, Principal of the General Assembly's Institution (now called the Scottish Church College, Calcutta) said about his pupil Narendaranath (future Swami Vivekananda): "Naren is really a genius. I have travelled far and wide, but I have never yet come across a lad of his talents and possibilities. He is bound to make a mark

in life." Disciples, p. 26 as cited in R.C. Majumdar, *Swami Vivekananda*, 10.

2. Narendranath studied the standard treatises on Western Logic and Philosophy. His deep studies of the Western philosophers like Mill, Hume, Descartes, Darwin and Spencer, and the scientific methods and discoveries in Europe led him to have a rationalistic outlook to life. See R.C. Majumdar, *Swami Vivekananda*, 10.
3. It is reported that, one day Narendranath met Ramakrishna Paramahamsa, a priest in the temple of goddess Kali at Dakshineswar, near Calcutta. Narendranath asked him: "Have you seen God?" "Yes, I have seen Him as I am seeing you", was the prompt reply of Ramakrishna. Ramakrishna further told Narendranath that he could make Narendranath see God. See R.C. Majumdar, *Swami Vivekananda*, 15-16.
4. See R.C. Majumdar, *Swami Vivekananda*, 25-26.
5. Ibid., 39.
6. See P.S. Daniel, *Hindu Response,* 120-178.
7. See *The Complete Works of Swami Vivekananda*, vol. 1, 318, 326.
8. Ibid., 468; also, vol. 4, 174.
9. Ibid., 2, 365; also, vol. 4, 191.
10. *The Complete Works of Swami Vivekananda*, vol. 9, 429.
11. Ibid., vol. 2, 381.
12. Ibid., vol. 5, 81.
13. Ibid., vol. 1, 393-403.
14. Ibid., vol. 5, 81-82.
15. Ibid., vol. 3, 324.
16. Ibid., vol. 6, 122.
17. Ibid., vol. 8, 141.
18. See P.S. Daniel, *Hindu Response,* 163.
19. *Speeches and Writings of Swami Vivekananda*, vol. 2, 430.
20. *The Complete Works of Swami Vivekananda*, vol. 2, 247.
21. See *The Complete Works of Swami Vivekananda*, vol. 3, 324.
22. *Speeches and Writings of Swami Vivekananda*, vol. 2, 453.
23. *The Complete Works of Swami Vivekananda*, vol. 6, 415.
24. *Speeches and Writings of Swami Vivekananda*, vol. 2, 427-428 (Emphasis added).
25. See *The Complete Works of Swami Vivekananda*, vol. 8, 137.

26. See P.S. Daniel, *Hindu Response,* 158.
27. Ibid., 136.
28. See *The Complete Works of Swami Vivekananda*, vol. 3, 432.
29. See P.S. Daniel, *Hindu Response,* 144.
30. Ibid., 147.
31. Ibid., 147, 149.
32. See *The Complete Works of Swami Vivekananda*, vol. 6, 103,105.
33. Ibid., vol. 4, 188,343.
34. Ibid., vol. 9, 429.
35. *Speeches and Writings of Swami Vivekananda*, vol. 2, 563.
36. See *The Complete Works of Swami Vivekananda*, vol. 4, 343.
37. See *Speeches and Writings of Swami Vivekananda*, vol. 2, 424.
38. Ibid., 526 (emphasis added).
39. *The Complete Works of Swami Vivekananda*, vol. 5, 81.
40. See *Speeches and Writings of Swami Vivekananda*, vol. 2, 556.
41. See D.V. Athalye, *Swami Vivekananda*, 9.
42. See *The Complete Works of Swami Vivekananda*, vol. 2, 199.
43. *Speeches and Writings of Swami Vivekananda*, vol. 2, 561-562.
44. Ibid., 563.
45. Ibid., *401.*
46. See D.V. Athalye, *Swami Vivekananda*, 10.
47. See *The Complete Works of Swami Vivekananda*, vol. 3, 432.
48. *The Complete Works of Swami Vivekananda*, vol. 3, 432.
49. See *The Complete Works of Swami Vivekananda*, vol. 1, 3; vol. 3, 274; vol. 5,190.
50. See D.V. Athalye, *Swami Vivekananda*, 10.
51. See *The Complete Works of Swami Vivekananda*, vol. 1, 24.
52. *Speeches and Writings of Swami Vivekananda*, vol. 1, 50.
53. See D.V. Athalye, *Swami Vivekananda*, 10-11.
54. *Speeches and Writings of Swami Vivekananda*, vol. 2, 557-558.
55. See A.L. Basham, "Hinduism", 253.
56. See G.M. Willims, *The Quest for Meaning*, 60.
57. See R. Rolland, *The Life of Vivekananda*, 92-94.
58. M.L. Burke, *Swami Vivekananda in the West,* vol. 3, 151.
59. Ibid., 518.
60. Ibid., 520.

61. See R. Rolland, *The Life of Vivekananda*, 93.
62. M.L. Burke, *Swami Vivekananda in the West,* vol. 5, 10.
63. Ibid., 37.
64. Ibid., 9.
65. Ibid., 9.
66. See P.S. Daniel, *Hindu Response,* 149, 151.
67. See *The Complete Works of Swami Vivekananda*, vol. 5, 233.
68. *The Complete Works of Swami Vivekananda*, vol. 5, 233.
69. See *The Complete Works of Swami Vivekananda*, vol. 5, 233-234.
70. *The Complete Works of Swami Vivekananda*, vol. 5, 233.
71. See P.S. Daniel, *Hindu Response,* 151-152.
72. See *The Complete Works of Swami Vivekananda*, vol. 3, 275.
73. Ibid., vol. 4,326.
74. *Speeches and Writings of Swami Vivekananda*, vol. 2, 544.
75. *The Complete Works of Swami Vivekananda*, vol. 5, 455.
76. See *Speeches and Writings of Swami Vivekananda*, vol. 2, 405.
77. *Speeches and Writings of Swami Vivekananda*, vol. 2, 490.
78. See *Speeches and Writings of Swami Vivekananda*, vol. 2, 467.
79. M.L. Burke, *Swami Vivekananda in the West,* vol. 5, 385.
80. Ibid., vol. 1, 132.
81. See *The Complete Works of Swami Vivekananda*, vol. 7, 43.
82. M.L. Burke, *Swami Vivekananda in the West,* vol. 1, 415.
83. *The Complete Works of Swami Vivekananda*, vol. 8, 212-213.
84. See *Speeches and Writings of Swami Vivekananda*, vol. 2, 545.
85. *Speeches and Writings of Swami Vivekananda*, vol. 2, 436-437.
86. M.L. Burke, *Swami Vivekananda in the West,* vol. 1, 221.
87. *The Complete Works of Swami Vivekananda*, vol. 3, 333.
88. *Speeches and Writings of Swami Vivekananda*, vol. 2, 445.
89. M.L. Burke, *Swami Vivekananda in the West,* vol. 1, 124.
90. *Speeches and Writings of Swami Vivekananda*, vol. 2, 549.
91. Ibid., 399-400.
92. See D.D. Pattanaik, *Hindu Nationalism*, vol. 2, 16.
93. Ibid., 22.
94. See P. Kanungo, *RSS's Tryst with Politics*, 51.
95. See W.K. Andersen and S.D. Damle, *The Brotherhood in Saffron*, 38.
96. Ibid., 137.

97. See P.C. Swain, *Bharatiya Janata Party*, 61.
98. See D.K. Rath, "A Centre for Dialogue on Civilisations", 17.
99. See *Speeches and Writings of Swami Vivekananda*, vol. 1, 303-304.
100. Ibid., 306.
101. See D.V. Athalye, *Swami Vivekananda*, 10.
102. See "Some Eminent Freemasons", 53.
103. P.S. Daniel, *Hindu Response*, 178, endnote 253.

• III •

Bal Gangadhar Tilak's Rationalisation of Violence through the Interpretation of the *Gita*

Bal Gangadhar Tilak was born on 23 July 1856 in an orthodox Chitapavan Brahmin family in the small town of Ratnagiri in Maharashtra. Tilak's father lived on a small salary, which he supplemented with earning from writing textbooks. His mother passed away when he was ten years old and his father when he was sixteen. He joined the Deccan College, Poona, in 1872, obtained his Bachelor of Arts (B.A.) degree in 1876 with Mathematics and Sanskrit, and completed his education with a Law degree in 1879. In the years that followed, he emerged as a formidable political leader, Sanskrit scholar, writer[1] and political philosopher with radical views. Tilak was greatly influenced by Western thought on politics and metaphysics[2] and was to a great extent a product of English education.

Tilak was foremost among the earlier generation of national leaders who had fought for the independence of India. He was accused of instigating people to violence, criticised for his extremist activities and rated among the most controversial leaders of India's struggle for independence. K.M. Panikkar, the noted historian, says: "He [Tilak] was the recognised leader of the 'Extremists' in India who considered it their duty 'to rise up and fight' foreigners in Indian soil."[3] In fact, together with Bipin Chandra Pal, Lala Lajpat Rai and Aurobindo Ghose he constituted an 'extremist' core within the Indian National Congress.[4] In spite of this, Tilak was respected and held in high esteem even by foreign intellectuals for his scholarship, but was feared for his extremism. As a wielder of a sharp pen he used his talent to promote extremism and oppose foreign rule, especially through his *Kesari* (in Marathi)[5] and *Mahratta* (in English), which were started in 1881 The columns in these newspapers unfold his compelling, strong and radical personality and militant political views. Jawaharlal Nehru in his autobiography wrote: "...the great and indomitable Tilak who would not bend though he break."[6] Tilak later came to be called 'Lokamanya' ('Honoured of the People'). However, as far as social questions were concerned, he was a conservative. Tilak died in Bombay on 1 August 1920.

Extremist tradition in India as an underestimated factor

The obscure role played by forces of militancy and extremism has often gone unnoticed in the course of the liberation of India due to the overwhelming impact of Mahatma Gandhi's non-violence (*ahimsa*). Thus, the militant tradition in India has not been fully explored and remains to a great extent underestimated. What one hears mostly is the non-violent Gandhi. But there are also personalities like Bal Gangadhar Tilak who professed a different ethics from that of Gandhi and followed a trend of extremism and violence, which earned him the appellation of the 'father of Indian unrest'.

The re-emergence of Hindu nationalist ideology in the recent decades, with its glorification of violence, militancy, extremism, communalism, religious fundamentalism and ethics of 'end justifies the means', has a long history. Tilak is among the prominent leaders of modern India who has significantly influenced the extremist form of Hindu nationalism. He advocated 'violence as the higher duty' based on his interpretation of the *Bhagavadgita* ('Song of the Lord'), the best read text among the Hindus,[7] dismissing in the process the popularly accepted commentaries of the *Gita* by Adi Sankara (8th century A.D.) and Ramanuja (1017-1133 A.D.) advocating renunciation and devotionalism respectively. Thus, Tilak became a forerunner to many new interpretations of Hindu scriptures, especially *Ramayana* and *Mahabharata*, from a militant point of view.

Tilak's commentary on the *Gita*

The *Gita* is an episode in India's great epic *Mahabharata*.[8] Tilak was taught that the *Bhagavadgita* contained all the principles and philosophy of the Hindu religion. Hence, he thought it necessary to find an answer in this book to his queries. Thus began his study of the *Gita*.[9] His commentary on the *Gita*, which came to be called *Gitarahasya* ('The Secret of the *Gita*') was a very influential one. In this work he expounded with a wealth of scholarship and unimpeachable orthodoxy the doctrine of 'energism' or action (*karma-yoga*). He started his commentary in November 1910 and completed it in March 1911 though he could publish it only in 1915. He claims that his commentary is an independent and original one investigating the purpose of the *Gita* and showing how the Hindu religious philosophy is applied to the solution of the ethical problems involved in everyday life. Hence, the *Gita* is a work of ethics, more specifically how Hindu religious philosophy is applied to solve ethical problems.[10]

Tilak claims that he approached the *Gita* with a mind pre-occupied by no previous ideas about any philosophy, and had no theory of his own for which he sought support in the sacred book. He says: "I believe I have succeeded in it, because having no theory of mine for which I sought any support from the book so universally respected, I had no reason to twist the text to suit my theory."[11]

In the *Gita*, Arjuna was perplexed about what his duty was, whether he should or should not take part in the *Kurukshetra* war. If he engages in war, the result would be committing heinous sins like the destruction of his own clan, though it was the duty of every *kshatriya* (warrior) to fight. Thus, on the one hand, the religion of the warrior was saying to him 'fight' and on the other hand, devotion to his ancestors, preceptors, love for his brethren, affection for his relatives, and other natural laws were urging him 'not to fight'. If he fought it would be a fight with his own people and he would incur the terrible sin of killing his ancestors, preceptors and relatives. If he did not fight, he would be failing in his duty as a warrior.[12]

Tilak argues that the *Gita* was expounded by Lord Krishna in order to induce Arjuna, who was dejected by the idea that it was sin to engage in war with one's own kith and kin. Tilak says that the conclusion he arrived after his study is that the *Gita* advocates the performance of action in this world even after the actor has achieved the highest union with the Supreme Deity by *jnana* (knowledge) or *bhakti* (devotion). This action must be done to keep the world going by the right path of evolution which the Creator has destined the world to follow.[13]

Thus, according to Tilak, what is expounded in the *Gita* is not the 'path of renunciation' (*jnana marga*) or the 'path of devotion' (*bhakti marga*) but the 'path of righteous action (*karma-yoga*).[14] By action (*karma*) Tilak means duty, and the duty for a *kshatriya* (warrior) like Arjuna, is to fight. It is his *karma-yoga* ('special device of performing actions').[15] The paths of renunciation and devotion advocate indifference to the world which in effect emasculates the devotees of the *Gita* and fill them with apathy. Thus, he was convinced that the original *Gita* did not preach the philosophy of renunciation but energism (*karma-yoga*).[16] Hence, he presents *karma-yoga* as superior to renunciation and devotion.[17] He says: "look upon your science of Proper Action (Karma-Yoga) as a most important science."[18] His conviction was strengthened by the study of the epic *Mahabharata*, the *Vedanta Sutras*, the

Upanishads and other Sanskrit and English treatises on the Vedanta.[19] When many outstanding commentators of the *Gita* considered the 'path of action' as inferior to other paths, Tilak staunchly advocated it. However, he says that there are also others who consider *karma-yoga* as the most excellent path, for example, the Marathi poet Vaman Pandit.[20]

Tilak maintained that the doctrine of *karma-yoga* is not a new theory. It is so ancient that not even Krishna was the great teacher who first propounded it. It is India's sacred heritage from time immemorial.[21] *Karma-yoga* is the method which leads to the attainment of both material and spiritual glory.[22] Finally, Tilak tells us that, though the *Gitarahasya* could be published only in 1915, the ideas contained in it he had in mind for over 20 years or more.[23]

Gita teaches warrior morality

Tilak argues that *Gita* has been narrated in order to induce Arjuna to do his duty, when he was on the point of giving up. Warfare was his lot according to his duty (*svadharma*).[24] Hence, Krishna explicitly asked Arjuna to fight in accordance with his caste duty (*dharma*).[25] Consequently, Arjuna did fight and in the course of it, he actually killed Bhishma, Karna, Jayadratha, and others as occasion arose.[26] Tilak argues that it is enshrined in the *Gita* that it is morally right to give measure for measure to immoral persons.[27] Thus, Tilak promotes a warrior-morality and a warrior-religion. In the *Gitarahasya* we read: "...there [in the *Gita*] the warrior-religion has been pronounced [by Sri Krishna] to be superior to the law of fraternity."[28]

Rationalisation of violence

In many Hindu leaders of recent past we can observe a discernible trend of Hindu self-assertion and aggressiveness, and Tilak is one such ideologue. The dilemma which many Hindus face today is how to be aggressive and militant and shed the garb of being non-violent and passive. Should one use violence or non-violence? How to justify it rationally? How to find foundations for it in Hindu scriptures?

Basing on the *Gita*, Tilak projects violence as a duty. He cites Krishna who declares that if everyone becomes harmless, warriorship cannot be continued and when once warriorship comes to an end, subjects will have no protectors and anybody will be in a position to destroy anybody else.[29] Krishna says: "Oh Kesava [Arjuna], that Ksatriya is truly law-abiding, who kills such persons as break laws, ethical principles, or rules of proper conduct, or is greedy or sinful, notwithstanding that they occupy the position of preceptors."[30]

In the *Gita* Krishna says: "Better one's duty (though) imperfect than another's well performed."[31] What is the duty is specified empirically, and it can even be expedience. The influence of Immanuel Kant who said 'duty for duty sake' as a categorical imperative is evident here. According to orthodox Hinduism, duties are determined by one's caste, and one's caste is hereditary. Since Arjuna belonged to the warrior caste (*kshatriya*), his duty was already determined by birth, i.e., to fight, or to engage in violence.

Tilak observes that the ethics of worldly life is very subtle.[32] Violence thus received a gallant endorsement from Tilak. But, he followed a subjective ethics delineated to suit his militancy and extremism. According to him, when needed, one should give measure for measure by way of retaliation and protect oneself.[33]

Tilak used the *Gita* to justify his violent and militant nationalist campaign and other activities connected with it. This attitude made Gandhi to say: "...he [Tilak] frankly differed from me in my extreme views on non-violence."[34]

Violence as the higher law

As we have seen, it is the authority of *Gita* which is at the foundation of Tilak's ethics. He argued for the justification of violence and termed it the *higher law*. As stated earlier, Tilak was known as the 'father of Indian unrest', an extremist and a relentless fighter. He saw it appropriate to retaliate with violence, and considered it as good, necessary and morally justified. Once in the course of discussion between Gandhi and Tilak on violence and non-violence, the latter upheld the principle of tit for tat[35] and considered the *satyagraha* of Gandhi as a weapon of the weak.[36] Militancy, and not mendicancy, was his call to defend Indian dignity. Hence, his concept of *swaraj* ('self-rule') endorsed the use of violence in its various forms including militancy and terrorism for the pursuit for national independence.

Tilak took as his model Shivaji (1627-1680), the great Maratha leader, whose ethics was at times ambivalent, as is evident especially from his treatment of Afzal Khan, the Mughal General, whom he treacherously murdered. Ivan Strenski maintains that in Tilak's case, his ambivalence in the matter of the assassination of colonial administrator Walter Charles Rand, seems to re-play the same ambivalence that affects Shivaji. Neither act can be said to have been honourable or forthright. Both relied on treachery, deceit and deception.[37] But they are considered justified since they come under the so-called violence as the higher duty.

Arjuna as the model in the use of violence as higher duty

Tilak says that in the *Gita*, Arjuna has been induced to fight since it has been declared as the best of all paths by the *Gita* and nowhere he has been asked to give up action.[38] Everywhere in the *Gita*, the only advice given to Arjuna by Krishna is that he should perform action.[39] Hence, Tilak asks: "If the *Gita* was preached to desponding Arjuna to make him ready for the fight – for the action – how can it be said that the ultimate lesson of the great book is Bhakti or Gnana alone?"[40] As is evident, utilitarianism and ethics of 'end justifies the means' are at the foundation of his interpretation of the *Gita*.

The result of Tilak's interpretation of the *Gita*, advocating the so-called violence as higher duty, was disastrous for the Indian society. Communal violence against Muslims increased rather than decreased with the rise of Tilak.[41] Many were influenced by Tilak's radical ethics based on the *Gita*. Damodar Chapekar, who was executed for the crime of assassinating a British officer, appealed to Tilak for a copy of the *Gita* on the eve of the execution, and the latter gave him his own copy of the sacred book, and the young man went to the gallows carrying it.[42] Roshan Lal, who was sentenced to death for his involvement in the Kakori Conspiracy Case (1925) in which revolutionaries successfully derailed a train near Kakori railway station and looted the government treasure it was carrying, went to the gallows carrying a copy of the *Gita* in his hands.[43]

K.M. Panikkar says that *Gitarahasya* makes no direct allusion to politics. But, the political meaning was clear enough because of the author's own background and political circumstances of the time in India.[44] To Tilak it was clear that it was only through the message of the *Gita* that India could save herself.[45]

Impact of Tilak's ethics: Rise of militant Hinduism and communalism

The manner in which a religion chooses to interpret its sacred scriptures in conflict resolution has far-reaching consequences. The ethics of *Gitarahasya* took the form of militant Hinduism and political extremism. It found practical expressions in a number of initiatives which promoted communalism and politics based on religion, like, the celebration of Ganesh[46] festivals, Shivaji festivals, Anti-Cow Killing Societies, Gymnastic Societies, extremist journalism and militant activities. They awakened Hindu consciousness among many Hindus, which resulted in increased anti-minority feelings and acts of violence and extremism in many parts of India.

Ganesh festivals

Tilak was perhaps the first Indian political leader who realised the strength of the masses. He evolved many programmes in order to bring people together. He argued that hero worship is at the root of nationality, social order and religion.[47] Nehru remarked that Tilak was the first political leader of the new India who reached the masses and drew strength from them.[48]

In 1895, Tilak inaugurated the Ganapati festivals.[49] Ganesh is one of the most popular of the deities worshipped by the Hindus. The Ganapati movement was inaugurated by Tilak as a counterpoise to the Muslim festival Muharram in which Hindus of the lower castes participated.[50] Till then, Ganapati festivals had nothing of a public character. But, Tilak succeeded in transforming a simple domestic rite into a public celebration.[51]

In 1894, Tilak with the help of the Natu brothers was responsible for making the festival a public event lasting ten days with music and an organised procession involving boys from schools and colleges.[52] Songs were sung in praise of Tilak and Shivaji. Boys were engaged in fencing and other physical exercises. The Natu brothers taught them sword and single stick exercises.[53]

Stanley A. Walport observes that through the Ganapati festivals Tilak succeeded in bringing together the hitherto ignored urban and peasant lower classes, indoctrinating them with political songs and speeches, drilling young men to march about town in militant groups and imparting to Hinduism a congregational character hitherto unknown to it.[54] During the processions they shouted: "O Heroes of Hind" and "Adore your country as God."[55]

Often, the Ganapati festivals provoked the Muslim community. Tilak wrote articles in a tone which was very offence to the Muslims, calling the Hindus to abstain from acting as the bearers of the corpses of Hassan and Hussain, that the weeping stories of the Muslims in their Muharram celebrations have nothing in them that would awake patriotism.[56] In 1894 and 1895 Tilak held special Ganapati meetings in his own house at Poona where songs were sung in which moderate Hindus and the British government were denounced, and Tilak approved these songs.[57]

David Smith observes that the worship of Ganesh was reinvented in Maharashtra by the great independent leader Tilak. Today, the Ganesh festival is the largest Hindu public religious performance in Maharashtra.[58] Yogendra K. Malik and V.B. Singh remind us that Tilak's use of the Ganesh festivals was an example of the use of traditional religious symbols to mobilise the Hindus in the cause of Hindu nationalism.[59] According to Walport, with the Ganesh festivals, militant Hinduism's first modern cadre was born.[60]

Shivaji festivals

Tilak was also instrumental in reviving the memory of Shivaji and setting in motion a great national propaganda which culminated in 1895 in the celebration at the chief centres of Brahmin activity in the Deccan of Shivaji's reputed birthday.[61] According to Tilak, the Shivaji festivals serve like manure to the seeds of enthusiasm and the spirit of nationalism.[62] He saw in this festival a peculiar value for the whole country, and argued that it is the duty of everyone to see that this character of the festival is not ignored or misrepresented.[63]

Shivaji festivals at times created tension between the Muslims and the Hindus. Some of the articles that appeared in *Kesari* prove this fact.[64] But Tilak said: "The Shivaji festival is not celebrated to alienate or even to irritate the Mahomedans. [....] We are not against a festival being started in honour of Akbar or any other hero from old Indian history."[65] The Shivaji festivals were also attempts to consolidate Hindu consciousness and Hindu militancy. Kushwant Singh adds that every time the Ganesh and Shivaji festivals were celebrated there were Hindu-Muslim riots.[66] Walport says that, with the revival of the Shivaji festivals, the next link in the organisational chain of militant Hinduism was developed.[67]

Shivaji as a role model for violence as higher duty

Shivaji, the Maratha leader, provided a kind of mythological exemplar for Tilak of his ethics of violence as higher duty, whose festivals he ardently promoted, though Mahatma Gandhi considered Shivaji as a misguided patriot. In 1896, Tilak lamented the neglect of the sites associated with the life and death of Shivaji. He said: "That the place of coronation and the tomb of that great man who gave the joy of independence to Maharashtra for two centuries should have been so utterly forgotten by the Marathas is indeed a misfortune."[68] On 24 June 1906 Tilak wrote an article in his *Mahratta* entitled "Is Shivaji not a National Hero?" [69] He called Shivaji '*swadeshi* hero'[70] and argued that "Shivaji is the only hero to be found in Indian history".[71] Tilak also began the modern projection of Shivaji as the leader of Maratha independence in Maharashtra. He urged children to read a portion of a historical novel entitled *Ushahkal* dealing with the times of Shivaji.[72] According to him, what makes Shivaji a national hero is the spirit which guided him throughout and not his deeds as such.[73]

But history tells us that Shivaji treacherously murdered Afzal Khan.[74] Ivan Strenski reminds us that Tilak's failure to bring about a method of controlled use of force must be seen at least partly as a failure of his political mythology. In a word, the myth of Shivaji sent all the wrong messages to those who might have wished for an ethic of justifiable use of force. Moreover, knowing about other ambivalent features of Tilak's political behaviour, one might conclude that Tilak chose the Shivaji myth precisely *because* it was ambivalent: it permitted him to appeal to chivalrous and heroic elements of the Maratha leader's lofty character, while at the same time permitting him to trade upon some of Shivaji's unsavoury qualities.[75]

Strenski argues that Shivaji's killing of the Mughal general Afzal Khan raises many ethical questions. The 'great chivalric hero' Shivaji arrived with concealed deadly weapons to meet Afzal Khan. At his first opportunity, Shivaji murdered Afzal Khan on the very spot where they had agreed to talk peace.[76] Walport describes the murder of Afzal Khan as follows:

> To all outward appearances clad innocently enough, Shivaji approached the Muslim in his plain cloth shirt, but under it he wore a vest of mail, and concealed in his right sleeve was a scorpion-shaped dagger, while the finger tips of his left hand were sheathed with metal tiger claws. The embrace with which he greeted Afzal evoked the death-pang outcry from the Muslim.[77]

What followed was the massacre of Afzal Khan's entire retinue. Now leaderless, the Mughal army dispersed and Shivaji won what Marathi patriots have celebrated as a great victory – a victory won by duplicity and deception. Shivaji's failure to keep his solemn word makes him seem cowardly and dishonourable, little better than a sneak thief. Put on to the balance with the rest of Shivaji's deeds, it weighs heavily against permitting any honest reader to see in him an honourable man. Hence, says Strenski, Shivaji cannot be a role model for anyone who wishes to found an ethic of the principled or controlled use of violence.[78]

It has been discovered that many years prior to the killing of Afzal Khan, Shivaji used the pretext of marriage to wrest control of a territory. After promising to marry the daughter of Chandra Rao More, the ruler of Javli, he killed More and took over Javli.[79] Strenski says: "...some of Tilak's own most notorious public deeds seem to indicate that his philosophy of political action was informed by the very moral ambivalence that characterises the myth of Shivaji."[80]

Anti-Cow Killing Societies

Tilak started and used Anti-Cow Killing Society, which in its original form was a religious movement founded on the fact that the Hindus regard the cow as a sacred animal.[81] Unfortunately, his Anti-Cow Killing Society was regarded as a direct movement to provoke Muslims.[82] Tilak did not take part in any anti-cow killing movement as such, but took advantage of the ill-feeling between the Hindus and Muslims for which this movement was a symptom.[83] Tilak took a prominent part in inflaming the minds of Hindus against the Muslims. In several of his articles appeared in *Kesari* he upheld the view that in the anti-cow killing riots, as in all other outbreaks, the Musalmans were the aggressors. He praised the spirit in which the Hindus had stood up to their assailants when attacked and blamed those who held that when assailed by Muslims the Hindus should flee.[84]

Gymnastic Societies

Tilak maintained that unless Hindus learned to employ force they must expect to be impotent witness of the gradual downfall of their ancient institutions. Therefore, he proceeded to organise Gymnastic Societies in which physical training and the use of more or less primitive weapons were taught in order to develop the martial instincts of the rising generation.[85] The Natu brothers were recognised leaders of Hindu orthodoxy. They carried Tilak's propaganda to schools and colleges proclaiming that unless they learned to employ force the Hindus must expect to be impotent witnesses of the gradual downfall of all their ancient institutions.[86]

His Gymnastic Societies sometimes resorted themselves into juvenile bands of dacoits to swell the coffers of *swaraj*. Young Hindus were taught to use arms and induced to believe it to be their duty to employ them against the enemy.[87] The teaching which he gave or caused to be given to the members of the said societies was of such an evil and demoralising nature that with his approbation the members of some such societies formed themselves into bands of robbers who committed murder and robbery with the object of obtaining money to pursue Tilak's political campaign.[88]

Extremist journalism

Tilak started two newspapers *Kesari* and *Mahratta*. He wrote incriminating articles to encourage terrorism. In several of his writings he spoke of the cheapness of bombs and the economy with which they could be manufactured.[89] He described the bomb as a charm and an amulet and a legitimate weapon of political reform.[90] He even considered terrorism as an expression of patriotism. He said: "There is an excess of patriotism at the root of the bombs in Bengal."[91] He went so far as to say that the Bengalee murders were 'beneficent murders' so that, in his opinion, there might be a beneficent murderer.[92]

Tilak used his newspapers to incite the Hindus to assert their rights. He vilified the Muslims and the British.[93]

From June through August of 1902, *Kesari* ran a highly provocative series of nine editorials entitled 'Guerrilla Warfare'.[94] Sometimes *Kesari* contained articles on methods of the Russian revolutionaries and the cult of the bomb in Bengal.[95] He openly advocated Russian methods of retaliation. Writing in *Kesari* on 16 July 1907 he exhorted Indians to follow the Russian methods of political agitation.[96] Tilak also wrote some articles proposing to the government to make gymnastics a compulsory subject in schools.[97]

In the *Kesari* of 28 May 1907 he exhorted Indian leaders to emulate the example of Russian democrats in their methods of political agitation.[98] He also spoke of how the Russians managed to evade press censorship.[99] On 27 July 1907 Tilak wrote in *Kesari*: "We find in Mr. Savarkar's book a true echo of the thoughts of Mazzini, his secret and the open attempts to bring about the unification of Italy."[100] "We find in Mazzini's writings a clear enumeration of the noble principles of democratic politics."[101]

When Tilak began *Kesari* and *Mahratta* he had stated that the aim of the two newspapers would be to give a fearless account of the existing condition in the country, to give reviews of Indian books and to give correct estimates of political affairs in Britain.[102] But, as is evident, his columns went beyond this scope and promoted extremism and militancy. They became vehicles for his radical political views and ethics of violence.

Militant activities

Tilak was the founder of the militant revolutionary school in the national movement.[103] He seems to have had connections with the secret societies at Nasik, Bengal and elsewhere.[104] He felt himself strong to capture the Congress organisation in 1907, though it was not successful.[105] The fight between the moderates and the extremists carried on in the political arena led to a split in the Indian National Congress. The extremists founded a party of their own. But Tilak said that the extremists of today will be the moderates of tomorrow just as the moderates of today were extremists yesterday.[106] In 1907, at Surat, Tilak and his revolutionary group were expelled from the Congress for their radicalisation of Indian politics, which included also Aurobindo Ghose.[107] The rift was only healed in 1914 when Tilak finalised a pact with the Muslim League for a joint front against the British.[108]

It has been argued that in the murder of Walter Charles Rand[109] and Charles Egerton Ayerst[110] at Nasik, the assassins were only giving effect to Tilak's teachings.[111] He played a leading role in inflaming the minds of the Hindus against the Muslims. During the anti-cow killing agitation of 1893, which caused disturbances throughout the country and much loss of life and property, he thus showed himself as an open advocate of violence and the cult of physical force.[112] Sometimes he advocated insurrection and argued that the Boer system of warfare which had been successful against the British, was that which had been adopted by Shivaji against the Muslims.[113] In 1908 Tilak was tried for sedition because of an attempt on the life of Kingsford, a British judge at Muzaffarpur. Though the intention was to murder Kingsford, the assassins missed the target and two ladies were killed. Tilak in his writings supported the bomb throwers.[114] This bomb outrage offered the government a golden chance to arrest Tilak. Tilak was sentenced for six years in prison.

Tilak was convicted for inciting disaffection against the British in his writings in Marathi. But he claimed that the English renderings were defective. The trial ended in his incarceration and he was sent to Mandalay (Myanmar) and it was there that he composed his influential commentary on the *Gita* – the *Gitarahasya.*

Anti-Muslim attitude

Tilak played a prominent part in inflaming the minds of the Hindus against the Muslims. Between 1880 and 1890, throughout India, there was an evident antipathy between Hindus and Muslims. There were numerous riots and encounters between the members of the two faiths in many parts of the county.[115] He promoted Ganapati festivals, in the first place, to prevent people from taking part in the Muslim festival Muharram.[116] He was accused of inciting the Hindus to assert their rights to play music in passing before mosques.[117] He even called the Muslims a savage race. He said: "...even a savage race like the Mohammedans did not disarm the Hindus while exercising their imperial sway over India."[118]

In High Court of Justice, Kings Bench Division accused Tilak of several crimes. For example, in 1893, during the Hindu-Muslim riots in Bombay, Tilak took advantage of the situation to stir up the feelings of the Hindus against the Muslims. He was accused of using the Anti-Cow Killing Societies as a means to provoke the Muslims.[119] According to the report of the Bombay government, on 16 July 1918, on the occasion of Shivaji's coronation festival, Tilak presided at a lecture on conscription. In his speech, he called the army a mercenary which consisted of Muslims and foreigners.[120] It has been observed that basically, Tilak's anti-Muslim attitude manifested itself in four things: the question of playing music before the mosques, the Ganapati celebrations, the Shivaji movement and the Anti-Cow Killing Societies.

Anti-Christian attitude

Tilak saw Christianity as an enemy of Hinduism. He said: "Now I turn to the forces that are arrayed against us. There are mainly two forces of (1) science, and (2) Christianity. If our religion is threatened with any hostile criticism, it comes from these two."[121] Once he took tea in a Christian missionary school and accepted to do penance for it.[122]

Tilak was vehemently opposed to the so-called conversion activities of the Christians. When Pandita Ramabai, a great Sanskrit scholar, who became a widow, converted to Christianity and then set up *Sharada Sadan* for educating destitute high-caste widows, Tilak alleged that it was being covertly used to promote conversion to Christianity.[123]

Tilak never really favoured social reforms.[124] On 30 July 1907 he wrote in *Kesari* against Christian involvement in social reform and human rights issues. He said:

> Though the correspondence with regard to the abolition of the customs of dedicating minor girls to the gods at Jejuri and Savantwadi is carried on under the leadership of Dr. Bhandarkar, it is the Missionaries who are as a matter of fact at the bottom of the whole affair. It was they who first brought to the notice of Government that such girls led an immoral life after attaining puberty and that the existing statutory resolutions were quite inadequate to remedy the [sic] evil. [....] It is not at all possible for the people to believe that the above suggestion of the Missionaries originated from disinterested motives. [....] Our hypocritical Missionaries do not seem to know that immorality is not a criminal offence in England and that the value of the chastity of women can be estimated there in damages. The missionaries needlessly interfered in the matter.[125]

Again, referring to Christianity, Tilak said: "Our enemies are fast disappearing before the teachings of modern science, take courage and work hard for the final triumph."[126] He envisaged a time when, instead of Christians preaching

Christianity in India, Hindus will see their preachers proclaiming *Sanatana Dharma* (Eternal Religion) all over the world.[127]

Critical attitude towards Buddhism and Jainism

Tilak did not even view benevolently the Buddhists and the Jains of India. He praised Adi Sankaracharya of Kaladi who aggressively fought against these two religions. Tilak says: "Buddhism flourished and attacks were made on Hindu religion by Buddhists and Jains. After 600 years of chaos rose one great leader, Shankaracharya and he brought together all the common philosophical elements for our religion and proved and preached them in such a way that Buddhism was swept away from the land."[128]

Promotion of Hindu nationalism

Koenraad Elst observes that Tilak was the first to connect Hindu symbolism with the freedom struggle and he interpreted the *Gita* in terms of political activism.[129] It was during the British rule that Hindu nationalism took birth. 'The father of Indian unrest' was in many respects one of the figures who nurtured it. Tilak was a Hindu nationalist to the core who made – as Walport says – no distinction between religion and politics.[130] He was anti-Muslim and anti-Gandhi. According to Tilak, religion is an element of nationality.[131] He buttressed the claims of Hindu chauvinism through his scholarship. He said: "The common factor in Indian society is the feeling of *Hindutva* (Hinduness)."[132] The Hindu religion provides to the Indian society a moral as well as social tie. During the Vedic times India was a self-contained country and a great nation united by a common culture. That unity disappeared and it brought upon the nation great degradation. But it is the duty of the leaders of India to revive that union.[133]

Tilak stood for the establishment of a Hindu *rashtra* in India. It is argued that Tilak had a part in the so-called 'Nepal plot'.[134] The idea presumably was to convince the king of Nepal to invade India, sparking in turn an uprising within the country in his support, since if the independent king of the only independent Hindu kingdom conquered India there would be one sovereign Hindu nation.[135]

Emulation of a great past is axiomatic to any cultural renaissance. Tilak argued that truths that are being discovered by the West were known to the *rishis* of India. Modern science is gradually justifying and vindicating the ancient wisdom of India.[136] He says: "Are not these common allegiances to the Vedas, the Gita and the Ramayana our common heritage? If we lay stress on it forgetting all the minor differences that exist between different sects, then by the grace of providence we shall [...] be able to consolidate all the different sects into a mighty *Hindu nation*. This ought to be the ambition of every Hindu."[137]

The *Gitarahasya* is essentially a work of nationalist literature than of philosophy. Through it Tilak made a stirring call to his countrymen to action in order to claim their birth right which is *swaraj* (self-rule). He argued that in that process it is legitimate to indulge in violence, in imitation of Arjuna and Shivaji. It is the motive rather than the action in itself that matters. In other words, end justifies the means.

Claim of the superiority of Hinduism

Tilak advocated the superiority of Hinduism over all other religions. In his address in Benaras in 1906 he said: "There is no other religion on the face of the earth except the Hindu religion wherein we find such a hopeful promise, a promise that God comes to us as many times as necessary. After Mohammed, no Prophet is promised, and Jesus Christ came once for ever. No religion holds such promise full of hope [....] A time will come when our religious thoughts and our rights will be vindicated."[138]

According to Tilak, all the different sects of Hinduism are in fact branches of the Vedic religion. He claims that the term *sanatana dharma* ('eternal religion') shows that Hinduism is very old – as old as history of the human race itself. Vedic religion was the religion of the Aryans from a very early time. Hindu religion as a whole is made up of different parts co-related to each other as many sons and daughters of one great religion.[139]

Tilak claims that all religions, except Hinduism, are partial truths. He says: "...they [non-Hindu religions] are partial truth while our Hindu religion is based on the whole, the Sanatana truth." [140] He adds: "Hindu religion is very comprehensive – as comprehensive as its literature itself; we have a wonderful literature. Wisdom, as is concentrated in the *Gita* and epitomised in about 700 verses, that wisdom, I am confident, cannot be defeated or overcome by any philosophy be it Western or any other."[141]

In many of his speeches Tilak asked for greater co-ordination of all the sections of Hinduism under the banner of *Bharata Dharma Mahamandala* ('All India Religious Association'). He also emphasised the value of numbers. He said: "Numerical strength also is a great strength. Can the religion which counts its followers by crores die? Never, unless the crores of our fellow-followers are suddenly swept away our religion will not die. All that is required for our glorious triumph and success is that we should unite all the different sects on a common platform and let the stream of Hindu religion flow through one channel."[142]

Tilak also proudly maintained that Hinduism is the most tolerant religion in the world. According to him, it tolerates all religions. He asks: "If there be any religion in the world which advocates toleration of other religious beliefs and instruct [sic] one to stick to one's own religion, it is the religion of the Hindus alone."[143] He adds: "Shri Krishna does not say that the followers of other religions would be doomed to eternal hell. I challenge anybody to point out to me a similar text from the scriptures of other religions. It cannot be found in any other religion."[144]

Indoctrination of the young through education

Tilak was convinced that the salvation of his motherland lay in education of the people, which for him had to be English education.[145] He was convinced that the mind arrives at a correct or incorrect decision according as it has been educated.[146] In a speech delivered in 1908 he spoke of the need for national education and religious education. He said: "We are not given such education as may inspire patriotic sentiments among us."[147] "We must have education on national lines, and for this there must be schools fully under the control of national leaders."[148] "Of the many things that we will do there, *religious education will first and foremost engage our attention.* Secular education only is not enough to build up character."[149]

According to Tilak, the want of religious education is one of the causes that have brought the Christian missionary influence all over the country.[150] For the promotion of national and religious education, he first thought of establishing private schools on the model of the missionary institutions. Then, he succeeded in founding the New English School without any help from the government, thereby establishing a model of education of the Indians for the Indians and by the Indians.[151]

Tilak envisaged a Hindu university for Hindus. He said: "The idea of a Hindu University where our old religion will be taught along with modern science is a very good one and should have the support of all."[152]

The success of Tilak's New English School paved way for its conversion into a public body called the Deccan Education Society under whose auspices the Ferguson College was founded in 1885 for training educational missionaries for all of Maharashtra. Later, due to a conflict related to the management, Tilak resigned.

A critical evaluation of Tilak's philosophy

Tilak created a revolution in the world of ethics with his *Gitarahasya*. It had far-reaching consequences in the field of religion, politics, relationship with religious minorities and national struggle for independence. Below we take a critical look at his ethical views and its impact on the Hindutva ideology which is in vogue. K.M. Panikkar observes that it is Tilak's *Gitarahasya* which marked the change in Indian political scenario. He showed for the first time that the message of the *Gita* was not renunciation as others had thought before, but it was essentially a scripture preaching a doctrine of social activism where action for human good without personal attachment is preached as the first imperative.[153]

Subjective interpretation of the Gita

Richard Charles Zaehner says that in interpreting the *Gita*, as in interpreting any sacred text, the danger is that the interpreter will quote all that is grist to his mill while failing to draw attention to what embarrasses him in other parts of the text.[154]

Tilak introduced a new trend in the reading of scriptures with his *Gitarahasya*, namely, that of giving a subjective interpretation to the Hindu scriptures in order to give foundation for his concept of violence as higher duty. It is said that "what one ought to do" is the problem of morality. The *Gita* says that what ought to be done is one's caste duty. If we follow Tilak's *Gitarahasya*, the caste duty consists in action, which may involve also violence, and it is fully justified. This is, of course, abuse of caste power.

The traditional Hindu texts like the *Gita* took on unprecedented importance with Tilak's *Gitarahasya*. The *Gita* became for the Hindu reformers a kind of counter Bible. Consequently, many translations of the *Gita* were sponsored throughout the subcontinent in various languages. Until the advent of Tilak, the interpretations given to the *Gita* never really advocated violence. Many of the great Hindu reformers felt compelled to compose their own 'reading' or commentary of it. Thus, not only do we hear from the more spiritual reformers such as Swami Vivekananda (1863-1902), Sarveppalli Radhakrishnan (1888-1975) or Vinoba Bhave (1895-1994) but also men of action like Gandhi. But their concept of *karma-yoga* differed from Tilak's.

The great commentators of the *Gita* preferred non-violence than violence. Some saw in the *Gita* action for social reform, others action for political independence, and some others saw in it a call to take up arms. For the most part, the overwhelming majority of commentators read the *Gita* non-violently, as a spiritual or moral allegory and the desire to avoid violence was ever present. Many made allegorical readings of the battle between the Pandavas and the Kauravas. Gandhi saw the *Mahabharata* itself as a 'great anti-war epic' and Krishna's conversation with Arjuna as imaginary. This interpretation became the dominant reading of the *Gita* during the 20th century. But with Tilak it was different.

In his own time Gandhi had rejected the views of Tilak. He said: "I do not find myself in agreement with everything he [Tilak] says."[155] "What we need to consider is whether Indians should accept the views of Mr. Tilak and his party. We submit, after great deliberation, that Mr. Tilak's views should be rejected."[156]

K.M. Panikkar tells us that the British government was not unaware of the dynamite that the *Gita* contained, for long before Tilak's *Gitarahasya* had been published, he had been preaching its message. The authorities even considered seriously the question of proscribing the *Gita*; but a holy book which the Hindu masses use as daily prayer and which has been translated into every Indian language could not be proscribed as a seditious volume.[157]

Divine sanction to violence

Tilak's interpretation of the *Gita* was an attempt to find justification for violence and militancy in the Hindu scriptures. An action may involve violence. But, when that action is seen as a duty, violence becomes unavoidable and necessary. Tilak goes a step further and gives it a divine sanction. He presents Krishna as the new law-giver. This makes his ethics even more dangerous and diabolic. Thus violence becomes a religious activity, an obligation (*dharma*) for all Hindus and salvation is to be achieved through it. This makes us raise two pertinent questions: Can a subjective interpretation of sacred scripture to rationalise violence be justified? Can such an interpretation be declared as divinely sanctioned? As we have seen above, according to Tilak, both are possible.

Tilak's ethics has been a great attraction for many Hindutva ideologues and organisations of modern and contemporary India. Hindu sacred scriptures like the *Bhagavadgita*, *Ramayana* and *Mahabharata* and even some *Puranas* are liberally interpreted in order to justify militancy, violence and extremism against both real and imaginary enemies in many parts of India. Ashis Nandy is correct to some extent when he says that South Asian gods and goddesses, like their Hellenistic counterparts, can sometimes be found on the wrong side of morality and law.[158]

Many modern and contemporary Hindutva ideologues were inspired by Tilak's interpretation of the *Gita*. For example, M.S. Golwalkar, who was the leader of the RSS from 1940 to 1973 said: "Our philosophy teaches us to fight with all our strength, [...] Sri Krishna commands Arjuna to fight, [...] and in a spirit of doing one's duty unwaveringly."[159]

Aurobindo said: "It is an error to think that the heights of religion are above the struggles of this world. The recurrent cry of Sri Krishna to Arjuna insists on the struggle: 'Fight and overthrow thy opponents'."[160]

Pravin Togadia, a prominent leader of the VHP says: "...during the Mahabharata, did God ask Arjuna not to fight, did God talk to Arjun about *ahimsa*? What had Krishna Bhagawan said? Fight. [....] He told Arjuna to kill Karna. This is what Kyshtriya [sic] blood is made up of. Karna was killed. Did anyone tell Krishna that he had followed a path of *adharma*?"[161]

There is nothing as dangerous as giving divine sanction to violence. It easily convinces the naive and the ignorant to indulge in violence as there is merit attached to it. It makes the criminals to commit violence with religious fervour.

Many instances of communal violence in India are justified by religion. In 1992 those who died during the *kar seva* in order to demolish the Babri mosque are considered as martyrs. On 6 December 1992 at Ayodhya in the midst of the hysterical cries of the *kar sevaks, Jai Siya Ram*, the Babri mosque was razed to the ground. The attack on a century-old Christian girls' school at Rajkot on 20 June 1998 was carried out amidst shouting slogans of *Jai Shri Ram*. The same slogan was heard when the Australian missionary Graham Staines and his two sons were burned alive in Orissa in 1999.[162] When the Muslims women were being gang raped at Godhra in Gujarat in early 2002 the rapists shouted, *Har Har Mahadev*.[163]

Religious sanction to violence helps militants and extremists to plan to the finest details the execution of their misdeeds. Thus acts of violence become a sort of sacred ritual, the criminals assume the role of high priests and what is promised to the accomplices in the crime is merit.

Justification of Hindu militancy

Tilak represented a militant version of Hinduism.[164] He argues that Hinduism is a warrior-religion with a warrior-morality. Lord Krishna did not send Arjuna to the woods as a mendicant or make a *sanyasin* out of him, filling his mind with apathy.[165] He did not place in his hands cymbals or drum or harp but bow and arrows.[166] His advice to Arjuna was to fight: "...therefore, O Arjuna, fight;"[167] "...therefore, determine to fight and rise;"[168] "...therefore, think of me [Krishna] and fight;"[169] "...the doer and the causer of everything is I myself [Krishna], and you [Arjuna] are only the tool; and therefore, fight and conquer your enemies."[170] Tilak reminds us that Arjuna did really fight, and in the course of the fight he actually killed Bhisma, Karna, Jayadratha, and others as occasion arose.[171] In other words, according to Tilak, in modern terms, a true patriot is one who holds the *Gita* on the one hand and pistol on the other.

Gandhi once remarked that Tilak seems to have said that in our language we have no word corresponding to conscience. Therefore, he rejected the idea of conscience.[172] Gandhi was of the opinion that Tilak missed the inner meaning of the *Gita* when he used it to justify violence. He says: "But I have often felt that he [Tilak] has not understood the age-old spirit of India, has not understood her soul,"[173] which according to Gandhi, is non-violence (*ahimsa*).

During the trial of Tilak the judge said the following about him in the sentence he delivered: "It seems to me that it must be a diseased mind, a most perverted mind, that could say that the articles which you have written are legitimate weapons in political agitation. They are seething with sedition; they breathe violence; they speak of murder with approval, and the cowardly and atrocious act of committing murder with bombs not only seems to meet with your approval, but you hail that advent of the bomb in India as if something had come to India for good."[174]

Violence is energy and talents wasted. The judge added: "...you [Tilak] are a man of undoubted talents and great power and influence. Those talents and influence if used for the good of your country would have been instrumental in brining about a great deal of happiness for those very people whose cause you expouse."[175]

Thus, as K.M. Panikkar observes, the terrorists and other political groups which worked for revolution believed frankly in violence and elevated it to a creed,[176] and with the beginning of the 20th century a new type of nationalism which believed in revolutionary methods emerged. The leaders of this new movement were Tilak in Western India and Aurobindo Ghose in Bengal.[177]

Ethical relativism and intrinsic goodness of violence

The *Gitarahasya* advocates ethical relativism. Tilak believed in the principle of 'end justifies the means' which implies only that one's *motives* should be untainted by selfish interest and passion.[178] The method does not matter. In other words, it is the motivation rather than the action in itself which is important in determining culpability. He says: "'The Reason (*buddhi*) is of greater importance than the Action' [....] If one considers only the external Action, it is often misleading."[179] Thus, an action may be sinful. But, from the fact that the external action is bad, one cannot draw the conclusion that the reason must also be bad.

Similarly, with regard to truth. Under certain circumstances one has a higher obligation to lie. Tilak says: "Telling a lie has been found, after mature deliberation, to be much better than speaking the truth."[180] "There is no sin in speaking the untruth on the following five occasions, namely, if in jock [sic] or while speaking with women or at the time of marriage, or if your life is in danger, or for protecting your own property."[181] It is stated in the Vedas that even gods themselves broke the pledges made by them.[182] There is then, in the strict sense, nothing called truth, justice, honesty, fairplay, charity, and the like. What exists is ethics of expediency. Everything is, therefore, relative. D.D. Pattanaik, a pro-Hindutva writer, admits: "Tilak was ready to condone occasional acts of terrorist violence on grounds of expediency."[183] But, the paradox is that, according to Tilak, even though one indulges in terrorist violence it may not be considered as sin so that one can still attain final liberation (*moksa*). He says: "...the Gita has propounded the device of performing action in such a way that one ultimately attains release without committing sin."[184]

Concerning the ethical problem involved in the killing Afzal Khan by Shivaji through treachery, Tilak said that great men are above the common principles of morality. Krishna preached in the *Gita* that we have the right even to kill our own *guru* and our kinsmen.[185] Tilak openly approved the use of bomb as a legitimate weapon in political agitation.[186] He wrote articles in defence and justification of political assassinations.[187] He was accused of the offence of forgery by fraudulently altering documents.[188] He came to be considered as the chief conspirator against the British government.

Here, it may be argued that the ethics of Tilak has a counterpart in Chanakya (Kautilya, 4th century B.C.), who wrote a treatise on statecraft entitled *Arthasastra*, which contained a code of conduct for rulers that justified force, cunning and ruthlessness and endorsed real politic and dismissed considerations of morality in public life, which ranged from spying to assassination.[189]

Gandhi could never agree with Tilak on an ethics of this kind. K.M. Panikkar says: "To Gandhiji it was not sufficient that the ideal should be *Lok Samgraha* or the welfare of all. It was even more important that the means should be ethically right [...] it must be uncontaminated not merely by selfishness but by anything which injures others."[190] Gandhi says: "After many a frank chat with the Lokamanya I had come to see that on some vital matter we could never agree [....] I only know that we fundamentally differed."[191] "I cannot claim the honour of being the follower of the late Lokamanya [....] I am conscious that my method is not Mr. Tilak's method."[192] According to Gandhi, both the end as well as the means to achieve it should be good and only then an action can be said to be good. He further stated that even if one's 'inner voice' tells him to do an evil act he should not do it: "If a voice told a thief, 'kill that girl, cut off her limbs and take away her jewellery', I would not say it was the still small voice within. It would be sheer wickedness."[193]

Ivan Strenski says that the ethic of action in the *Gita* is employed to guide the use of public violence in political matters. The *Gita*, and the *Mahabharata*, of which it forms a portion, are about war. The straightforward literal injunction of the *Gita* is to fight, and to fight to death. Thus, Krishna urges the reluctant Arjuna to rally his courage and fight. This will surprise those familiar only with the more 'spiritual' interpretations of the *Gita*.[194]

Tilak's ethics propounded in the *Gitarahasya* is subjective, relative, dubious, ambivalent and machiavellian. He harbours on the idea that violence is a simple thing, a mere performance of caste duty. But violence in any form is self-defeating and it always involves irrationality, however lofty the motives may be. Violence simply works on the principle that 'end justifies the means'. This was the ethics of the Nazis.[195]

Often violence is motivated and pre-meditated and carefully planned. It is irrational in the domain of motivation as well as in the results it produces. The best example of this is the Godhra pogrom of February-March 2002 in Gujarat. Kushwant Singh says that during the Godhra massacre armed mobs were out in different parts of Gujarat with detailed lists of Muslim homes and establishments. Several hundred Muslims were hacked to death or burnt alive, women raped, homes and shops looted and burnt. Not only did the police remain inert, when the army arrived on the scene it was not deployed. Officers who tried to do their duty and foil the plans of the mobs were transferred out.[196] Arundhati Roy says about the Gujarat massacre: "The leaders of the mob had computer-generated cadastral lists marking out Muslim homes, shops, business and even partnerships. They had mobile phones to co-ordinate the action. They had trucks loaded with thousands of gas cylinders, hoarded weeks in advance, which they used to blow up Muslim commercial establishments. They had not just police protection and police connivance, but also covering fire."[197] If Tilak were to be alive today, he would have, in all likelihood, endorsed the communal pogrom of Gujarat, which was meticulously planned and executed.

Influence on the Hindutva movement

In Tilak, Hindu religion invaded the domain of politics. He was an icon of religio-centric politics in his time. But, he was eclipsed by Gandhi in the leadership of the Congress Party. This political displacement of Tilak corresponded with what *seemed* the virtually final eclipse of his reading of the *Gita* as well.[198] But it was not so. On 30 January 1948 Nathuram Godse (1912-1949) fired three shots at point blank range at Gandhi. The assassin after firing the shots raised his hand with the gun and called for the police. He voluntarily surrendered to the authorities.[199] The Hindu Mahasabha celebrated the event by distributing sweets.[200] Godse later said that he had done his duty like Arjuna in the Mahabharata whom Krishna advised to kill his own relatives because they were evil.[201] He had also read Tilak's writings.[202]

Godse exhibited a surprisingly serene composure after the murder and showed his legal skill and self-confidence in the way in which he argued his case in English, a language he supposedly did not know well. Ashis Nandy says that it was as if the assassination gave meaning and drive to a life which otherwise was becoming increasingly prosaic.[203] Godse was extremely religious. He read into the *Gita* with his martial background. For him Krishna was speaking to Arjuna about *real battles* and not allegorical battles fought in the inner self. Tilak's ethics of intrinsic goodness of violence had once again come back to life. It was once again seen as a sacred duty of the patriots of the Hindu *rashtra*.

Gandhi was denounced by Hindutva ideologues for preaching and practising the doctrine of *ahimsa* (non-violence) in the most 'perverted form'. He was killed by a Hindu for having undermined and betrayed Hindu India.[204] Gopal Godse, brother of Nathuram Godse says: "Our motive was not to achieve control of the government; ... we were simply trying to rid the nation of someone who had done and was doing great harm to it. He had consistently insulted the Hindu nation and had weakened it by his doctrine of *ahimsa*."[205] Patrick Nair reports that at Nagpur the RSS has built a shrine in honour of Godse. While visiting Nagpur in the 1980s he wandered into the RSS complex and found a shrine dedicated to Nathuram Godse. It had a plaque with the message that one day when the Hindu nationalists come to power a far more fitting memorial would be erected.[206]

Prior to 30 January 1948, there had been five known unsuccessful attempts to kill Gandhi, all of them except one in Maharashtra – the land of Tilak. The first was in Poona in June 1934 when Gandhi was engaged in an anti-untouchability campaign there. The second, in July 1944, at Panchgani where Nathuram Godse, dressed in a Nehru shirt, pyjama and jacket, rushed towards Gandhi brandishing a dagger in his hand and shouting anti-Gandhi slogans. But, he was overpowered by the people around Gandhi. The third, in September 1944, at Sevagram which also involved Godse along with some others. The fourth, in June 1946, near Poona when some unknown persons tried to derail the train in which Gandhi was travelling. The fifth, on 20 January 1948 in New Delhi which involved a bomb attack.[207]

The unprecedented growth of the RSS and its affiliates and the upsurge of militancy among the Hindus should be seen as one of the effects of the re-reading of Tilak's interpretation of the *Gita*. Following Tilak's example many Hindutva ideologues and organisations are now giving new interpretations not only to the *Gita* but also to other sacred books of the Hindus like the *Ramayana* and *Mahabharata* and even *Puranas* in order to rationalise violence as a means to promote Hindu cultural nationalism. Referring to *Mahabharata* – of which the *Gita* forms a part – Rajmohan Gandhi says that the epic is a story of unending revenge and violence.[208]

In his own time Tilak became the guru of V.D. Savarkar (1883-1966), especially in his extreme ideology of nationalism. It was Tilak who recommended the case of Savarkar for a scholarship to go to London for studies. In London, Savarkar was busy with production of bombs, eventually sending a manual on this subject back to Tilak, publication of revolutionary pamphlets, books, etc. [209] The founder of the RSS, Keshav Baliram Hedgewar (1889-1940) also came under the influence of Tilak.[210] Another prominent RSS leader, who was influenced by Tilak, was Balkrishna Shivaram Moonje (1872-1948), the founder of the Bhonsle Military School in Nasik.[211] Madhav

Kashinath Damley, the founder of *Lokhandi Morcha* or *Iron Front*, a Fascist movement, was also a follower of Tilak.[212] Tilak's thoughts have influenced the Hindu Mahasabha,[213], the Jan Sangh[214] and the RSS.[215] The RSS subscribes to Tilak's understanding of *karma-yoga* and the *swayamsevaks* are advised to read the *Gita* regularly.[216] Krishna Kumar, writing about the revival of Hindu nationalism in India, says: "...the RSS was a blossom of the vigorous seed of revivalist nationalism that Tilak had sown."[217] Almost all those convicted in the trial of Gandhi murder case had a connection, past or present, with either the Hindu Mahasabha or the RSS and they were believers in violence.

Many Hindutva ideologues make strenuous effort to popularise the view that the Hindu gods and goddesses are 'weapon wielding deities'. In 1966, N.N. Banerjee, president of the Hindu Mahasabha, on the occasion of the golden jubilee of the organisation, told the Hindus that all their deities, such as Siva, Vishnu, Durga, Kali, Kartikeya, Shri Ramachandra, Shri Krishna, are warriors and they carry weapons. Hence, Hindus need to realise their significance and should become their dynamic worshippers.[218] Aurobindo reminds us that in the *Mahabharata*, Krishna says that God created battle and armour, the sword, the bow and the dagger.[219]

Describing Goddess Kali, V.S. Naipaul says: "Kali, 'the black one', the coal-black aboriginal goddess, surviving in Hinduism as the emblem of female destructiveness, garlanded with human skulls, tongue forever out for fresh blood, eternally sacrificed to but insatiable."[220] Ashis Nandy states that Kali is the new symbol of a treacherous cosmic mother, eager to betray and prone to aggression, fierce, violent, associated with robbers, thieves, thugs, prostitutes, and in some of her incarnations she was associated with certain dangerous diseases.[221] B. Walker says that Kali holds in two of her hands a sword and a dagger and in the other two are severed heads dripping with blood. Her long tongue hangs out of her mouth and blood trickles down her chin and neck as she gorges herself at her cannibal feasts. In one hideous image a headless Kali holds her own severed head, while the mouth greedily drinks the blood spurting from her neck.[222]

Rama of *Ramayana* is depicted as wielding a bow and arrow. In fact, the symbol of the Shiv Sena is Ram's bow and arrow. He is also projected as the national hero of the Hindu nation.[223] Hanuman is the monkey-god who served Rama with steadfast devotion. But he is also a symbol of irrational destruction. He went to Lanka in search of Sita. Before he left he destroyed everything in sight, razing houses and uprooting trees as though they were grass until he was captured by Indrajit, son of Ravana. In a bid to humiliate Hanuman and send him back to Ram, an oil-soaked cloth was tied to his tail and set alight. But Hanuman, charged through the city and the surrounding countryside causing untold havoc and burning all the crops with his fiery tail.[224] Today, Hanuman is the model for the Bajrang Dal activists – the Indian version of the Nazi Stormtroopers (SA, *Sturmabteilung* 'storming department'). Durga Vahini cadets emulate the Goddess Durga, the demon-killing protective mother,[225] who is actually supposed to be the Goddess Kali. Many Hindutva ideologues now speak of militant Hinduism as the 'Third Eye' of the Hindu.[226]

M.M. Ahluwalia maintains that the Hindu revolutionaries were influenced by the European revolutionaries on the one hand and the militancy of Hindu gods and goddesses and historical heroes on the other.[227]

Many Bengali secret societies were inspired by Tilak's interpretation of the *Gita*. The members of the *Anushilan Samiti* took an oath of allegiance to the organisation before an image of Goddess Kali with the *Bhagavadgita* in one hand and a revolver in the other.[228] Aurobindo envisaged *karma-yoga* as a means of legitimising violence as a form of sacrifice.[229] He believed in an aggressive Hinduism.[230] According to him, open attack, unsparing criticism, the severest satire, the most wounding irony, are all methods perfectly justifiable and indispensable in politics.[231] In 1951, N.C. Chatterjee, as president of the Hindu Mahasabha, said: "The greatest task of the Mahasabha is to create Hindu character on the basis of the Geetha [sic]." In 1960, V.G. Deshpande, in his presidential address of the 45th Annual Session of the All India Hindu Mahasabha, spoke of the need to resort to guerrilla and mountain warfare.[232] The *karma-yoga* expounded in the *Gita* is practised by the RSS *pracharaks* ('preachers') which is described as a matter of inner sacrifice. They maintain that action, even when violent, can constitute a means of renunciation when it is undertaken without regard to personal advantage and in the service of Hindu nation (*rashtra*) and Hindu *dharma*.[233]

Many Nazis of Germany took inspiration from the *Gita*. For example, Heinrich Himmler (1900-1945), the chief of Hitler's security service (SS, *Schutzstaffel* = *security guard*) constantly carried with him this sacred book, cited from it, compared Hitler to Lord Krishna and wanted his SS troop to be like the Kshatriya caste of India which saw war as part of their spirituality.[234] Savitri Devi (1905-1982), a staunch Nazi (popularly known as 'Hitler's Priestess'), was the first woman writer who regarded Adolf Hitler as a divine incarnation equal of Rama and Krishna in the *Gita*.[235] She justified the elimination of millions of Jews in Nazi Germany by quoting from the *Gita*. Devi also considered the *Schutzstaffel* of Hitler as the incarnation of the Indo-Aryan Kshatriya caste.[236] According to Victor and Victoria Trimondi, the *Gita* spiritualises cruelty (*skralisierung der Grausamkeit*). All imaginable forms of cruelty were practised in the fratricidal war described in the *Gita*. In addition, Hitler envisaged cruelty as a virtue of the new generation of Nazi youth.[237]

Writing in the 1960s K.M. Panikkar said that the *Gita* has become the scripture of the new age, the main foundation on which its ethic, its social doctrines and even its political action depends.[238] The Rama myth is a help to rationalise the aggressiveness and violence of the Shiv Sena, VHP, BJP, RSS, Bajrang Dal and the Sangh Parivar as a whole. Rama is the new icon of the anti-Muslim movement in India as was Shivaji in Tilak's time. *Mahabharata* is seen as a scripture of war. The televising of *Ramayana* (1987-1989 in 91 weekly episodes) and *Mahabharata* (1988-1990 in 94 episodes) helped the Hindu masses to imbibe the spirit of violence from their favourite sacred books, gods and goddesses.[239] Today, the sacred books of Hinduism – which are meant to guide the everyday religious code of the Hindus – are often used to extol violence for a so-called 'greater cause'. The saffronised NCERT school textbook of Social Sciences for Class IX extols revolutionaries like Tilak, Aurobindo, V.D. Savarkar, G.D. Savarkar, Swami Shraddhananda, Sister Nivedita, and militant organisations like *Anushilan Samiti* (Bengal), *Yugantar* Party (Bengal, led by Barindra Ghose brother of Aurobindo Ghose), *Abhinav Bharat* (in Maharashtra, led by Savarkar brothers), Baroda Secret Society (Maharashtra), etc. [240]

In 1991, the BJP campaigned vigorously for the extension of a Sunday morning television serial depicting the life of the famous Indian political philosopher, Chanakya or Kautilya (the word 'Kautilya' means 'crookedness and treachery'),[241] the reputed author of *Arthasastra*, a hand book of totalitarian, ruthless and cynical stagecraft characterised by depravity in standards of morality.[242] The serial portrayed Chanakya's struggle to assist Chandragupta Maurya (320-297 B.C.) in ancient India in a way to suggest its similarities to the struggle waged by the BJP then to seize political power in New Delhi.[243] But those who are familiar with the functioning of the BJP knows that much of its ethics is 'chanakyan' where 'end justifies the means'. Its 'India Shining', 'Feel Good', 'Super Power India' slogans were founded on chanakyan cut-throat ethics of lies, crookedness and ruthlessness with the desire to win 300 seats in the Indian Parliament during the general elections of 2004 – a dubious heritage from Tilak's ethics of expediency.

Conclusion

The *Gita* is perhaps the highest expression of the ethical religion of the Hindus. But Tilak interpreted it in the interest of his political expediency and twisted its message to justify violence, extremism and militancy. Today, some Hindutva ideologues consider him as the person who freed the Indian National Congress from the so-called scourge of moderation.[244] Tilak selectively cited from the *Gita* in order to justify his ethical stand and he believed in the intrinsic goodness of violence. This might be the reason why he said that politics is a game of worldly people and not of *sadhus*.[245]

Tilak's experiment of combining religion and politics became a model for the Hindutva ideologues of contemporary India. Communal violence in India today is frequently and almost ubiquitously justified by using Hindu scriptures, especially the *Gita*, *Ramayana* and *Mahabharta*. Many interpret them literally, and indulge in the most eccentric forms violence against their enemies without qualms of conscience. Arvind Sharma remarks that it was more than a mere curiosity that both Mahatma Gandhi and his assassin Nathuram Godse swore by the *Bhagavadgita* – one by its figurative interpretation and the other by its literal.[246] S.C. Sen Gupta observes that the *Gita* is patently a call to arms, an exposition of the doctrine of violence when it becomes a duty.[247] B.R. Ambedkar, criticising Hinduism and it's the tendency towards violence, observes that the *Gita* is about the justification of war; Krishna offers a philosophical defence of war and killing in war.[248]

During the *rath yatra* of L.K. Advani in 1990, in many places the most common offering was traditional weaponry: arrows, dices, maces, swords, trident and *kripans*. At Jetpur in Gujarat 101 Kshatriya youths offered him a bowl containing their blood.[249] No wonder why V.S. Naipaul says: "I think religion is the greatest curse of mankind. It has killed more people, destroyed more property, than any other thing."[250]

Tilak's ethics is not for any right thinking person to emulate. All violence is destructive. Jesus Christ has said: "One who takes the sword will perish by the sword"; "blessed are the meek they shall inherit the earth". There is nothing called 'good violence' as such. Can we speak of a 'good murderer' or a 'good terrorist' or a 'good rapist'? Violence is the product of diseased minds. Violence can go out of control especially if it is mob violence since with the mob one cannot any more speak of rationality and right proportion. Tilak's ethics of violence, which he justifies by interpreting the *Gita*, provides us another reason to question the claim that Hinduism is a tolerant religion and that it upholds *ahimsa* (non-violence). Finally, his interpretation of the *Gita* is subjective, distorted, far-fetched, deviant, perverse and dangerous. The ethics of intrinsic goodness of violence will create anarchy, intolerance and destruction, as it has been confirmed by the recent past in India.

Notes

1. Tilak's major works are: *The Orion* (1893), *The Arctic Home of the Vedas* (1903) and *The Gitarahasya* (1915).
2. Tilak was particularly fond of Hegel, Kant, Spencer, Mill, Bentham, Voltaire and Rousseau. See "Tilak, Balgangadhar (1856-1920)", 118.
3. See K.M. Panikkar, "Hindu Revival", 14.
4. See D.D. Pattanaik, *Hindu Nationalism*, vol. 2, 38.
5. At one time *Kesari* had a circulation of 20,000 copies, which was a large circulation for India at the time of Tilak. It also had a Hindi version published from Nagpur. See B.G. Tilak, *Selected Documents*, vol. 1, 90.
6. J. Nehru, *An Autobiography*, 388.
7. Franklin Edgerton observes that the *Gita* is the chief devotional book of the Hindus. It has been for millions of Indians the principal source of religious inspiration and it is to the Hindus what the New Testament is to the Christians. See F. Edgarton, *The Bhagavad Gita*, 103.
8. The *Gita* constitutes Book VI, chapters 25-42 of the epic *Mahabharata*. Probably the *Gita* received its first outlines in the first and second centuries AD and acquired its present form about AD 300. Many Hindu commentators and critics have devoted themselves to the study of the *Gita*, like, Adi Sankara, Ramanuja, Madhva, Vallabha and Nimbarka. Among the moderns mention may be made of Tilak,

Aurobindo, Gandhi, C. Rajagopalachari and Vinoba Bhave. However, their views differ widely. See B. Walker, *Hindu World*, vol. 1, 34. S. Radhakrishnan is another noted interpreter of the *Gita*. See S. Radhakrishnan, *The Bhagavadgita* (1948), 1993.

9. See B.G. Tilak, *Selected Documents*, vol. 4, 61.
10. Ibid., vol. 2, 118.
11. Ibid., vol. 3, 59. But this claim does not seem to be entirely true. He quotes thinkers like Kant, Hegel, Green, Mill and others in his work. Tilak says that to a certain extent his line of argument runs parallel to the line of thinking followed by Green in his *Prolegomena to Ethics*. See B.G. Tilak, *Selected Documents*, vol. 2, 118. Prior to Tilak, Swami Vivekananda (1863-1902) interpreted the *Gita* insisting on action. See D.D. Pattanaik, *Hindu Nationalism*, vol. 2, 16.
12. See B.G. Tilak, *Gitarahasya*, introductory, 34.
13. See B.G. Tilak, *Selected Documents*, vol. 4, 61.
14. *Karma-yoga* can have a variety of meanings, such as, 'path of action', 'way of action', 'righteous action', special way of performing actions', 'energism', etc. Basically, it implies the 'way of action' which is one of the three classical ways to liberation propounded by orthodox Hinduism.
15. Tilak describes 'yoga' as some special skill, device, intelligent method, or graceful way of performing actions. See B.G. Tilak, *Gitarahasya*, 77. A *karma-yogi* is one who performs skilfully. See *Ibid*., 79.
16. See B.G. Tilak, *Gitarahasya*, Author's Preface, xviii.
17. Tilak says: "This I hold is the lesson of the Gita. Jnanayoga there is, yes. Bhaktiyoga there is, yes. Who says not? But they are both subservient to the Karmayoga preached in the Gita." See B.G. Tilak, *Selected Documents*, vol. 4, 61.
18. B.G. Tilak, *Gitarahasya*, 103.
19. See B.G. Tilak, *Gitarahasya*, Author's Preface, xviii.
20. See B.G. Tilak, *Gitarahasya*, introductory, 27. Elsewhere he says that a certain Brooks also maintained that the *Gita* advocated *karma-yoga*. See B.G. Tilak, *Selected Documents*, vol. 2, 127-128.
21. See B.G. Tilak, *Selected Documents*, vol. 3, 64.
22. Ibid., 65.
23. Ibid., vol. 2, 118.
24. See B.G. Tilak, *Gitarahasya*, 1171.
25. Ibid., 89.

26. Ibid., 36-37.
27. Ibid., 94.
28. Ibid., 53.
29. Ibid., 44.
30. Ibid., 61.
31. *Gita* 3,35.
32. See B.G. Tilak, *Gitarahasya*, 68.
33. Ibid., 42.
34. See *The Collected Works of Mahatma Gandhi,* vol. 20, 371.
35. Ibid., vol. 32, 195.
36. Ibid., vol. 15, 32.
37. See I. Strenski, "Legitimacy", 11.
38. See B.G. Tilak, *Gitarahasya*, 1173.
39. Ibid., 1172.
40. B.G. Tilak, *Selected Documents*, vol. 3, 60.
41. See I. Strenski, "Legitimacy", 9.
42. See S.A. Walport, *Tilak and Gokhale*, 89.
43. See B.S. Parakh (ed.), *Contemporary India*, 38.
44. See K.M. Panikkar, "Hindu Revival", 14.
45. K.M. Panikkar, "Hindu Revival", 14.
46. He is the elephant-headed son of Siva and Parvati. In some legends he is the son of Siva and Durga or is created by Parvati alone. See B. Walker, *Hindu World*, vol. 1, 176.
47. See *Kesari*, 17: 22, 1 June 1897, 3 as cited in S.A. Walport, *Tilak and Gokhale*, 81.
48. See J. Nehru, *Glimpses of World History*, 441.
49. See B.G. Tilak, *Selected Documents*, vol. 1, 133.
50. Ibid., vol. 2, 230.
51. Ibid. According to P. Kanungo, Tilak not only tried to organise Hindu nationalism around Ganapati festivals, but also used it as a vehicle for anti-British, anti-Muslim and anti-social reform propaganda. See P. Kanungo, *RSS's Tryst with Politics*, 108.
52. See B.G. Tilak, *Selected Documents*, vol. 3, 6.
53. Ibid.
54. See S.A. Walport, *Tilak and Gokhale*, 68.
55. These songs have been translated and are preserved in the National Archives, New Delhi, History of the Freedom Movement Materials,

R II ½ as cited in S.A. Walport, *Tilak and Gokhale*, 70, 319, endnote 20.

56. See B.G. Tilak, *Selected Documents*, vol. 2, 230.
57. Ibid., vol. 3, 6.
58. See D. Smith, *Hinduism and Modernity*, 182.
59. See Y.K. Mailk and V.B. Singh, *Hindu Nationalists in India*, 216-217.
60. See S.A. Walport, *Tilak and Gokhale*, 69.
61. See B.G. Tilak, *Selected Documents*, vol. 3, 7.
62. Ibid., vol. 4, 39.
63. Ibid., vol. 4, 27.
64. Ibid., vol. 2, 231
65. Ibid., vol. 4, 27.
66. See K. Singh, *The End of India*, 43-44.
67. See S.A. Walport, *Tilak and Gokhale*, 79
68. As cited in A. Sharma, *Modern Hindu Thought*, 210-211.
69. B.G. Tilak, *Selected Documents*, vol. 4, 26-28.
70. Ibid., 26.
71. Ibid.
72. Ibid., vol. 1, 53.
73. Ibid., vol. 4, 27.
74. Ibid., vol. 3, 6.
75. See I. Strenski, "Legitimacy", 9.
76. Ibid., 10.
77. S.A. Walport, *Tilak and Gokhale*, 85-86. According to a report published in October 2004, the VHP, which is an extremist Hindutva organisation, has started an agitation aimed at demolishing the 17th century tomb of Afzal Khan. See V. Ramakrishnan, "BJP's Failing Tactics", 5-6. See also A. Katakam, "A Tomb as Target", 11-13.
78. See I. Strenski, "Legitimacy", 10.
79. See A. Katakam, "A Tomb as Target", 13.
80. I. Strenski, "Legitimacy", 10.
81. See B.G. Tilak, *Selected Documents*, vol. 3, 5.
82. Ibid., vol. 2, 225.
83. Ibid., 227.
84. Ibid., 227-228.
85. Ibid., 232.

86. Ibid.
87. Ibid.
88. Ibid.
89. Ibid., vol. 1, 74.
90. Ibid., vol. 3, 15.
91. B.G. Tilak, *Selected Documents*, vol. 1, 105.
92. See B.G. Tilak, *Selected Documents*, vol. 1, 74.
93. Ibid., vol. 2, 229.
94. See S.A. Walport, *Tilak and Gokhale*, 150.
95. See B.G. Tilak, *Selected Documents*, vol. 2, 244.
96. Ibid., vol. 1, 49-50.
97. Ibid., vol. 2, 235.
98. Ibid., vol. 1, 42.
99. Ibid.,45.
100. B.G. Tilak, *Selected Documents*, vol. 1, 50-51.
101. Ibid., 51.
102. See D. Keer, *Lokamanya Tilak*, 29.
103. See Menon, P.K.K, *The History of Freedom Movement*, vol. 2, 29.
104. See B.G. Tilak, *Selected Documents*, vol. 1, 133; also *Ibid.*, 237.
105. See B.G. Tilak, *Selected Documents*, vol. 1, 136.
106. Ibid., vol. 4, 29-30.
107. Ibid., vol. 1, 139.
108. See A. Sharma, *Modern Hindu Thought*, 195.
109. Rand was the chairman of the Plague Committee, appointed by Governor Sandhurst. He was based at Poona and was known as a stern disciplinarian. Prior to this appointment he had served as magistrate of Satara district and had passed a sentence convicting eleven Brahmins to jail. Because of this he was also regarded with hostility by orthodox Hindus. See S.A. Walport, *Tilak and Gokhale*, 83.
110. Ayerst was a Lieutenant who was accompanying W.C. Rand when they was attacked and killed by the Chapekar brothers Balkrishna and Damodar. See S.A. Walport, *Tilak and Gokhale*, 89.
111. See B.G. Tilak, *Selected Documents*, vol. 2, 240. For a detailed account of the murder see S.A. Walport, *Tilak and Gokhale*, 88-91.
112. See B.G. Tilak, *Selected Documents*, vol. 1, 133.
113. Ibid., 135.
114. Ibid., 76.

115. Ibid., vol. 2, 226.
116. Ibid., 230.
117. Ibid., 228.
118. B.G. Tilak, *Selected Documents*, vol. 1, 106.
119. See B.G. Tilak, *Selected Documents*, vol. 3, 5.
120. Ibid., 102.
121. As cited in A. Sharma, *Modern Hindu Thought*, 207.
122. See "Tilak, Balgangadhar (1856-1920)", 118.
123. See A. Sharma, *Modern Hindu Thought*, 193.
124. To some extent, Tilak was against untouchability. He said: "if God were to tolerate untouchability I would not recognise Him as God at all. [...] I do not deny that it was the Brahmin rule that introduced the practice of untouchability. This is a cancer in the body of Hindu society and we must eradicate it at all costs". *Bal Gangadhar Tilak: His Writings and Speeches*, Madras 1922[3] as cited in A. Sharma, *Modern Hindu Thought*, 201. But it is also true that on 24 March 1918 an All India Depressed Classes Conference was held under the presidentship of Sayajiro Gaikwad, the Maharaja of Baroda. Although Tilak spoke of the removal of untouchability, he refused to sign a manifesto declaring that the signatories would not observe untouchability in their day-to-day life. See "Tilak, Balgangadhar (1856-1920)", 118. Again, Tilak differed on the question of widow remarriage. See *The Collected Works of Mahatma Gandhi*, vol. 20, 371.
125. B.G. Tilak, *Selected Documents*, vol. 1, 51-52.
126. A. Sharma, *Modern Hindu Thought*, 207
127. See A. Sharma, *Modern Hindu Thought*, 208.
128. As cited in A. Sharma, *Modern Hindu Thought*, 206.
129. See K. Elst, *Decolonising the Hindu Mind*, 111.
130. See S.A. Walport, *Tilak and Gokhale*, 68.
131. See A. Sharma, *Modern Hindu Thought*, 205.
132. As cited in A. Sharma, *Modern Hindu Thought*, 211.
133. See B.G. Tilak, *Selected Documents*, vol. 4, 28.
134. The 'Nepal plot' was a plan by some Hindus in India to convince the King of Nepal to invade India so that there would be one sovereign Hindu nation. In 1901 Tilak attended the Calcutta Congress with his business associate Vasudev (alias Vasukaka) Ganesh Joshi (1856-1944), and after the Congress they met and talked with a Maharashtrian school mistress named Mataji, then living in Calcutta. Mataji

suggested that Tilak and Joshi visit Nepal, where she had lived for many years. She offered to introduce them to the King of Nepal. Starting the journey to Patna in early 1902, their intention was to enter Nepal with the Saivite pilgrims allowed free transit across the border in February to visit the temple of Siva during the festival. However, because of a plague the Nepalese border was closed and Tilak and Joshi were obliged to return to Poona. Later in April of the same year, Tilak deputed Vasukaka and K.P. Khadilkar to Nepal where they were to set up a tile factory, as a respectable front for arms and munitions plant designed to supply the invading Nepalese army. But the incredible plot was never realised. See S.A. Walport, *Tilak and Gokhale*, 148-149.

135. See S.A. Walport, *Tilak and Gokhale*, 148.
136. See A. Sharma, *Modern Hindu Thought*, 207.
137. B.G. Tilak, *Selected Documents*, vol. 4, 28 (emphasis added).
138. Ibid., 29.
139. See A. Sharma, *Modern Hindu Thought*, 205.
140. As cited in A. Sharma, *Modern Hindu Thought*, 207
141. Ibid.
142. Ibid.
143. B.G. Tilak, *Selected Documents*, vol. 4, 50.
144. As cited in A. Sharma, *Modern Hindu Thought*, 206-207.
145. See D.V. Tahmankar, *Lokamanya Tilak: Father of Indian Unrest and Maker of Modern India*, London, 1956, as cited in A. Sharma, *Modern Hindu Thought*, 193.
146. See B.G. Tilak, *Gitarahasya*, 177.
147. B.G. Tilak, *Selected Documents*, vol. 4, 49.
148. Ibid., vol. 1, 34.
149. B.G. Tilak, *Selected Documents*, vol. 4, 50 (emphasis original).
150. See B.G. Tilak, *Selected Documents*, vol. 4, 48.
151. See D.V. Tahmankar, *Lokamanya Tilak: Father of Indian Unrest and Maker of Modern India*, London, 1956 as cited in A. Sharma, *Modern Hindu Thought*, 193.
152. As cited in A. Sharma, *Modern Hindu Thought*, 208.
153. See K.M. Panikkar, "Hindu Revival", 4.
154. See R.C. Zaehner, *The Bhagavad Gita*, 4.
155. *The Collected Works of Mahatma Gandhi*, vol. 88, 173. But Gandhi had the magnanimity to say: "He [Tilak] lived for swaraj and he died

muttering the swaraj mantra". *Ibid.*, vol. 19, 510; "Though Mr. Tilak and other great Indians like him differ from us, we should continue to hold them in the highest esteem [....] Since they are great patriots, we must consider no honour too great for them". *Ibid.*, vol. 8, 419.

156. *The Collected Works of Mahatma Gandhi*, vol. 8, 418.
157. See K.M. Panikkar, "Hindu Revival", 15.
158. See A. Nandy, *Bonfire of Creeds*, 142.
159. M.S. Golwalkar, *Bunch of Thoughts*, 342.
160. Aurobindo, *India's Rebirth*, 51.
161. "Against the Law", 10. (From the video recording of Pravin Togadia's entire speech in Hindi, translated into English by Teesta Setalvad).
162. See S. Sarkar, "Hindutva and the Question of Conversions", 74-75. See also P. Sahgal and K. Walla, "Losing Control?", 18.
163. See P. Bidwai, "For Justice in Gujarat", 122.
164. See Y.K. Mailk and V.B. Singh, *Hindu Nationalists in India*, 218.
165. See B.G. Tilak, *Gitarahasya*, introductory, 35.
166. Ibid., 36.
167. *Gita*, 2,18 as in B.G. Tilak, *Gitarahasya*, introductory, 36.
168. Gita, 3, 37 as in B.G. Tilak, *Gitarahasya*, introductory, 35.
169. *Gita*, 8,7 as in B.G. Tilak, *Gitarahasya*, introductory, 36.
170. *Gita*, 11, 33 as in B.G. Tilak, *Gitarahasya*, introductory, 36.
171. See B.G. Tilak, *Gitarahasya*, introductory, 37.
172. See *The Collected Works of Mahatma Gandhi*, vol. 37, 267.
173. *The Collected Works of Mahatma Gandhi*, vol. 37, 261.
174. B.G. Tilak, *Selected Documents*, vol. 1, 83.
175. Ibid.
176. See K.M. Panikkar, "Impact of Europe", 21.
177. See K.M. Panikkar, "A Primer of India", 27.
178. See B.G. Tilak, *Selected Documents*, vol. 3, 65
179. B.G. Tilak, *Gitarahasya*,120.
180. Ibid., 47.
181. Ibid., 51.
182. See B.G. Tilak, *Gitarahasya*, 53.
183. D.D. Pattanaik, *Hindu Nationalism*, vol. 2, 37.
184. B.G. Tilak, *Gitarahasya*, Author's preface, xx.

185. See *Kesari* 17, 24, 15 June 1897, 3, as cited in S.A. Walport, *Tilak and Gokhale*, 86-87.
186. See B.G. Tilak, *Selected Documents*, vol. 1, 138.
187. Ibid., vol. 3, 12-13, 15.
188. Ibid., 3, 11.
189. See T.J.S. George, *The Enquire Dictionary*, 28.302. See also S.R. Goyal, *The Kautilya Arthasastra*, 166-174.
190. K.M. Panikkar, "Hindu Revival", 16.
191. *The Collected Works of Mahatma Gandhi*, vol. 22, 461-462.
192. Ibid., vol. 20, 369.
193. Ibid., vol. 88, 173.
194. See I. Strenski, "Legitimacy", 2.
195. For example, Joseph Goebbels, Adolf Hitler's right hand man, said: "*jedes* Mittel recht ist, diese Ketten der Sklaverei zu zerbrechen"('any means is right to break the shackles of slavery [of the German nation]. *Goebbels Reden 1932-1939*, Band 1, 1.
196. See K. Singh, *The End of India*, 28-29.
197. A. Roy, "Gujarat, Fascism and Democracy", 32.
198. See I. Strenski, "Legitimacy", 7.
199. See N. Godse, *Why I Assassinated Mahatma Gandhi*, 5.
200. See "At Last they Got Him", 31.
201. See Godse, *Gandhihatya ani Mee*, 46, 221 as cited in A. Nandy, *Bonfire of Creeds,* 87.
202. See T. Ghosh, *The Gandhi Murder Trial*, 25.
203. See A. Nandy, *Bonfire of Creeds,* 73.
204. See V.S. Naipaul, *India: A Wounded Civilisation,* 156.
205. Interview with Gopal Godse in Pune on 13 May 1969 as cited in W.K. Andersen and S.D. Damle, *The Brotherhood in Saffron*, 50-51
206. See P. Nair, "RSS' Godse Shrine", 47.
207. "At last they Got Him", 29-31. See also Nandy, *Bonfire of Creeds*, 70.
208. See R. Gandhi, *Revenge and Reconciliation*, 1,6.
209. See S.A. Walport, *Tilak and Gokhale*, 169.
210. See Baxter, *The Jana Sangh*, 3 2. See also H.V. Seshadri (ed.), *Dr. Hedgewar: The Epoch-Maker*, 35.
211. See B.G. Tilak, *Selected Documents*, vol. 2, 207; 216-217; 219-222.
212. See K. Elst, *The Saffron Swastika*, vol. 1, 497-498.

213. In 1951 N.B. Khare said in his presidential address of the Hindu Mahasabha: "Hindu Sabha stands for the Tilakite policy or the Gita policy". N.B. Khare, *Presidential Address* (1951), 23.
214. See P.C. Swain, *Bharatiya Janata Party*, 61. See also D.D. Pattanaik, *Hindu Nationalism*, vol. 2, 60.
215. P. Kanungo says: "The RSS has certainly borrowed from Tilak the technique of militant mobilisation to assert and consolidate Hindu identity." P. Kanungo, *RSS's Tryst with Politics*, 108.
216. See P. Kanungo, *RSS's Tryst with Politics*, 109.
217. See K. Kumar, "Hindu Revivalism", 545.
218. See N.N. Banerjee, *The Golden Jubilee* (1966), 6.
219. See Aurobindo, *India's Rebirth*, 46.
220. V.S. Naipaul, *India A Wounded Civilisation*, 92.
221. See A. Nandy, *Bonfire of Creeds*, 42, 142.
222. See B. Walker, *Hindu World*, vol. 1, 509.
223. A.G. Noorani, in his review article of the book by Manjari Katju entitled *Vishva Hindu Parishad and Indian Politics*, reminds us that the traditional depiction of Ram in lithographs has been accompanied by a mood of tranquillity and serenity, and he rarely assumes an angry disposition. However, Ram was made a weapon by the VHP all of a sudden in 1984 after the *Ekatmata Yagna* years of 1983. It is a political symbol which helps the VHP politically. See A.G. Noorani, "The BJP and the VHP", *Frontline*, 28 March 2003, 77. For similar ideas see also D. SMITH, *Hinduism and Modernity*, 41, 190-191.
224. See B. Walker, *Hindu World*, vol. 1, 425. The same Hanuman foolishly carried the whole mountain, unable to locate the magical drug Vishalyakarani that he was told to find on the hills for the treatment of Lakshman's war wounds. See A. Nandy, *Bonfire of Creeds*, 138.
225. See A. Nandy, *Bonfire of Creeds*, 42.
226. See G.M. Jagtiani, *Militant Hinduism ("Third Eye" of the Hindu)*, (1993). Notice the reference to 'third eye'.
227. See M.M. Ahluwalia, *Freedom Struggle in India*, 324, as cited in D.D. Pattanaik, *Hindu Nationalism*, vol. 2, 74.
228. See U. Mukherjee, *Two Great Revolutionaries: R.B. Bose and J.N. Mukherjee*, Calcutta, 1966, 17 as cited in C. Jaffrelot, *The Hindu Nationalist Movement*, 35.
229. See C. Jaffrelot, *The Hindu Nationalist Movement*, 41 footnote 124.
230. See Aurobindo, *India's Rebirth*, 131.

231. Ibid., 20.
232. See V.G. Deshpande, *Hindu Socialism Explained*, 15.
233. See C. Jaffrelot, *The Hindu Nationalist Movement*, 40-41.
234. See Trimondi, V. and Trimondi, V., *Hitler, Buddha, Krishna*, 26-27, 31,83.
235. See N.G. Clarke, *Hitler's Priestess*, 1-6; Trimondi, V. and Trimondi, V., *Hitler, Buddha, Krishna*, 342-360.
236. See Trimondi, V. and Trimondi, V., *Hitler, Buddha, Krishna*, 88.
237. Ibid., 89.
238. See K.M. Panikkar, "Hindu Revival", 14.
239. According to a popular view, the *Mahabharata* and the *Ramayana* revolve around a struggle between good and evil forces. In the former the 'good' Pandavas vanquish the 'bad' Kauravas in the Kurukshetra war, and in the latter the evil Rakshasas led by Ravana are defeated by Rama.
240. See B.S. Parakh (ed.), *Contemporary India*, 29-30.
241. See B. Walker, *Hindu World*, vol. 1, 540.
242. Ibid., 542.
243. See K. Kumar, "Hindu Revivalism", 555. P. Kanungo observes that the teleserial 'Chanakya' (1991-1992), though its theme appeared to be different from the epic serials 'Ramayana' and 'Mahabharata', in reality it was a mere continuation. See P. Kanungo, *RSS's Tryst with Politics*, 207.
244. See D.D. Pattanaik, *Hindu Nationalism*, vol. 2, 39.
245. See B.G. Tilak, *Selected Documents*, vol. 4, 17.
246. See A. Sharma, "Gandhi or Godse?", 24.
247. See S.C.S. Gupta, *Swami Vivekananda and Indian Nationalism*, 53.
248. See V. Rodrigues (ed.), *The Essential Writings of B.R. Ambedkar*, 193.
249. See P. Kanungo, RSS's *Tryst with Politics*, 203. Advani reportedly did not approve of this gesture and advised them to donate blood in the nearby hospital. See *Ibid.*, 220, note 103.
250. V.S. Naipaul, *India A Million Mutinies Now*, 418.

• IV •

Vinayak Damodar Savarkar as a Narrow Visionary and a Hindutva Hardliner

Vinayak Damodar Savarkar (1883-1966) was born on 28 May 1883 in the Chitpavan Brahmin family at Bhagur, a village near Nagpur in Maharashtra. After his matriculation in December 1901, he joined the prestigious Ferguson College, Pune, in 1902, where he excelled as a good speaker, powerful writer and organiser. He founded a secret society called *Mitra Mela* (Friends' Group) which later became *Abhinav Bharat* (Young India Society) on the model of the Italian revolutionary Giuseppe Mazzini's 'Young Italy'. After graduating in 1905 he moved to Bombay to study law. In the meantime, he received a scholarship to study in England, and set sail for London in 1906. During his student days in England, he started the 'Free India Society' and organised Indian students for revolutionary activities and spread his revolutionary ideas through pamphlets, booklets and books. He translated the life of Mazzini into Marathi, and some consider him as the personification of Mazzini.[1]

Savarkar was a congenital preacher of violence. There were conspiracy cases against him both in India and England. In 1910 he was charged with murdering an Englishman and was tried and sent to the Andamans in the same year. The ship carrying him stopped at Marseilles, where he jumped into the sea and swam to the shore to claim asylum on French soil. But he was captured and was transported to the Andamans.[2] In 1921 he was transferred to Ratnagiri Jail in Maharashtra. After his release from Ratnagiri Jail in 1937 he dedicated his time to organising the Hindu Mahasabha – a political party of Hindus with strong militant and communal leanings – as its president till 1942. He was the accused no. 7 in the Gandhi murder case[3] and though he was acquitted on technical grounds,[4] there are many, especially scholars, who strongly believe that Nathuram Godse who assassinated Gandhi was inspired by Savarkar's ideology and that the latter had approved the murder as a political weapon.[5] It has also been observed that Savarkar who propounded Hindutva was a 'non-believer' until he was converted to Buddhism late in life.[6] He died on 26 February 1966 at the age of 83, practically forgotten by all.[7]

Savarkar is one of the most controversial figures of modern India. For the Hindutva ideologues he is a celebrated 'hero', the 'father' of their ideology and a Hindu nationalist *par excellence.* For others he is a 'villain'[8] for whom violence was a way of life and who opposed the Indian National Congress and Mahatma Gandhi in the struggle for the independence of India.

Savarkar as a controversial figure

In recent years, it has become fashionable among Hindutva ideologues to pay blind obeisance to V.D. Savarkar as a 'freedom fighter' and a 'national hero'. Savarkar has been for a long time *veer* ('brave hero') in the Rashtriya Swayamsevak (RSS) folklore and in the school textbooks sponsored by them. A few years ago, the RSS attempted to have his statue erected in Marseilles, France, to commemorate his 'anti-British' stand in the early 1920s. The plan had to be abandoned after a worldwide protest campaign to the French President and the Mayor of Marseilles.

More recently, the former BJP-led government in New Delhi had the audacity to propose his name for the *Bharat Ratna* ('Jewel of India') award – the highest civilian award! In September 2001, a film was produced on Savarkar projecting him as a great freedom fighter. "On 4 May 2002, the Port Blair Airport, in the Andamans, was re-named after him – 'Veer Savarkar Airport!"[9] On 26th February 2003, amid a raging controversy, the President A.P.J. Abdul Kalam unveiled the portrait of Savarkar in the central hall of parliament in New Delhi, facing the painting of Mahatma Gandhi, which some people argue was done for the purpose of denigrating Gandhi. As the President unveiled the portrait, the BJP and the Shiv Sena MPs and their supporters shouted, *Swatantrya-Veer Savarkar Amar Rahe* (Long live Savarkar, the brave warrior of freedom).[10] In early 2004 the BJP-led government commissioned to set up a plaque dedicated to Savarkar on the *Swatantra Jyoti* ('Freedom Torch') monument in the Cellular Jail of Andamans.[11]

But does V.D. Savarkar really merit the epithet *swatantrya-veer* ('brave worrier of freedom')? Was he such a great, dedicated, brave revolutionary hero and freedom fighter throughout his life? These are questions that require close examination. Much has already been written against him being considered as a national hero and a freedom fighter. We examine afresh the 'Savarkar case' in order find the truth about him.

Attempts to create national heroes

One of the major problems faced by the contemporary Hindutva ideologues is that they lack respectable nationalist heroes. The Hindutva protagonists never possessed at any point of their history a person of national standing and acceptance. So, today, they are desperately seeking affiliations to recognised leaders of Indian nationalism. Through countrywide grassroots level campaigns, 'invention of historical evidences' and re-interpretation of history, and the use of print and electronic media, the Hindutva ideologues are trying to project that their leaders participated in the freedom struggle.[12] And one such figure is V.D. Savarkar, the 'father' of the modern Hindutva, who provides the ideological foundation for much of the present-day communal tensions in the country.

There are many Hindutva ideologues who use all possible means at their disposal to claim that the contribution of Savarkar in the freedom struggle has been as great as that of Mahatma Gandhi.[13] They also lament that Savarkar has not been given due recognition as a freedom fighter. In order to remedy this problem, recently, the combined efforts of the BJP, RSS, Vishva Hindu Parishad (VHP) and the Sangh Parivar have 'conferred' on him – much to the dismay of many reasonable Indians – the epithet '*swatantrya-veer*' ('brave worrier of freedom').[14] Some even claim that the two terms 'swatantrya veer' and 'Savarkar' are inseparable like flower and its fragrance, the lamp and its light.[15]

Reasons for questioning Savarkar's *veerata* (bravery)

It seems that those who have 'thrust' upon Savarkar the epithet *swatantrya-veer* has conveniently concealed the inconsistencies in his involvement in the freedom struggle, the fact of his servile surrender to the British colonial government, and his non-cooperation with Gandhi and the Indian National Congress in their struggle for freedom.

Savarkar underwent a serious metamorphosis during his years in jail in the Andamans between 1911 and 1921. He subjected himself to the British and pleaded clemency on *their* conditions and agreed to give full co-operation to them. Many documents to this effect are available in the national archives. He also worked against Gandhi and the Indian National Congress, which were the symbols of Indian national movement. Further, he actively promoted the Hindutva ideology, communalism, re-conversion, Hindu *rashtra* (nation) and 'xenophobia' towards such minorities as the Muslims, Christians, Communists, Secularists, Liberals, etc. Thus, Savarkar broke away from the mainstream freedom movement and adopted a public position expressing this break. He died in 1966, at the age of eighty-three, practically forgotten by the people of India because they knew that there was no real *veerata* (bravery) in the so-called *Veer* Savarkar.

Because of these reasons many right thinking people in India and outside have protested against the epithet *swatantrya-veer* being given to Savarkar. Documents that were available but were kept under cover for nearly eight decades show his true personality, not as *veer* but as a *coward*. Scholars have taken pain to research into the original documents and the writings of Savarkar himself in order to arrive at this conclusion. Today, he stands exposed as a 'hero' with a clay-feet – much to the embarrassment of the Hindutva ideologues who have assiduously attempted to promote him as a national hero.

Savarkar's flirt with Indian Nationalism

Savarkar's initial anti-British struggle was no doubt impressive and it commands respect. His *Abhinav Bharat* (Young India) drew its inspiration from Giuseppe Mazzini's *Giovani Italia* (Young Italy). Savarkar had gone to London to study law. While in England he formed the 'Free Indian Society' with a commitment to overthrowing British rule in India. His group learned the art of bomb-making from a Russian revolutionary in Paris. Because of his anti-British stance he was denied his barristership. He also secretly sent to India firearms and literature on bomb-making.

The patriotism of 'early' Savarkar is epitomised in his *The War of Independence 1857* in which he named the revolt of Indian soldiers against the British – the so-called 'Sepoy Mutiny' – 'the War of Indian independence'. It is this 'early' phase of Savarkar's life alone that the contemporary Hindutva protagonists highlight when they present him as a 'hero' of India's struggle for independence. They conveniently hide his subsequent life which was marked by pro-British attitudes and total non-involvement in any major activity aimed at Indian nationalism.

Savarkar's surrender to the British

The conditions in the prison of the Andamans were no doubt harsh but not a few patriots faced it courageously. But Savarkar was not one among them. He appealed for clemency, first in 1911[16] and then again in 1913,[17] the latter during the visit of Sir Reginald Craddock. In a letter dated November 14, 1913, Savarkar wrote to the Home Minister of the Government of India:

> I hereby acknowledge that I had a fair trial and just sentence. I heartily abhor methods of violence resorted to in days gone by and I feel myself duty bound to *uphold law and constitution* [British] to the best of my powers and am willing to *make the reform* [i.e., the Montague-Chelmsford reforms of 1919 which did not satisfy the demands of the nationalist movement] *a success* in so far as I may be allowed to do so in future.[18]

We read again:

> If the government in their manifold beneficence and mercy release me, I for one cannot but be the *staunchest advocate* of constitutional progress and *loyalty to the English government* which is the foremost condition of that progress [...] Moreover, my *conversion* to the constitutional line would bring back all those mislead young men in India and abroad who were once looking up to me as their guide [...] The Mighty alone can afford to be merciful and therefore where else can the *prodigal son* return but to the parental doors of the government.[19]

In response to the petition, the British government released him under the condition that he will stay in Ratnagiri district and will seek the permission of the British government to leave the district and also that he will not engage in any public or private political activities without the consent of the government. The period of conditions lasted till 1937.

It is important to note here that Savarkar in his letter *acknowledged that he had a fair trial*. He also accepted the conditions set by the British without any compunction. He stated that *if released he would be a staunch advocate of the British policies*. The language of his letter is clearly *servile* and it brings out the *coward* in him.

In 1920, Gandhi wrote in *Young India* about Savarkar's attitude towards the British: "They [the Savarkar brothers] both state unequivocally that they do not desire independence from the British connection. On the contrary, they feel that India's destiny can be worked out in association with the British."[20] Thus, Savarkar 'forfeited' his claim to be a revolutionary freedom fighter and bartered the country's independence to obtain his own personal freedom. This act of surrender to the British alone is sufficient to obliterate all the revolutionary feats attributed to him by his contemporary followers.

Savarkar as an advocate of Hindu nationalism

During his detention in the Andamans, Savarkar's views underwent a great change. He renounced the struggle against British imperialism and transformed himself from being a revolutionary nationalist to a staunch proponent of Hindu fascism. In the ideological front Savarkar came to be greatly influenced by German racism. He studied with care Bluntschli's *The Theory of the State* – a book which he had not only read but also used when teaching his fellow prisoners. Bluntschli was an exponent of German ethnic nationalism and his writings influenced many other Hindu nationalists, including M.S. Golwalkar.[21] Savarkar also took inspiration from other Western architects of ethnic nationalism.

Savarkar was a changed person after his jail term in the Andamans. Then on he never associated with anything even remotely sounding as anti-British. In 1923, he published his controversial *Hindutva: Who is a Hindu?* which won him the title 'Father of Hindutva'.[22] Again, soon after his release from the Andamans, K.B. Hedgewar, the founder of the RSS, met him in Ratnagiri prison to obtain his support for the founding of the RSS, inaugurated in 1925.

Savarkar joins the Hindu Mahasabha

In 1937, the conditions of Savarkar's release were removed completely. On release he was invited to join the Congress. But he refused and joined the Hindu Mahasabha (The Great Hindu Conference). J.D. Joglekar comments: "The man who wrote *Hindutva* and also many newspaper articles about the 'Hindu Nation' was surely not likely to join the Congress."[23]

In the same year Savarkar was elected president of the Hindu Mahasabha – the political wing of the Hindutva ideologists. R.C. Majumdar states that Savarkar was re-elected year after year and the organisation developed into a political and communal body.[24] About the communal nature of the Hindu Mahasabha, Nehru said: "The chief Hindu communal organisation is the Hindu Mahasabha, the counterpart of the Muslim League [...,] It is as aggressively communal as the League."[25]

Savarkar then began openly heaping abuses on Mahatma Gandhi and the Congress leaders. He branded Gandhi as an appeaser of Muslims. He also stated that *the struggle for supremacy would begin after the British have left* and that the Christians and Muslims were the *real enemies* who could be defeated only by Hindutva. He also had close contacts with the RSS – today's apex organisation of Hindu nationalists. Nathuram Godse, who assassinated Mahatma Gandhi in 1948, was an ardent follower of Savarkar. Savarkar himself was a co-accused in the murder of Gandhiji but was acquitted only due to lack of sufficient evidence.

Withdrawal from mainstream nationalism

A clemency letter in itself does not make Savarkar any less of a hero. But, we must also see what he did *in the prison* and what was his major concern *after the release*. His interest was in winning the friendship of the Hindus and the British. The old antagonism against the British imperialists did not exist any more. The Hindu Mahasabha actively campaigned to recruit

Hindu young men into the British army and the Congress activists used to call Savarkar a 'recruiting officer'. When Gandhi launched the 'Quit India Movement' asking people to renounce government jobs, Savarkar gave a counter-order saying: "I issue this definite instruction to all Hindu Sanghatanists in general holding any post or position of vantage in the government service, should stick to them and continue to perform their regular duties."[26]

Gandhi tried in vain to woo Savarkar into the mainstream nationalism. He says: "I have tried to woo him [V.D. Savarkar] and his friends. I have walked to Savarkar's house. I have gone out of my way to win him over. But I have failed."[27] Thus, Savarkar and his followers deliberately dissociated themselves from the gigantic struggle for national liberation from the colonial rule.

The strategic plan of the Hindu Mahasabha was to take on the reign of India after the independence. Savarkar's intention was to establish a Hindu *rashtra* out of India, and those who opposed it were branded as pseudo-nationalists. He said: "The demand for a Hindu Raj, these pseudo-nationalists say, is communal, stupid, mediaeval, theocratical, a menace to the progress of mankind itself."[28] He publicly asked the Hindus to oppose the efforts of Gandhi and the Congress. He stated: "I warn the Hindu Electorate categorically for the thousandeth [sic] time that unless they remove these Pseudo-nationalist leaders from the helm of our state: the Gandhistic Indianism will allow Moslems inside India to capture key posts in the army, the police, the state."[29] Such an attitude led Gandhi to say: "I find that the Hindu Mahasabha has made it their *dharma* to oppose Congress candidates everywhere."[30] As president of the Hindu Mahasabha, he urged his followers to boycott the Indian National Congress, asked them never to vote for a Congress candidate in any election but vote only for confirmed and merited Hindu nationalists.[31]

Father of modern Hindutva ideology or Savarkarism

Savarkar wrote *Hindutva* in 1922 while still in prison in Ratnagiri and published it in Nagpur in 1923, and it became and remains the basic text that defines this politico-religious concept. Since then, his 'enemy' was not the British imperialists but the minority religious groups and the secularists of India.

The Hindutva, according to him, rests on three pillars: *geographical unity*, *racial unity* and *common culture*. Those who regard India as their 'fatherland' and 'holyland' are the people to whom India belongs. This automatically excludes the Indian Christians and Muslims because, according to him, their holy places are in Jerusalem and Mecca respectively, and not in India.

The primary aim of his *Hindutva* was to reconstruct and mobilise the Indian Hindus through a process of Hindu identity-building based on exclusivism, xenophobia, violence, aggression and the ethics of 'end justifies the means'. He built the foundation for this on the rudimentary evidences of prejudice and conflict and by concocting false propaganda against the minorities.

Savarkar had strong links with some of the Nazis of his time. For example, the influence of Savitri Devi, the 'Hitler's Priestess', on the *Hindu Mahasabha* is an established fact.[32] Savarkar's oft-repeated slogan was "Hinduise all politics and militarise Hinduism".[33] One can find the same exhortation in the last part of Savitri Devi's pamphlet *A Warning to Hindus* published in 1939.[34] Some of the methods that Savarkar suggested for the spread of Hindutva were borrowed from the Nazis. In August 1938, he spoke to a crowd of 20,000 in Pune saying that Germany has every right to resort to Nazism and Italy to Fascism and events have justified that those 'isms' and forms of government were imperative and beneficial to them under the conditions that existed there. Savarkar's love of the Nazis was born out of his obsession with the idea of the 'dictatorship of the majority' and xenophobia. About Savarkar and his collaborators Gandhi commented: "Very few, if any, member of the Hindu Mahasabha are believers in non-violence. Neither Shri Savarkar nor Dr. Moonje nor Bhai Paramanand are".[35] "Those Hindus [...] like Dr. Moonje and Shri Savarkar, believe in the doctrine of the sword."[36]

Campaign for Hindu *rashtra*

Savarkar aimed at establishing a Hindu *rashtra* in India and he passionately appealed to the communal instincts of the Hindus. His oft-repeated slogan was *Hindustan Hinduonka* (India belongs to the Hindus).[37] He defined India as one "who regards this land of Bharatvarsha, from the Indus to the Seas as his Father-Land and as well as his Holy-Land that is the cradle land of his religion."[38] He advocated that India is to be a Hindu nation. His cry was: "Dravidians or Aryans [...] Hindus first and everything else next."[39] He added: "The Hindu Sanghatanist ideology alone can therefore, save our nation and re-establish an Akhand Hindusthan from Indus to the Seas."[40]

On the nature of the Hindu nation Savarkar said: "the Hindus, they being the people, whose past, present and future are most closely bound with the soil of Hindusthan as Pitribhu (fatherland), as Punyabhu (holyland), they constitute the foundation, the bedrock, the reserved forces of the Indian state."[41] Hence, he argued that the Hindus are a nation by themselves because of their religious, cultural, racial and historical affinities and geographical unity and these bind them together to form a homogenous nation.[42]

Savarkar envisaged a Hindu nation that is founded on pseudo-secularism, force, violence, threat of the 'other' and military might. He said: "...our state must raise a mighty force exclusively constituted by Hindus alone, must open arms and ammunition factories exclusively manned by the Hindus alone and mobilise everything on a war scale."[43] He asked the Hindus to elect only Hindus to represent them in the legislatures as they alone can, according to him, safeguard, defend and promote the interests of the Hindus.[44] Hence, he urged the Hindu *Sanghatanists* to capture political power wherever possible – in municipal boards, legislatures, provincial and central governments – and boycott the Indian National Congress[45] and vote only for confirmed Hindu nationalists.[46]

But Savarkar knew that such a state of affairs was not to be contemplated as long as Gandhi, Nehru and other secular leaders led the national movement. Nehru emphatically said: "...if you think in terms of any kind of a communal state, a Hindu Rashtra, etc. you are not going to get it, however much you may try."[47] Such a view led Savarkar to assert: "As [...] neither the Gandhistic ideology nor the pseudo-nationalistic ideology of the Congress can ever cope with this Islamic offensive and as the *Hindu Sanghatanist ideology alone* can and will be able to fight out this danger successfully, the Government should consist of such Ministers alone who are pledged to the Hindu Sanghatanist ideology alone."[48]

Savarkar nurtured a narrow-minded nationalism based on Hindu religion and Hindu culture. He said: "To us, Hindus, Hindustan and India mean one and the same thing."[49] The resolution 13 passed by Hindu Mahasabha session held from 17 December 1936 to 7 January 1937 spoke of Savarkar as one who is engaged in the *cause of Hinduism*. It read: "It [Hindu Mahasabha] notes with gratefulness the splendid services which Mr. Savarkar has been rendering to the cause of Hinduism and urges the government to remove all restrictions imposed upon him at present so as to enable him to serve more fully and completely his religion, community and country."[50]

Savarkar accused Nehru saying that he had been indulging in furious denunciations against the demand for a Hindu nation as if the mere demand for a Hindu nation constitutes a danger to his government.[51] He said: "Pandit Nehru swaggers on that if the Hindu Sanghatanists persist on in their efforts to establish a Hindu Raj, they would meet with the fate of Hitler and Mussolini."[52] He questioned those who stood for a secular nation saying: "How is it then that the very mention of the name of Hindustan or the Hindu State alone takes your breath out as if you were smitten by a snake bite?"[53]

Advocate of pan-Hinduism

Savarkar advocated the concept of pan-Hinduism. In 1937, as president of the Hindu Mahasabha, he stated in his presidential address in Ahmedabad: "...the Hindu Mahasabha is not in the main a Hindu Dharma Sabha, but it is pre-eminently a Hindu Rashtra Sabha and is a pan-Hindu organisation shaping the destiny of the Hindu nation in all its social, political and cultural aspects."[54]

To Savarkar the calling of the Hindu Kingdom of Nepal as a foreign country was intolerable. He held that the brave and warlike Gurkhas were part and parcel of Hinduism and any move to keep them segregated from India was strongly and relentlessly opposed by him. In fact, under his guidance, the Ratnagiri Hindu Sabha initiated a movement to bring them back to pan-Hinduism.[55]

Against the co-existence of Hindus and Muslims

When 'early' Savarkar wrote his *The War of Independence 1857*, he upheld Hindu-Muslim unity. He also remained unflinchingly opposed to the British. But, after his conversion to the Hindutva ideology, on several occasions he gave hints concerning the impossibility of a co-existence of Hindus and Muslims. He accused the Indian Muslims of being anti-Hindu, anti-Indian with extra-territorial allegiance.[56] According to him, the entire Muslim community in India is communal.[57] In 1939 he said that nationality did not depend so much on a common geographical area as on unity of thought, religion, language and culture. For this reason the Germans and the Jews could not be regarded as a nation. Later, in the same year, he made a statement in the 21st session of the Hindu Mahasabha that the Indian Muslims are on the whole more inclined to identify themselves and their interests with Muslims outside India than Hindus who live next door, like the Jews in Germany. He said: "I warn the Hindus that the Mahommedans are likely to prove dangerous to our Hindu nation."[58]

Savarkar staunchly advocated the two-nation theory and the partition of India. He said: "I have no quarrel with Mr. Jinnah's two-nation theory. We, Hindus are a nation by ourselves and it is a historical fact that Hindus and Muslims are two nations."[59] He accused the Muslims of staying away from the national struggle for independence but reaping fruits of that struggle.[60] It was his conviction that a Muslim remains a Muslim first and Muslim last and Indians never.[61]

Muslims and Christians are foreigners

Savarkar's Hindutva propounded the theory that Muslims and Christians are foreigners and, therefore, they have no place in India. He said: "Mohammadens and Christian communities possess all the essential qualifications of Hindutva but one and all that is that they do not look upon India as their holyland."[62] He affirmed again: "Their holyland is far off in Arabia and Palestine. Their mythology and Godmen, ideas and heroes are not the children of this soil. Consequently, their names and their outlook smack of foreign origin. Their love is divided."[63] He further noted: "But besides culture the tie of common holyland has at times proved stronger than the claims of a Motherland. Look at the Mohammedans [...] Mecca to them is a stronger reality than Delhi or Agra. Some of them do not make any secret of being bound to sacrifice all India if that be to the glory of Islam [...] The crusades again attest to the wonderful influence that a common holyland exercises over peoples widely separated in race, nationality and language, to bind and hold them together."[64]

Re-conversion (*shuddhi*) activities

One of the most sensitive activities in which the Hindu Mahasabha indulged in was the re-conversion or *shuddhi* movement. Savarkar fought tooth and nail against any Hindu changing his religious allegiance. According to him, foreign faiths like Islam and Christianity convert millions of Hindus by force and fraud in the length and breadth of India.[65] The British colonial government lend political support to Christian missionaries in India in their conversion activities.[66] Hence, Savarkar ardently advocated re-conversion with the spirit of a fanatic. When he returned to Ratnagiri, one of his principle activities was re-conversion. As president of the Hindu Mahasabha, he exhorted the Hindus to re-convert the Christians and carry on the *shuddhi* movement.[67]

In his memories and diaries of the prison days Savarkar glorified his years in the prison by claiming that he contributed to the political education of the prisoners. But, the writings pertaining to those years are not bereft of communal poison. He engaged himself in re-conversion activities. For instance, while in the Andamans, his fanaticism led him to the extent of performing *shuddhi* thereby reclaiming the Hindus who were converted to Islam.[68]

On several occasions Savarkar spoke disparagingly of Muslims and Christians: "The scandalous activities of Bengal Moslem gundas and proselytisers, working hand in hand have become so persistent and so notorious that one cannot understand how the Hindus in East Bengal have grown so incredibly emasculated."[69] "The Moslem shopkeepers, those who visit Hindu ladies for selling glass bangles, Moslem servants in Hindu houses – all try to seduce or kidnap boys and girls and generally force them to accept Mahommedanism."[70] "The Christians also are making great progress in this state. If things go on like that Sambhar would cease to contain a Hindu home."[71]

J.D. Joglekar notes that the first re-conversion at Savarkar's instance took place in 1925, when one Jadhav, who had become a Christian, was brought back to the Hindu fold. The next year, a whole Brahmin family converted to Christianity, was re-converted.[72]

Savarkar believed that conversions from Hinduism are a direct attack on India's nationhood. B.K. Kelkar, commenting on the philosophy of Savarkar, says that he played a triple role of a *thinker* of Hindutva, a *protector* of it and the *organiser* of

Hindus. He also held the view that to change one's religion meant to change one's nationhood and culture. According to him, the proselytisation carried on by Christians and Muslims weans the people away from the cultural mainstream of the nation, and ultimately they no longer remain a part of the nation.[73]

Advocate of militancy and terrorism

Savarkar advocated violence, terrorism and militancy. Ashis Nandy calls Savarkar the non-believing father of Hindu nationalism.[74] According to Savarkar, Hindutva is not only a means of Hinduising the polity but also of militarising the effeminate, disorganised Hindu.[75] In fact, he scoffed at Gandhi's concept of non-violence and said that it is steel and gun-powder that decide the destiny of nations.[76]

Right from his early years Savarkar was inclined towards violence, terrorism and militancy. He founded the secret society *Mitra Mela*, which later known as the *Abhinava Bharat.* His recruits were primarily college students. The various units of this group promoted traditional forms of physical exercise and popularised nationalist ballads and poetry to serve as tools in spreading their message among the masses. The *Abhinava Bharat* advocated armed revolution in order to throw off the shackles of foreign rule. It had links with the *Anushilan Samiti* of Bengal, which was also a revolutionary party.[77]

Savarkar, during his stay in England, recruited Indian students into an underground unit, which smuggled into India anti-British literature, manuals on the manufacture of explosives, guns and nationalist books.[78] He translated the life of Giuseppe Mazzini, the Italian fascist, into Marathi and 20,000 copies of it were distributed. His *Joan of Arc* also gained popularity among his followers. His article entitled "A Call to Arms" appeared in *Hindustan Review* in 1906 incited revolutionary activities. He concluded his version of the Cawnpore massacre with the prayer that "Mother Ganges, who drank that day the blood of Europeans may drink her to fill again".[79]

The armed Sinn Feiner movement[80] of Ireland, led by De Valera is said to have influenced the Indian revolutionaries. Valera, was an occasional visitor to V.D. Savarkar at India House, London.[81] In London, on 1 June 1909, Madan Lal Dhingra, a close associate of Savarkar, shot and killed Sir William Curzon-Wyllie.[82] Rajmohan Gandhi remarks that Dhingra's deed had been inspired and perhaps aided by a certain Shyamji Krishnavarma and Savarkar, and both of them eluded the British Police. The statement that Dhingra read at his trial was drafted by Savarkar.[83] In 1910, Savarkar was tried and convicted as a conspirator in the murder of a British official in India, and was sentenced to life imprisonment on the Andaman Islands. But, the saffronised NCERT school textbook for Social Sciences for Class IX conveniently 'forgets' to explain *why* Savarkar was arrested and sentenced to transportation for life. It simply states: "Shyamji Krishna Varma's close associate V.D. Savarkar was also arrested and sentenced to transportation for life in April 1910."[84]

In 1921, Savarkar was removed from the Andamans to a prison at Ratnagiri, India. At Ratnagiri Jail, in 1922, he wrote *Hindutva*. Copies of the tract were reproduced by hand and distributed among Maharashtrian nationalists and Hedgewar, the founder of the RSS read one of these hand-written copies.[85] It has been observed that when Nathuram Godse left the RSS[86] and formed the Hindu Rashtra Dal (1943), a paramilitary organisation, it received the blessing of Savarkar.[87] Nathuram Godse, who murdered Gandhi, was a close associate of Savarkar.[88] Speaking in the context of the assassination of Gandhi, the then Home Minister Sardar Patel wrote: "It was a fanatical wing of the Hindu Mahasabha directly under Savarkar that [hatched] the conspiracy and saw it through."[89]

Larry Collins and Dominique Lapierre in *Freedom at Midnight* (1976, chapter 16) claim, on the basis of the authors' interviews with Gopal Godse (brother of Nathuram Godse) that Nathuram Godse and his political mentor Savarkar had had a homosexual relationship. This may or may not be true, and Gopal Godse has denied that he had ever mentioned his brother's homosexuality while being interviewed.[90]

Implementation of Savarkarism today

The militant Hindutva ideology of Savarkar or 'Savarkarism' dominates Indian political and religious scene today. When the political power in New Delhi was in the hands of the Hindutva ideologues, they engaged in re-writing the Indian history along fascist lines, and persons like Savarkar, Golwalkar, Hedgewar, Moonje and Godse emerged as 'national heroes'. In the process, the memories of collective struggle for independence and its true symbols and landmarks were being forgotten, and its towering personalities were replaced by dwarfs and cowards.

Even after the fall of the BJP-led NDA government in New Delhi in 2004, there are many in the Indian Parliament and the state governments who have been schooled in Savarkarism. Savarkar believed in a strong militarised India, and in consonance with it the BJP-led government made sure that India's nuclear and missile programmes went ahead without any break.

Lal Krishna Advani learned Hindutva from Savarkar and many of his policies are literal implementation of the ideas of his ideological mascot. Atal Bihari Vajpayee who headed the previous right-wing BJP-led government, Murali Manohar Joshi who directed the saffronisation of Indian education and the re-writing of history along the Hindutva lines as the HRD minister, Sita Ram Goel, Ram Swarup and Arun Shourie who gained notoriety for maligning the minorities of India through their pen pushing, Narendra Modi who is called the cave man of Gujarat, a 'modern day Nero' and an adept in the use of political language *without* refinement or restraint, Bal Thackeray, the Hitler admirer, the RSS, the VHP, the Bajrang Dal and other members of the Sangh Parivar who indulge in violence, crime, communalism and show of muscle power and so on, are some of those who are schooled in Savarkarism and who consider Savarkar as their 'national' hero. But Savarkar cannot be the hero of any true patriotic Indian who values secularism and the pluralistic culture of India. Thus, Savarkar remains as an icon only for the Hindutva ideologues.

No '*veerata*' in the so-called 'Veer Savarkar'

Savarkar started his public career as a large-hearted revolutionary patriot and anti-British. But his flirtation with freedom struggle did not last long. He renounced his principles in the Andaman jails and after his release from prison he stayed away from all anti-British activities. With his aggressive anti-Gandhi, anti-Congress and anti-minority propaganda, he ended up helping the British in their policy of divide and rule.

The defence of Savarkar and projecting him as a national hero are result of a reaction to strong criticism from secular and democratic Indians. It is true that some credit should be given to him for his contribution to Indian nationalism in his early years *prior* to his arrival in the Andamans. But, on no account does he deserve the honour of being called *swatantrya-veer* Savarkar! Any attempt in popularising this epithet will automatically legitimise the fascist doctrine of the Hindutva. It will strike at the very root of India's secularism and veritably destroy the edifice of Indian religious and cultural pluralism.

Therefore, in order to assess the merit of Savarkar, it is not enough to limit oneself to the study of his life and activities *prior* to his deportation to the Andamans – as the contemporary Hindutva ideologues are doing. It tells us only the half truth about Savarkar. The other half is a story of cowardice, fanaticism, fascism, racism, militancy, terrorism, servitude to the British and Hindu sectarian nationalism. Those who indulge in such activities cannot be freedom fighters. Again, the truth about Savarkar is that he accepted the humiliating terms from the British, openly opposed Gandhi's policies, the Civil Obedience Movement and the Indian National Congress. He recruited Indians for the British Army. He did not participate in any anti-British agitation. He preached the ideology of Hindutva, Hindu communalism, pseudo-secularism, hatred of the minorities and practice of re-conversion. He advocated the two-nation theory and pan-Hinduism and allegedly participated in the conspiracy to murder Mahatma Gandhi and was one of the accused.

Thus, Savarkar showed little *veerata* (bravery) as a freedom fighter and patriot. He was the embodiment of cowardice, selfishness, non-patriotism, narrow nationalism, communalism, and one who worked against true national interests. He betrayed the trust of the Indians and their aspirations by arraying himself against his own motherland and by co-operating with the British. He opposed the great leaders of India's freedom struggle like Gandhi and Nehru. Against the policies of the Indian National Congress he cultivated the politico-communal organisation called the Hindu Mahasabha. Mahatma Gandhi said: "There are only two parties – the Congress and those who side with the Congress, and the parties who do not."[91] How could then such a person as Savarkar deserve the epithet '*swatantrya-veer*'?

Conclusion

Throughout his life Savarkar was obsessed with violence, bloodshed, revenge and retribution, and he considered them as legitimate means for achieving his ends. He ardently promoted the communal Hindu Mahasabha, collaborated with the British and was a major conspirator in Gandhi's assassination and was acquitted only on technical grounds. The various political stances he took after his arrest and deportation to the Andamans and after his release from prison, prove beyond doubt the absurdity of placing him on the pedestal along with the great freedom fighters and patriots of India. Hence, the claim that Savarkar was a true patriot and a brave freedom fighter is a myth without any foundation, and consequently he does not deserve the epithet *swatantrya-veer.* As Praful Bidwai says, the effort to elevate him to a national icon is utterly despicable and repugnant and must be categorically rejected. Savarkar was no *veer* (hero) and must not be glorified and his name does not deserve to adorn Port Blair Airport or the Central Hall of Parliament.[92] We may conclude with the words of M.S. Golwalkar: "Strange, very strange, that traitors should sit enthroned as national and patriots heaped with ignominy. This is the point. We have learned to call a class of people patriots, saviours of the nation."[93] This can aptly be applied to V.D. Savarkar.

Notes

1. D. Keer, *Veer Savarkar*, 54.
2. For a detailed account of Savarkar's escape and capture and the judicial procedure which followed between the French and the British see File 847 V.D. Savarkar; arrest and extradition, escape and recapture at Marseilles (18 March – 7 October 1910), L/P&J/6/994, India Office, British Library, London; File 359 Savarkar case; Cases, Counter Cases and Replies, etc. (15 December 1910-10 March 1911), L/P&J/6/1060, India Office, British Library, London; File 778 Savarkar Case, trial and conviction, question of extradition in the case of failure at the Hague (9 December 1910-23 February 1911), L/P&J/6/1069, India Office, British Library, London; File 1131 Savarkar Case; Proceedings at the Hague (including result) (28 January - 21 April 1911), L/P&J/6/1077, India Office, British Library, London.
3. Savarkar was arrested on 11 March 1948 and was made an accused in the conspiracy case. See S. Godbole, "Congress Loves to Hate Savarkar", 15.
4. Savarkar was acquitted because there was no corroborative point to confirm Digamber Ramachandra Badge's crucial testimony. But twenty years after the assassination the Justice Jivan Lal Kapur Commission of Inquiry found that Badge's evidence was being corroborated by Savarkar's bodyguard Appa Ramachandra Kasar and Gajanan Vishnu Damle. See R. Ramachandran, "The Mastermind", 35.
5. For a discussion on this issue see R. Ramachandran, "The Mastermind?", 33-35; "'Please don't' Get Angry with your Shishya'", 1. It is reported that on 31 January 1948 a mob of some 1500 people attacked Savarkar's house in Mumbai and his younger brother

Narayanrao Savarkar was seriously injured in the attack. See S. Godbole, "Congress Loves to Hate Savarkar", 15.

6. See "Aiyarspeak", 25.
7. That Savarkar was a national and political 'non-entity' in independent India is evident especially from the following. It is said that the Maharashtra Government had kept spies outside Savarkar's house till the very end of his life; since Savarkar was championing militarization, some thought that it would be fitting if his mortal remains were to be carried on a gun-carriage. A request to that effect was made to the then Defence Minister Y.B. Chavan. But Chavan turned down the proposal; not a single minister from the Maharashtra Cabinet showed up in the cremation ground to pay homage to Savarkar; in New Delhi, the Speaker of the Parliament turned down a request that it pay homage to Savarkar; after the independence of India, Jawaharlal Nehru had put forward a proposal to demolish the Cellular Jail in the Andamans and build a hospital in its place; when Y.B. Chavan, as the Home Minister of India, went to the Andamans, he was asked whether he would like to visit Savarkar's jail. Chavan was not interested; when Morarji Desai went as Prime Minister to the Andamans, he too refused to visit Savarkar's cell. See S. Godbole, "Congress Loves to Hate Savarkar", 15.
8. See the cover story of *Indian Currents*, 15 September 2004 with the caption 'Hero or Villain? Or does it matter at all'.
9. See A.G. Noorani, "Savarkar and Gandhi", 34.
10. See "Kalam Unveils Savarkar Portrait", 1. The BJP General Secretary Pramod Mahajan, defending Bal Thackeray who made certain derogatory remarks about Mahatma Gandhi, said that Gandhi could at best be regarded as India's *suputra* ('a great son') but not *rashtra pita* ('father of the nation'): a country which is over 5,000 years old does not need a father. See *The Times of India*, 4 January 1997 as cited in P. Kanungo, *RSS's Tryst with Politics*, 216, note 49.
11. When the Congress-led UPA government came into power after the general elections of April-May 2004, under the order of Mani Shankar Aiyar, the Union Minister for Petroleum, the plaque carrying quotes from Savarkar was removed from *Swatantra Jyoti* and were substituted by words of Mahatma Gandhi. This of course led to a political controversy.
12. A.G. Noorani observes that it took the Sangh Parivar long to own up Savarkar. The Jan Sangh never spoke of him or of Hindutva from 1951-1977. The BJP, formed in 1980, took up Hindutva only in 1990

and Savarkar in 2000, through Atal Bihari Vajpayee. See A.G. Noorani, "Savarkar and Gandhi", 36.

13. A.G. Noorani says that the unveiling of Savarkar's portrait in Parliament House on 26 February 2003 shows that Hindutva ideologues are prepared to stoop very low in order to accomplish their sordid ends. It will replace the national ideology of secularism with Hindutva and the national hero Gandhi as the Father of the nation, with Savarkar. See A.G. Noorani, "Savarkar and Gandhi", 36.
14. See, for instance, H.V. Seshadri, "The Swatantrya-Veer", 367-375.
15. See J. Trehan, "Savarkarism', 500.
16. A.G. Noorani says that Savarkar was brought to the Andamans on 4 July 1911. Before the year ended he sent his first petition for clemency. See A.G. Noorani, "Savarkar and Gandhi", 35.
17. But these were not all. A.G. Noorani observes that Savarkar has a sustained record of abject apologies. He says: "Which other freedom fighter has so sustained a record of abject apologies and undertakings?. They were given in 1911, 1913, 1925, 1948 and 1950. The last was given in the Bombay High Court on July 13, 1950 to secure release from preventive detention." A.G. Noorani, "Savarkar and Gandhi", 36.
18. From the facsimile of Savarkar's letter, *Frontline*, 7 April 1995 (emphasis added).
19. R.C. Majumdar, *Penal Settlement in Andamans*, 213. For the complete text of Savarkar's mercy petition dated 14 November 1913 see *Mainstream* 25 September 2004, 14-15.
20. *The Collected Works of Mahatma Gandhi*, vol. 17, 462.
21. See C. Jaffrelot, *The Hindu Nationalist Movement*, 32.
22. Some scholars argue that, for writing *Hindutva Who is a Hindu?* Savarkar borrowed from one of a number of writers and thinkers of nineteenth century Bengal who had used this definition in roughly the same form. See P. Kanungo, *RSS's Tryst with Politics*, 129 note 23. Others see it as a Brahmanical effort of appropriation of non-Brahmanical schools of thought from Jainism down to Virashaiva movement. See *Ibid.*, 134 note, 106.
23. J.D. Joglekar, "Veer Savarkar: Profile of a Prophet", 324.
24. See R.C. Majumdar, *The History and Culture*, 611-612.
25. J. Nehru, *The Discovery of India*, 425.
26. Quoted by A.G. Noorani "The Collaborators", *Frontline*, 1 December 1995.

27. *The Collected Works of Mahatma Gandhi*, vol. 70, 348.
28. V.D. Savarkar, "Nehru's Nightmare – Hindu Raj?", 171.
29. Ibid., 173.
30. *The Collected Works of Mahatma Gandhi*, vol. 82, 26.
31. See V.D. Savarkar, *Hindu Sanghatan*, 100-101.
32. See Trimondi, V. and Trimondi, V., *Hitler, Buddha, Krishna*, 344.
33. See V.D. Savarkar, *Historic Statements*, 1,2,76,98.
34. See Trimondi, V. and Trimondi, V., *Hitler, Buddha, Krishna*, 345.
35. *The Collected Works of Mahatma Gandhi*, vol. 73, 311.
36. Ibid., vol. 76, 389.
37. See V.D. Savarkar, *Hindu Sanghatan*, 116.
38. V.D. Savarkar, *Hindutva*, 116.
39. V.D. Savarkar, "Then Who is Who, Pray", 169.
40. V.D. Savarkar, "Nehru's Nightmare: Hindu Raj?", 173.
41. V.D. Savarkar, *Hindutva*, 140.
42. See V.D. Savarkar, *Hindu Sanghatan*, 84.
43. V.D. Savarkar, "Problems before Hindudom", 177.
44. See V.D. Savarkar, *Historic Statements*, 1.
45. Ibid., 21-22.
46. See V.D. Savarkar, *Hindu Sanghatan*, 101,103.
47. *Selected Writings of Jawaharlal Nehru*, vol. 7, 404.
48. V.D. Savarkar, "Problems before Hindudom", 177 (emphasis added).
49. V.D. Savarkar, *Hindu Sanghatan*, 83.
50. File 50 Hindu Mahasabha Resolutions passed at the 18th session, held at Lahore (17 December 1936-7 January 1937), Resolution No. 13, p.8, L/P&J/71186, India Office, British Library, London.
51. See V.D. Savarkar, "Nehru's Nightmare: Hindu Raj?", 170.
52. V.D. Savarkar, "Nehru's Nightmare: Hindu Raj?", 171.
53. Ibid., 172.
54. Quoted in C. Gupta, "Life of Barrister Savarkar, 297.
55. See C. Gupta, "Life of Barrister Savarkar", 291.
56. See V.D. Savarkar, *Hindu Sanghatan*, 17, 23.
57. Ibid., 76.
58. V.D. Savarkar, *Hindu Sanghatan*, 31.
59. V.D. Savarkar, *Hindutva*, 140. A.G. Noorani notes that Savarkar propounded the two-nation theory first in 1923 in his *Hindutva* and

next in 1937 in his presidential address to the Hindu Mahasabha. See A.G. Noorani, "Savarkar and Gandhi", *Frontline*, 28 March 2003, 36.

60. See V.D. Savarkar, *Hindu Sanghatan*, 21.
61. Ibid., 68.
62. V.D. Savarkar, *Hindutva*, 113.
63. Ibid., 113.
64. Ibid., 135-136.
65. See V.D. Savarkar, *Hindu Sanghatan*, 46.
66. Ibid., 56.
67. Ibid., 91.
68. See C. Gupta, "Life of Barrister Savarkar", 277.
69. V.D. Savarkar, "Facts Without Comment", 182.
70. Ibid., 180.
71. Ibid.
72. See J.D. Joglekar, "Veer Savarkar: Profile of a Prophet", 323.
73. See B.K. Kelkar, "Savarkar: A Three-Dimensional View", 363.
74. See A. Nandy, *Bonfire of Creeds*, 131.
75. Ibid., 126.
76. See V.D. Savarkar, *Hindu Sanghatan*, 206.
77. See W.K. Andersen and S.D. Damle, *The Brotherhood in Saffron*, 17.
78. Ibid., 60, note 45. See also File 2286, Report on V.D. Savarkar imprisoned for importing weapons to India; treatment of prison in the Andamans (12 June 1914-24 September 1914) L/P&J/6/1314, India Office, British Library, London.
79. See D.D. Pattanaik, *Hindu Nationalism*, vol. 2, 71.
80. Sinn Fein is an Irish nationalist movement which began in 1902 under the leadership of Arthur Griffith.
81. See D.D. Pattanaik, *Hindu Nationalism*, vol. 2, 67.
82. See B.S. Parakh (ed.), *Contemporary India*, 29.
83. See R. Gandhi, *Revenge and Reconciliation*, 204.
84. B.S. Parakh (ed.), *Contemporary India*, 29.
85. See W.K. Andersen and S.D. Damle, *The Brotherhood in Saffron*, 60, note 45.
86. But Gopal Godse, the younger brother of Nathuram Godse argues that the latter did not leave the RSS. See "Gopal Godse", 27.
87. See W.K. Andersen and S.D. Damle, *The Brotherhood in Saffron*, 43-44.

88. Gopal Godse admits that for all the Godse brothers – Nathuram, Dattatreya, Gopal and Govind – Savarkar was their *guru*, a political *guru*, that they read all his writings and that they understood Savarkar to the fullest. See "Gopal Godse", 27-28.
89. Home Minister Sardar Vallabhabhai Patel's letter dated 27 February 1948 as cited in W.K. Andersen and S.D. Damle, *The Brotherhood in Saffron*, 68, note 131.
90. See L. Collins and D. Lapierre, *Freedom at Midnight*, New Delhi, 1976, Chapter 16 as cited in A. Nandy, *Bonfire of Creeds*, 79.
91. R.C. Majumdar, *The History and Culture*, 695.
92. P. Bidwai, "Caught in Historical Cliches", 103.
93. M.S. Golwalkar, *We*, 2.

• V •

Madhav Sadashiv Golwalkar on Hindu *Rashtra*, Indian Muslims and Christians

Madhav Sadashiv Golwalkar,[1] popularly known as Guruji, was born at Nagpur, Maharashtra in 1906. After graduating from the Hislop College, Nagpur, he joined the Banaras Hindu University for his Master's degree in Science during which period he came under the influence of Madan Mohan Malaviya (1861-1946), the founder of the University, who prodded the young Golwalkar to work for the Hindu cause. Later, he served as a professor at the same university. When he returned to Nagpur in 1933, he came under the influence of Keshv Baliram Hedgewar (1889-1940), who founded the Rashtriya Swayamsevak Sangh (RSS) in 1925. From 1937 onwards, Golwalkar plunged himself heart and soul into the RSS work and from 1940 to 1973 he guided the destiny of the RSS as *sarsangchalak* (chief guide of the association).[2]

Golwalkar's main philosophy was built around the concept of Hindu *rashtra* (nation). Under his leadership, the RSS organisation grew and established itself in most parts of India. He was also responsible for the concept of *Sangh Parivar* (affiliates of the RSS family).

Golwalkar, together with Vinayak Damodar Savarkar, is greatly responsible for developing the concept of Hindu nationalism in the 1920s and 1930s as an instrument to promote the interests of Hindu society, religion and culture. Today, he is acknowledged as one of the systematisers of the ideology of Hindutva and one of its main theorists. His noted work *We, Our Nationhood Defined* (1939)[3] is radical in its outlook and controversial and inflammable in content, and because of which the RSS itself withdrew it from circulation for a time.[4] His another important work is *Bunch of Thoughts* (1966, 1996).[5] Golwalkar died on 5 June 1973.

Golwalkar's concept of Hindu *rashtra* (nation)

Golwalkar's political and religious philosophy is centred around the concept of India as a Hindu *rashtra* (nation). It is the cornerstone of his ideology and is founded on the principle of *one nation* (Hindu), *one culture* (Sanskrit) and *one religion* (Hinduism). This necessarily implies a negation of cultural and religious pluralism and true secularism. In fact, Golwalkar openly declared that the Muslims, Christians and Communists of India are internal threats to the nation.[6]

India is a Hindu rashtra from time immemorial

According to Golwalkar, India is a Hindu *rashtra* from time immemorial and it is a historical truth and it is so under all conditions, even in dreams.[7] He says: "We thus say that our Hindu Nationhood is a truth, borne out by logic, experience and history. It is the supreme solid fact of our national life and not any fleeting 'ism' born out of political and economic theories or exigencies."[8] In fact, all well-meaning and patriotic Muslims and Christians of India do accept it as a fact.[9]

Golwalkar claims that the concept of Hindu *rashtra* is not a mere bundle of political and economic rights. It is essentially cultural.[10] For him, the word *rashtriya* naturally means 'Hindu' and therefore, the word 'Hindu' need not be used at all.[11] He notes: "the thought for which we stand is correctly and unambiguously described by the word 'Hindu'."[12] He says that the British colonisers never realised that India was 'One Country, One People and One Nation'.[13] Therefore, it is the duty of all Indians to proclaim unhesitatingly the truth of India as a Hindu nation. He observes: "It is our sacred duty, therefore, to re-establish the truth of our Hindu Nationhood, to remove all the debris of falsehood and make every Hindu realise his proud heritage of being a living limb of this great Hindu Nation."[14] The Rashtriya Swayamsevak Sangh (RSS) – whose head he was for more than three decades – is dedicated to the rejuvenation of the Hindu way of life and the promotion of the Hindu *rashtra*.

Hindus are the real children of the Hindu rashtra

Golwalkar considers India as the mother of all Hindus. For him, Hindus are the *real* children of the Hindu *rashtra* and they have been living here since time immemorial. Adherents of all other religions found in India are either guests or refugees or mere residents in the country. Thus, he spoke of the Muslims, Christians and Parsis as residents in India.[15] He argues that a handful of Muslims came to India as enemies and invaders, followed by a few foreign Christian missionaries. But today, he alleges, the Muslims and the Christians have enormously grown in number. But they did not grow just by multiplication but through converting the local population. Thus, a portion of the population taken from the Hindu-fold became Muslims and another Christians. The rest could not be converted and so they have remained as Hindus.[16]

According to Golwalkar, some people may claim that no man is born as Hindu or Muslim or Christian but as a simple human being. This may be true of others but not for Hindus. A Hindu gets the first *samskar* when he enters the mother's womb, and the last when his body is consigned to the flames. Hindus are Hindus even before they emerge from the womb of their mothers. A Hindu is born as a Hindu. But all others are born to this world as simple unnamed human beings who are later on either circumcised or baptised, and thus they become Muslims or Christians, respectively.[17]

Hindu religion and politics are inseparable

Golwalkar maintains that the very interpretation of the concept of *dharma* includes religion and politics. If anyone asks should we bring religion into politics, it stems from a misunderstanding of the concept of *dharma* and confusing it with the Western concept of religion. The Western countries suffered for centuries because of their dogmatic concept of religion and the control of state by the Church. The Hindu concept of *dharma* is as different from that as cheese is from chalk. *Dharma* or spirituality is not a dogma but a view of life in its totality. It is not a separate sphere of national life just as political or economic spheres. In his view, Hindu spirituality is a comprehensive vision of life that should inform and elevate and correlate all fields of society for the fulfilment of human life in all its facets. It is the sap of our national tree, the life-breath of our national entity.[18]

Golwalkar's views on Indian Muslims and Christians

Golwalkar had a very negative attitude towards the minority religions of India, especially Islam and Christianity. He categorised them as *enemies, invaders, aliens* and *internal threats* of the Hindu nation. According to him, the so-called minority religions are bound to become disruptive elements to the Hindu nation. Hindus are, therefore, at war at once with the Moslems on the one hand and British (who are Christians) on the other.[19]

All Semitic religions are intolerant

Golwalkar alleges that all Semitic religions – Judaism, Christianity and Islam – are intolerant. The Semitic concept of faith breeds intolerance and divides people in the name of religion.[20] The first Semitic religion was Judaism, which was an intolerant faith. Then came Christianity, the child of the former, which was equally intolerant, though Jesus Christ was a great saint. But later, what went on in the name of Christ had nothing to do with him. It was not Christianity but only 'Churchianity'.[21] Christianity was followed by another Semitic religion, namely, Islam, which is also an intolerant faith.

In Semitic religions a single way of worship is prescribed for all. These faiths have one prophet, one scripture and one God and if anyone follows any other religion, there is no salvation for him, which Golwalkar says, is an absurd claim.[22]

Golwalkar's accusations against Islam

According to Golwalkar, there are several hostile elements within India, which pose a far greater menace to national security than aggressors from outside. The first such case is the Muslims.[23] He presents the story of Islam as one of 'Sword and Koran' written in the tears and blood of millions of innocent human beings.[24] The Islamic invasions were replete with instances of massacre, devastation, destruction, loot and arson, violation of sacred places, desecration of religion and culture and forced conversions.[25]

Accusation: Muslims are anti-nationals

According to Golwalkar, everywhere the Muslims are being abetted in their separatist and subversive activities by the governments and political parties.[26] Even today, Muslims, whether in high positions of the government or outside, participate openly in rabidly anti-national conferences. Their speeches carry the ring of open defiance and rebellion. The Muslim League in India is not only contesting elections but also raise slogans like 'Pakistan Zindabad' in their public meetings and processions. For them, only those areas in which their unbridled sway is established are *pak* (holy) and the rest of India where they are living and flourishing is *na-pak* (unholy).[27]

Golwalkar argues that all the pro-Pakistani elements did not go to Pakistan at the time of the independence of India in 1947. Many of them remained back in India even after the partition of the country.[28] Those who have remained back hardly seem to have changed their mind. He asks:

> Have those who remained here changed [...] Has their old hostility and murderous mood, which resulted in widespread riots, looting, arson, raping and all sorts of orgies on an unprecedented scale in 1946-47, come to a halt at least now? It would be suicidal to delude ourselves into believing that they have turned patriots overnight after the creation of Pakistan. On the contrary the Muslim menace has increased a hundredfold by the creation of Pakistan which has become a springboard for all their future aggressive designs on our country.[29]

Golwalkar alleges that the direct aggression of Muslims first resulted in the creation of Pakistan. Then, one-third of Kashmir went into their hands. Now, Pakistan is trying to gobble up the rest of Kashmir.[30] All over the country, wherever there is a mosque or a mullah, the Muslims feel that it is their own independent territory.[31] They have been systematically flooding Assam, Tripura and parts of Bengal with Muslims since long.[32] There is a conspiracy to make Assam a Muslim-majority area and later to join it to (East) Pakistan[33] (today's Bangladesh).

Golwalkar claims that there were Indian Muslims who garlanded their radio sets when Pakistan hockey team won over the Indian team in the Olympics.[34] Practically, there are Muslims who are in constant touch with Pakistan over the transmitter enjoying not only the rights of an average citizen but also some extra privileges and extra favours because they are 'minorities'. Such Muslims are a serious threat to the nation, according to Golwalkar. Within the country there are many Muslim pockets, which are like miniature Pakistans that can destroy the Indian national life altogether and such pockets have become centres of a widespread network of pro-Pakistanti elements in India.[35] Hence, Golwalkar says: "Let us cry a halt, before it is too late, [...] and come to grips with the cruel realties of the situation keeping the interests of national security and integrity as the one supreme consideration."[36] He even advocated the total liquidation of Pakistan as a nation for so much was his hatred towards that country. During an interview, he said: "Give one crushing defeat to the Pakistani army. Then, the people there will themselves do the rest. They will also revolt and Pakistan will cease to exist."[37]

Accusation: Muslims are destroyers of Hindu religion

Muslims came to India as invaders and settled down in the country as rulers and carried out a systematic destruction of Hindu religion and national honour. They demolished Hindu temples and places of pilgrimage, desecrated Hindu womanhood, converted large numbers to their faith at the point of sword or with the lure of material pleasures.[38] Whatever the Hindus believed in, the Muslim was wholly hostile to it. If they worship in the temple, the Muslims would desecrate it. If the Hindus engage in *bhajans* and festivals, that would irritate the Muslims. If the Hindus worship cow, the Muslims would like to eat it. If the Hindus glorify woman as a symbol of sacred motherhood, the Muslims would like to molest her. The Muslims were tooth and nail opposed to the Hindu way of life in all aspects – religious, cultural and social.[39] Golwalkar asks: "Who had broken the temple of Somnath? Clearly, the Muslims. To whom was it a point of honour and devotion? The answer is very clear – to the Hindus."[40] Hence, according to Golwalkar, the antagonism of the Muslims against the Hindus was more than political.

Accusation: Muslims did not participate in the freedom struggle

It has been the contention of Golwalkar that Muslims and Christians did not participate in the freedom struggle, and India won freedom mainly due to the effort of Hindu patriots. He often considered the Muslims and Christians as people who belonged to the hostile camp as far as the struggle for the independence of India is concerned. Golwalkar says: "They

[Muslims and Christians] have also developed a feeling of identification with the enemies of this land."[41]

Once in Nagpur there was a conference of some persons calling themselves non-Brahmins. Golwalkar was surprised to find Muslims and Christian speakers also addressing the conference. He said: "Hindus, whatever their denominations of caste or sect, formed a single society, and the Muslims and Christians belonged to an alien and often hostile camp!"[42]

According to Golwalkar, the Muslim League is an organisation which is anti-national and rabidly communal.[43] Maulana Mohammad Ali (1878-1931), the right hand man of Mahatma Gandhi in the early days of the freedom struggle, repeatedly said that the worst sinner and debauchee among the Muslims was, in his eyes, far superior even to Mahatma Gandhi.[44] The greatest 'nationalist Muslim' Maulana Azad (1888-1958) also in his last days betrayed his mind in the book *India Wins Freedom*. He considered all leading leaders of India like Mahatma Gandhi and Jawaharlal Nehru (1889-1964) as simpletons and Sardar Vallabhabhai Patel (1875-1950) a communalist.[45]

Accusation: Islam converts by sword

Golwalkar speaks of the blood stained pages of history of expansion of Islam. He claims that the overwhelming majority of the Muslims in India were those who were converted to Islam from Hinduism at the point of sword or by temptations of power and pelf.[46] The followers of Islam also inflate their numbers and it has tragic repercussions on the affairs of the country.[47] Sikhism came into being in order to contain the spread of Islam in Punjab.[48] Golwalkar reminds the Muslims of India that their forefathers were Hindus. Hence, according to him, Muslims should belong to the Hindu fold as self-respecting persons, give up their aggressive mode of the Moghul days and wake up to the realities of the present times and merge with the national life.[49]

Accusation: Islam is an inferior religion

Golwalkar argues for the superiority of Hindu religion and the inferior status of Islam. It is true, he says, the founder of Islam was a powerful man. But even he met only angel Gabriel and felt that he heard some divine voices, and nothing more. He did not see God face to face.[50] Then, he says with his usual Hindu pride: "It was given to the great sons of this soil [Hindus] to see and realise God in His full effulgence."[51] There is no parallel in the rest of the world literature that can match the doctrine of supreme self-confidence and self-realisation as in Hinduism. Nowhere else can one find the parallel of a Sri Krishna who speaks in the first person 'I' as God Himself as in the *Bhagvadgita*.[52]

Accusation: Muslims are a pampered minority

Golwalkar considers the Muslims of India as a pampered minority. The government overtly and covertly supports the Muslims. Hindustan ['land of Hindus'] came to be called India to appease the Muslims.[53] Whenever the Muslims slaughtered cows to insult Hindu feelings, the Hindus were told that it was the religious right of Muslims, and that being tolerant to other religions they should not object to it. Jawaharlal Nehru gave the Muslims a written assurance that on the advent of *swaraj* (self-rule) cow-slaughter would not be banned keeping in view their religious sentiments.[54] Portions of *Vande Mataram* were dropped to appease Muslim fanatics.[55] During the freedom struggle, Pandit Nehru had once undertaken in his home province a big campaign of 'Muslim mass contact' to win them over. But, the result was that Muslim League began to grow there in leaps and bounds. However, unfortunately, the more the leaders tried to appease the Muslims, the more their separatist and aggressive appetite was whetted.[56]

Golwalkar's accusations against Christianity

Golwalkar adopted a similar attitude towards Christianity as Islam. Though some of his views were clearly false and evidently damaging to the Christian community, they were frequently made use of in order to indoctrinate the Hindu minds, especially the members of the RSS and the Sangh Parivar. For example, Golwalkar says that Christianity is an *inferior religion*. Even in the case of Jesus Christ, nowhere there is any reference that he had actually seen God. He had only come across angels and Satan. When put on the cross, he doubted the mercy of God and exclaimed, "My God, My God, why have you forsaken me?"[57] Golwalkar made use of every opportunity in order to *sow seeds of suspicion, prejudice and intolerance towards Christianity*. Below we examine some of his major accusations against the Christian religion.

Accusation: Christians are internal threats to India

Golwalkar says that the Indian Christians - together with the Muslims and the Communists - are internal threats to India.[58] According to him, the Christians and the Muslims had agreed to join together and between themselves partitioned the country.[59] Communism is a crude revival of some tenets of Christianity.[60] The movement for a separate Dravidanad in South India owes its origin to the scheming brain of a foreign missionary. Writing in the 1960s Golwalkar claimed that it was a foreign Christian missionary who first toured every town and village in Tamil Nadu about eighty years ago and carried on an incessant and vicious propaganda that Tamil culture, Tamil language and everything Tamil differed fundamentally from the rest of the Indian culture, language, etc., and that the Tamilians formed an independent nation by themselves.[61]

Accusation: Christian social service has ulterior motives

Golwalkar says that Christian missionaries came from far off lands and worked among the poor with ulterior motives.[62] To a superficial observer the Christians appear not only as quite harmless but also as the very embodiment of compassion and love for humanity. They run many schools and colleges, hospitals and orphanages. Their speeches abound in words like 'service' and 'human salvation' as though they are specially deputed by God Almighty to uplift humanity. The people of our country are simple and innocent as they are taken up by all these things. But there is an ulterior motive attached to Christian social and humanitarian works.[63] It is through such tactics that Christians are swelling their numbers day in and day out.[64]

According to Golwalkar, Christians enter a place in the alluring grab of bringing peace and brotherhood to mankind. But wherever they have gone, they have proved themselves to be not blood-givers but blood-suckers. Wherever they have entered, they have drenched those lands with the blood and tears of the natives and have totally liquidated many races.[65] The Christian missionaries have nothing of the nobility of Christ. Golwalkar asks: "Are we not aware of the atrocious history of Christian missionaries in our own country of how they carried sword and fire on Goa and elsewhere?"[66]

A great number of Christian missionaries are working in India to convert Hindus. In every part of India there are areas where people are ill-fed, ill-clothed, illiterate and devoid of any opportunities to cultivate religious devotions. All this is exploited by the Christian missionaries for conversion. Even in the advanced parts of India we find that Christian missionaries have spread into deep interiors.[67] A majority of our poor people – for example, the hard-hit fishermen in our southern coast – have become Christians not so much because of faith in Christianity but due to their poverty.[68]

Golwalkar quotes with pleasure the controversial Niyogi Committee Report (1956)[69] and agrees with it that all the philanthropic acts of the Christian missionaries are simply a mask for carrying on their proselytising activities, sometimes by intimidating and tempting the simple folk. At the root of their activities is the ambition to carve out a Christian State for themselves on the strength of their numbers and they are spending millions of rupees for this purpose.[70]

But here it may be recalled that the Niyogi Committee Report had been so thoroughly refuted that no right thinking person would base his opinions on it.[71] Besides, Hindus do have, as Vishal Mangalwadi says, genuine difficulty in understanding Christian charity because Hinduism does not have a similar tradition.[72]

Accusation: Primary aim of Christianity is to convert

According to Golwalkar, the principal aim of Christian humanitarian activities is summed up in one word 'conversion' and towards that end they feel that any tactics, however foul, is fair.[73] Conversion of Hindus into other religions is nothing but making them succumb to divided loyalty in place of having an undivided and absolute loyalty to the nation. Hence, conversion is dangerous to the security of the country and is necessary to put a stop to it.[74] In other words, becoming Christian is not merely a case of change of faith, but a change even in national identity.[75]

Often conversion is done through fraud.[76] Golwalkar calls conversion the Christian mischief, and the various superstitious and mean tactics they employ for conversion are well known.[77] Sometimes a piece of beef or a loaf used to be thrown into the water tank of the village, and the villagers ignorant of what had happened, used to take water as usual. On the next morning the missionary would come and declare that since they had used the polluted water they had all lost their religion and that the only way left for them was to join his fold. In this way whole villages have been converted to Christianity on the West Coast.[78]

Accusation: Christianity has political ambitions

According to Golwalkar, the proselytising activity of the Christians is part of furthering their political ambitions.[79] The Christian missionaries are out to demolish not only the religious and social fabric of the Hindus but also to establish political domination in various pockets, and if possible, all over the country.[80] He says that many leading Christian missionaries have often declared unequivocally that their one single aim is to make India a province of the Kingdom of Christ. Once the Archbishop of Madurai said, as reported in *Vedanta Kesari* of Madras, that their sole aim is to fly the flag of Christ in the whole of India. Even during the Eucharistic Congress at Bombay in 1965, Cardinal Gracias bewailed that in spite of their centuries of proselytising in India, the Catholics were only six million and the overwhelming majority remained Hindus. Hence, he exhorted his followers in the cause of proselytisation. It means that all the people of India should be converted to Christianity. That is, their hereditary religion, philosophy, culture and way of life should be demolished and they should become absorbed in a world federation of Christianity.[81]

Golwalkar says that the Christians demanded a separate Hill State for themselves around Shillong, and it was inspired by the Christian missionaries. They agitated for a separate Jharkhand in Bihar. But such demands are fanatical and anti-national.[82] According to him, Congress rule in the state of Kerala was a *de facto* Christian rule.[83] During the people's agitation against the Communist government in that state, the Christian leaders used to say that it was a life and death struggle for the Christian missions in Kerala. They also went to the extent of saying that, "Kerala shall be ruled either by the Catholics or by the Communists", and they said they want to rule.[84] Golwalkar adds: "In our own country, is it not significant that the province where the Christian population and influence is the greatest, Kerala, is also the biggest Communist pocket?"[85]

Accusation: Insurgency in northeast is a creation of Christians

Golwalkar claims that the open rebellion going on in the Naga Hills in Northeast India is engineered by Christians. He accused the Christian missionaries of engaging in various forms of illegal and nefarious activities. For example, he said that the American arms which come to Pakistan are handed over to the

Christian missionaries in Northeast.[86] Phizo, the rebel Naga leader, reached England and was given asylum by the noted Christian missionary Michael Scott.[87] Writing in the early 1960s, Golwalkar said: "...it will be little wonder if at no distant date Nagaland is separated and formed into an independent State ridden and dominated by the Christian fanatics."[88] Hence, he advised the authorities to deal with the Christians with an iron hand.[89]

Accusation: Christianity is an intolerant religion

Golwalkar argues that Christianity is the child of Judaism and like the latter, the former is also equally intolerant.[90] Christians argue that there is no real Saviour other than Jesus Christ, that the Hindu religion is only a mass of superstitions, that without taking to Christianity they would all be doomed to eternal damnation and so on.[91] He says that even to this day, the same insidious indoctrination of young minds is carried on in the Christian converts. Again, it is the same Christian fanatics who smashed the Vivekananda Memorial Tablet on the Vivekananda Rock at Kanyakumari. Such are the men who come to us to preach that Christianity would shower bliss of peace and milk of human kindness upon humanity.[92] The Christian missionary Francis Xavier (1506-1552) experienced the highest joy of his life when he used to see the new converts trampling upon their former gods and goddesses, razing their temples to the ground and insulting their own parents and elders who remained Hindus.[93] Christians committed all sorts of atrocities on the Jews. Golwalkar says that Hitler is not an exception but a culmination of the 2,000-year long oppression of the Jews by the Christians.[94]

According to Golwalkar, the world has yet to see a generous Western conqueror. Even after nearly two thousand years of the much boasted Christian training, the 'generosity' that is shown by them to their own brother-Christians in the conquered nations of the West makes hair-raising reading.[95]

Accusation: Christians kept aloof from the freedom struggle

Golwalkar alleges that, in general, the Christians kept themselves aloof from the freedom struggle.[96] According to him, Christians are not merely irreligious but also anti-nationals.[97] Christians think that once the Hindu faith is knocked out from the Hindu hearts, their nationalism will also be destroyed. Thus, a void is created in his mind and it becomes easy for them to fill it with Christianity.[98]

During the War of Independence in 1857 some bishops in India had raised platoons to help the British government in suppressing the uprising. Since then, they were on the side of the British who, after all, belonged to their own faith. The British too were helping the Christian missionary to realise their pet projects and hidden agendas. Vast jungle and hill areas were specially chosen, as for example, the Chota Nagpur area and the Naga Hills, where only the Christian missionaries were sent and their borders sealed to all other religious preachers. There was a natural co-ordination between the local Christians, the Christian missions and the British government.[99] Golwalkar claims that there are Christian institutions in India, which even today fly the Union Jack (national flag of the United Kingdom) on 15 August as a sign of their allegiance to the British.[100]

Accusation: Christianity is an agent of a world strategy

Christians are agents of the international movement for the spread of Christianity. So long as the Christians in India indulge in such activities and consider themselves as agents of the international movement for the spread of Christianity, and refuse to offer their first loyalty to the land of their birth and behave as true children of the heritage and culture of their ancestors, they will remain here as hostile elements and will have to be treated as such.[101] Golwalkar says that, a few years ago, there was an All-India Conference of Christians wherein they were called upon to pledge themselves to establish

Christian Empire in India.[102] But he says: "...if anybody cherishes extra-territorial loyalties, we call him a traitor. Would it not then be a greater disloyalty to our country if a person derives inspiration from extra-territorial ideals?"[103]

Golwalkar's accusations against Buddhism

Golwalkar's anti-'other' attitude was also directed against Buddhism. He calls Buddhism a religion of fanatics, enemies of the cultural values and nationalist traditions of India. They are anti-nationals who sided with the invaders. He says: "...the Buddhist fanatics invited and helped the foreign aggressors who wore the mask of Buddhism. The Buddhist sect had turned a traitor to the mother society [Hindu society] and the mother religion [Hinduism]."[104]

Buddhist influence had the baneful effect of effacing from the minds of the masses their tenacious adherence to their faith. It over-individualised religion and the consequence was that the individual became more prominent than the society and the nation.[105] For example, where the influence of Buddhism had disrupted the caste system, it fell an easy prey to the onslaught of Muslims.[106]

According to Golwalkar, Adi Sankara (8th century A.D.) was an incomparable philosopher and a unique organiser of Hindu religion. He fearlessly roamed on foot from one end of the country to the other, conquering people to the Hindu faith and rekindling the ebbing flame of ancient Hindu culture. His activities aroused a national consciousness and threw out the treacherous elements of Buddhism as a distinct sect.[107]

Golwalkar's accusations against Jews and Parsis

Golwalkar maintains that the Jews and the Parsis in India are guests in the Hindu *rashtra*.[108] He practically ignored the Jews because they are numerically very small. But, the Parsis, though small in number, are an intelligent, industrious and prosperous community. To a large extent they have merged themselves with the mainstream of the Hindu life.[109] Therefore, they are not a serious threat to India.

The need to do away with the concept of minority

It was Golwalkar's conviction that the minorities in India are a pampered group. As a 'minority' happens to have certain political privileges in India, everyone wants to prove that he is a 'minority' and claim those privileges. This cuts the whole country into so many fragments, which will mean ruin for the nation.[110] In India, says Golwalkar, whoever disclaims his Hindu roots and parades himself as a non-Hindu minority finds a special favour with our government. The Indian political leaders go to the extent of granting special political status to non-Hindu and anti-Hindu communities.[111]

Golwalkar argues that in a secular country all citizens are equal and this principle should be strictly adhered to. Hence, the custom to think and talk in terms of 'minorities' and 'communities' should be totally abolished.[112] The committee formed in the name of national integration has, by giving a scope for several disgruntled groups to air their demands and complaints, roused in them a hope that their divisive demands would be conceded. Therefore, it is necessary to dissolve it forthwith.[113] He asks the Muslims and the Christians of India to shed the notions of their being 'religious minorities' and their 'foreign mental complexion' and merge themselves with the common national stream of India, which is Hindu.[114]

Muslims and Christians are non-patriots

It was Golwalkar's contention that only those who glorify the Hindu race are true patriots and Muslims and Christians obviously do not figure in this list. He says: "Those only are nationalist patriots, who, with the aspiration to glorify the Hindu race and Nation next to their heart, are prompted into activity and strive to achieve that goal. All others are either traitors and enemies to the national cause or, to take a charitable view, idiots."[115] He adds: "Mere common residence or birth and growth in our land cannot imply that the same loyalties, qualities and pattern of life exist among all its residents."[116]

Golwalkar alleges that when a person becomes a Muslim or a Christian, his patriotism and devotion to nation vanishes or at least diminishes considerably. He asks: "...what is the attitude of those people who have been converted to Islam or Christianity? They are born in this land, no doubt. But are they true to their salt? Are they grateful to this land which has brought them up? Do they feel that they are the children of this land and its tradition, and that to serve it is their great good fortune? Do they feel it a duty to serve her? No! Together with the change in their faith, gone is the spirit of love and devotion for the nation."[117]

Muslims and Christians should merge with Hindu religion

According to Golwalkar, so long as Muslims and Christians do not merge with Hindu religion, they are to be treated as foreigners. He says: "...all those, who fall outside the five-fold limits of that idea [Hindu *rashtra*, Aryan race, Hindu religion, Hindu culture and Sanskrit language], can have no place in the national life, unless they abandon their differences, adopt the religion, culture and language of the Nation and completely merge themselves in the National Race. So long, however, as they maintain their racial, religious and cultural differences, they cannot but be only foreigners, who may be either friendly or inimical to the Nation."[118] Mere common residence in a particular territory cannot forge a unified national society with common character and qualities. The newcomers should bring about a total metamorphosis in their life-attitudes and take a rebirth, as it were, in that ancient national lineage.[119] He says: "...all that we say is that the Muslims and Christians here should give up their present foreign mental complexion and merge in the common stream of our national life."[120] "There are only two courses open to the foreign elements, either to merge themselves in the national race and adopt its culture, or to live at its mercy so long as the national race may allow them to do so and to quit the country at the sweet will of the national race. This is the only sound view on the minorities [sic] problem. That is the only logical and correct solution."[121] "*...the foreign races in Hindustan must either adopt the Hindu culture and language, must learn to respect and hold in reverence Hindu religion, must entertain no idea but those of the glorification of the Hindu race and culture [...] or may stay in the country, wholly subordinated to the Hindu Nation, claiming nothing, deserving no privileges, far less any preferential treatment – not even citizen's rights.*"[122]

A critical evaluation of Golwalkar's views

The worldview of Golwalkar contains many things that are clearly controversial and inflammable. Many of his allegations against the Muslims and Christians are false and misleading and detrimental to the peaceful co-existence of peoples belonging to different faiths and the pluralistic ethos of India. Below we attempt a critical evaluation of some aspects of Golwalkar's ideology.

The Nazi influence on Golwalkar

Golwalkar was influenced by Adolf Hitler and his Nazi ideology. His Hitlerian leanings are evident in his writings and pronouncements. K.K. Gangadharan finds a striking similarity of ideas between Hitler and Golwalkar. Comparing 'Hitlerism' with 'Golwalkarism' he concludes that the ideology of the RSS – whose main ideologue he was – is 'Hitlarism under Hindu garb'.[123] Asit Krishna Mukherji, who was a Hitler sympathiser, also found a parallel between the *Hitlerjugend* (Hitler youth) and the RSS youth organisation.[124] Golwalkar glorified the concept of pure Aryan race and saw Germany as a model to be followed. In fact, he was an open admirer and emulator of Hitler. Several scholars are unanimous in stating that Golwalkar's concept of 'pure' race was essentially a Nazi idea, and for him the Hindus are the pure Aryan race.[125] Sudip

Mazumdar, writing in the *Newsweek* of 27 May 1996, described Golwalkar as a supreme racist who openly admired some of Hitler's ideas.[126] Victor and Victoria Trimondi, in their scholarly work *Hitler, Buddha, Krishna Eine unheilige Allianz vom Dritten Reich bis heute* (2002), reiterates the same view.[127] Golwalkar said: "To keep up the purity of the Race and its culture, Germany shocked the world by her purging the country of the semitic Races [sic] – the Jews. Race pride at its highest has been manifested here. Germany has also shown how wellnigh [sic] impossible it is for Races and cultures, having differences going to the root, to be assimilated into one united whole, a good reason for us in Hindustan to learn and profit by."[128]

Golwalkar's tendency to repeat frequently falsehood against people of other religions and secular groups smacks of the influence of the Nazi concept of 'big lies'. Creating 'big lies' and repeating them frequently was fundamental to the Nazi strategy. Hitler and his propaganda minister Joseph Goebbels made full use of this method during the height of their power. Golwalkar is evidently a believer in the efficacy of this strategy. He says: "Even falsehood if repeated incessantly will have its effect on weak minds."[129] Thus, in Golwalkar, we see the Nazi concept of 'big lies' put into profitable use for the indoctrination of the Hindus in order to create prejudice and suspicion against the minority religious groups and secularists of India. Thus, as S. Yechury says, Golwalkar relied heavily on the experience of Hitleraite fascism and Hitler emerged as 'Guruji's guru' (Golwalkar's teacher).[130]

Those who are familiar with the writings of Golwalkar will notice his ethics of relativism and the conviction that end justifies the means. He frequently engages in double talk, which is a species of the 'big lie'. In other words, many of his ideas lack coherence and was often led by opportunism in his pronouncements. In the following pages we shall examine some of the 'big lies' propagated by Golwalkar. It is necessary that in order to grasp the full import of the 'big lies' we contrast what follows with what has been said above.

India is a Hindu rashtra

The claim that India is a Hindu *rashtra* is fundamental to Golwalkar's philosophy and that of the RSS which he headed for more than three decades. Thus, his no.1 big lie is that India is a Hindu *rashtra* from time immemorial. What is implied here is that Hindu *rashtra* was born with Hinduism and that it moves and develops with Hinduism so that one cannot exist without the other. Consequently, all the members of other religions found in India are either foreigners or converts from Hinduism.

But, the historical fact is that India was never a Hindu nation at any time in its long history. The territorial boundaries of the India of today did not exist in ancient times. Until some years ago India was highly fragmented politically, culturally, linguistically, geographically and religiously. All the great emperors of India who had a certain concept of 'pan-India', like Chandragupta Maurya, Ashoka and Akbar, were not Hindus, nor were the British colonisers Hindu: Chandragupta became a Jain,[131] Ashoka was a Buddhist, Akbar was a Muslim and the British were Christians. Golwalkar even invented the myth of Aryans as the indigenous people of India,[132] which no historian of standing accepts. It is only a fabricated theory with a clear ideological bias.[133]

The Indian renaissance of the 18th and 19th centuries may have created a certain degree of Hindu consciousness among the Hindus but definitely not a consciousness of India as a Hindu nation, though some splinter groups within Hinduism may have propagated such an idea, it had few takers.

The renowned historian Romila Thapar says that the term 'Hindu' as referring to a religion was initially absent in the vocabulary of Indian languages and only slowly gained currency after it came to be used in Arab and Persian writing.[134] The Vedic *dharma* to which modern Hinduism attempts to trace its roots was not in reality Hinduism. It will become evident when we compare the beliefs and practices of the Vedic *dharma* with that of modern Hinduism. Hinduism of today is an umbrella term for many religions and sects that are loosely related to each other. Today, under the name of 'Hinduism', there are many religious communities with their distinct identities, differences, antagonisms and conflicts so that we cannot speak of one religion or one culture. Ninian Smart says: "Even to talk of a single something called Hinduism can be misleading."[135] V.S. Naipaul observes that the Hindu religion is a conglomeration of some 500 religions or faiths.[136]

Hence, the claim of Golwalkar that India is a Hindu *rashtra* from time immemorial is false and misleading. The very concept is a myth. Considering Hinduism as the national religion of India is equally a myth. Thus, we need to ask where is the so-called Hindu *rashtra* existing from time immemorial of which Golwalkar speaks? His claim is obviously a case of *imagined* history.

Hindu rashtra is most open towards minority groups

Golwalkar claims that the Hindu *rashtra* has the most catholic and rational approach towards the so-called minority groups of India. There are some who imagine that the concept of Hindu nation is a challenge to the very existence of the Muslims and Christians in India. He says that it is an insult to the great and all-embracing Hindu cultural heritage.[137] The fear that Hindu *rashtra* will imperil the existence of other religious groups arises from applying the Semitic yardstick to the Hindu *rashtra*.[138] In India, there can be no objection to God being called by any name whatever because love and respect for all faiths and religious beliefs is ingrained in Hindu hearts.[139]

Golwalkar says that Muslims in India are enjoying all the rights and privileges due to a citizen.[140] The RSS makes no demands and it does not fight for special rights or privileges. It does not compete in electioneering politics, nor has it any desire to share political power. Being positively Hindu in its outlook, it has equal respect, love and tolerance towards all faiths.[141]

Golwalkar says that Hindustan is the land of the generous Hindus.[142] Consequently, the Hindu in Bharat can never be termed 'communal'.[143] History bears testimony to the fact that Bharat is the cradle of religious generosity and has always welcomed and assured all religious groups a free, honourable and secure life.[144] All individuals are equally sacred and worthy of our service. Any sense of discrimination among them is reprehensible.[145] Hence, the so-called minorities living in India have nothing to lose but everything to gain by the rejuvenation of the Hindu *rashtra.*

If we compare these statements of Golwalkar with what he has said elsewhere about the minorities, it becomes obvious that he is indulging in double talk.

Hindus were never intolerant

The oft-repeated rhetoric of Hindu tolerance is made use of also by Golwalkar in his discussion on Hinduism. He says that the Hindus have always been showing due respect to all other beliefs. They do not look upon diversity in worship as something incompatible with national unity.[146] The Vedas are a storehouse of knowledge par excellence. All types of faiths are accommodated in that.[147]

Golwalkar says that Hindu tradition goes far beyond the Western concept of mere tolerance; it respects all faiths as equally sacred.[148] Hence, the expression 'communalism of the Hindu majority' is totally wrong and misconceived.[149] If by secularism is meant that the state should not be tagged to any particular creed and that all faiths should be equally respected, then this again would be another name for Hindu tradition.[150] Golwalkar says: "He cannot be a son of this soil at all who is intolerant of other faiths."[151] "We, in the Sangh [RSS], are Hindus to the core. That is why we have respect for all faiths and religious beliefs."[152] "There has never been any quarter for such a conflict or intolerance in our country either in the past or in the present."[153] "He cannot be a Hindu at all who is intolerant to other faiths."[154] "We never discriminated against any on the score of religion in any sphere of our national life."[155] What Golwalkar has said here is another instance his 'big lies' and double talk.

Hinduism does not proselytise

Golwalkar's next big lie is that Hinduism is a non-proselytising religion.[156]

But it was the same Golwalkar who said that the Hindus are a great people charged with a World Mission, that it is their sacred duty to bring home to the entire humanity the sublime truths embedded in the Hindu religion.[157] He also asked the Hindus not to remain ignorant of the potency of numbers. They should all, without fail, register themselves with the census as Hindus. He says: "Our brethren in the far Eastern region – they may be Naga, Khasi, Jayantia, Mikir, Mizo, etc. – all should designate their community as Hindu only."[158] He also advised the Sikhs to register themselves as Hindus.[159]

Golwalkar was aware of the potency of numbers for the creation of the Hindu *rashtra*. Hence, he was willing to go to any extent and make any concession provided they are willing to place themselves under the umbrella of Hinduism. When some of the Sikhs, Jains, Lingayats and Aryasamajists declared that they are separate from Hindus, he said: "It is clearly written in our Constitution that the term 'Hindu' includes Sikhs, Jains and Buddhists."[160] According to him, the expression 'Hindus and Harijans' is also a mistaken use.[161] Re-conversion is returning to one's ancestral faith and it is not conversion into Hinduism at all. It is merely home-coming.[162]

In the above cases there may not be an insistence on formal conversion to Hinduism as such, but definitely a conversion *de facto* is implied in Golwalkar's wish that all should register themselves as Hindus with the census. Again, if we consider the modern religious scenario of India, terms like *shuddhi* ('purification'), *ghar vapasi* ('returning home'), *paravartan* ('turning back'), 're-conversion', 'sanskritisation', 'cultural integration', etc., are indigenous labels for what people generally understand by proselytisation and conversion, and the RSS is one of the frontline organisations that plans and executes such programmes. In addition to these, there are several Hindu organisations, especially in the Western countries, which are actively engaged in proselytisation. The International Society for Krishna Consciousness (I.S.K.CON) is a typical example of it. Hence, Golwalkar's claim that Hinduism does not proselytise is a big lie.

Insurgency in northeast is instigated by Christian missionaries

Another 'big lie' of Golwalkar is that Christian missionaries are responsible for the insurgency and secessionist movements in Northeast India. Following his lead, the RSS and the Sangh Parivar accuse the Christians of the same. The same accusation is orchestrated by Arun Shourie of the BJP.[163]

In the first place, it needs to be examined whether the government in New Delhi ever seriously asked the question why Northeast India is in a condition of unrest. What has the government at the Centre done for the educational, social, cultural, economic and human development of the region? Vishal Mangalwadi, who visited Nagaland some years ago, was told by a Hindu from the Hindi belt who was an officer in the Indian Army about the real condition of Nagaland. There is, he said, only one railway station and only one airport for the whole state. It has no rivers, no major industries, no mineral wealth and no commerce. In fact, the Government of India has done much to damage Nagaland's trade and tourism by enacting various travel restrictions.[164] Much of what is said about Nagaland is true also for most of the other states of Northeast India.

The root cause of the problem of 'political unrest', 'insurgency' and 'secessionism' in Northeast India lies mainly with the fact of long standing neglect of the region by the various governments in New Delhi, and not with the Christian missionaries. Is the ULFA which is a powerful secessionist group of Assam a Christian's mission? No. Its members are Hindus. There are over 19 major secessionist groups in Manipur and most of them are led by Hindus. If we look at India as a whole, we would discover that, as Mani Shankar Aiyar says, the Naxalites of Andhra Pradesh are Hindus, the Hurriyat gang in Kashmir are Muslims, and the Khalistanis are Sikhs.[165] Hence, to blame the Christians for all the troubles of Northeast India is unfair. Here, the words of Archbishop Thomas Menamparampil of Guwahati seems appropriate: "*...missionaries are often accused for the political unrest in the North-East. In fact, there are only a small number of Christians among the political activists there. An unfair share of blame is put on the Christians.*"[166]

Christian mission was a conspiracy of British imperialism

Another accusation of Golwalkar is that the Christian's mission in India was a conspiracy of British imperialism. According to him, the Christian missionaries sided with the British colonialists and the British in turn helped them to carry out their nefarious agenda of converting Hindus to Christianity. This 'big lie' is systematically utilised to indoctrinate the young minds of India so that they may grow with a prejudice against Christianity. For example, in the saffronised NCERT school textbook of Social Sciences for Class IX, we read: "Trade led to political conquest and political power was used to propagate Christianity [...] The English East India Company in the name of religious neutrality was giving maximum support and encouragement to Christianity."[167]

But Mangalwadi has exposed the 'big lie' that the British colonial government helped the Christians missionaries and vice versa. He argues that the missionary movement was not a product of British imperial conspiracy. Englishmen in the British East India Company were not missionaries but mercenaries who came to India in search of money. Mangalwadi reminds us that, first of all, as far as the British colonisers were concerned, they were driven by five major interests: (a) individual greed to make money for the British East India Company; (b) need for a trading base for the Directors of the same Company; (c) conquest of territory for the British military heroes; (d) Indology for the British secular scholars, and (e) improvement of Hindus for the social reformers.[168] Missionary activity did not figure anywhere in their agenda.

Secondly, Mangalwadi says that during the entire 17th century only one Indian is known to have been baptised by the chaplains of the British East India Company. Again, during the entire 18th century, not a single British missionary was permitted to work in the British territories. The only Protestant mission that existed in India was pioneered by the Danes in the non-British territory of Tranquebar. A few German missionaries were later tolerated in some British centres because they had earned great respect from the Hindus and the Muslim kingdoms around them. In 1793, when it was discovered that William Carey was travelling to India to serve as a missionary, he was transferred from the British ship and he arrived on a Danish boat, and then worked as a manager in an indigo plantation, partly in order to evade arrest. Finally, in order to work as a missionary, he had to settle in the Danish territory of Serampore.[169]

Charles Grant started his campaign for the mission in 1786-87. But it was only 46 years later in 1833 that the British Parliament allowed missionaries from the West to operate in India, although in 1813 a law had been passed that missions could operate in India but only under licence. Many contemporaries of William Wilberforce, Macaulay and Trevelyan thought that Christians were fighting against the British interest and for the exclusive interest of India.[170]

Mangalwadi further observes that while the Christian missions did not receive any money from the Company or from the government, until 1858, at lest 26,589 Hindu temples were receiving financial support from the Company in the

Bombay Presidency alone, the biggest beneficiary being the Jagannath Temple at Puri. The Company also was investing huge sums in public education and for the promotion of Sanskrit, Persian and Arabic.[171] Many British people did not see that the missionaries would strengthen the empire. Rather, they feared that education and Christianity would be dangerous and that it would hurt the cause of the British empire.[172] The British Christians had to struggle against their government to get permit for missionaries to enter India.[173]

But Hindus were willing to enlist help from the British against the Muslims. Yechury says that the urge to establish the Hindu *rashtra* drove the RSS to be a virtual ally of the British.[174] B.S. Moonje, a prominent Hindu Mahasabha leader and a staunch advocate of Hindu *rashtra* and the founder of the Bhonsle Military School, wrote to the Viceroy of India on 26 September 1940 soliciting the favour of the British colonial government. We quote from the letter of Moonje now preserved in the British Library, London. He says: "Hindustan surrounded as it is on the Western and the North-Western Frontier by its traditional enemies [Muslims] of the last more then one thousand years, is the one stable factor in its choice of its allies for its permanent safety and prosperity. *It will naturally lead the Hindus to look up to Britain,* in spite of its quarrels with it for constitutional powers, however bitter at times they may be. *Thus, Hindustan and Britain are allied together in unshakeable bond of union for long years to come.*"[175]

Christians did not participate in the freedom struggle

According to Golwalkar, Christians in India are not merely irreligious but also anti-nationals.[176] He accused the Christians that, in general, they kept themselves aloof from the freedom struggle.[177] But, the true history of the Indian independence movement presents us with a different picture than that which Golwalkar provides. In discussing about Christian contribution we should keep in mind that we are speaking of Christians who at the time of the freedom struggle constituted around 2 per cent of the total population of India. In spite of their insignificant number, they did contribute their share to the freedom struggle as the analysis that follows, though not exhaustive, will show.

Felix Wilfred, an internationally renowned theologian, notes that those who look objectively at the history of the freedom struggle in India, would admit that there were Christian missionaries who gave full support to the nationalist cause to the embarrassment and indignation of the British colonial government. Among these missionaries the more well-known names are: Stanley Jones, C.F. Andrews, J.C. Winslow, Verrier Elwin, Ralph Richard Keithahn and Ernest Forrester-Paton. Some missionaries were even deported from India for their support to nationalist cause. Given this situation, missionary sources do not speak about the political and nationalist involvement of missionaries for fear of having to come under the censure of the government. In spite of this, there were numerous Christians who involved themselves in the freedom struggle.[178]

Likewise, George Thomas, a well-known Church historian maintains that the Indian Christian community played an influential role, especially in the early phase of the Indian National Congress – founded in 1885 – which was the premier instrument of political nationalism. According to him, the influence of Christians was impressive in the various sessions of the Indian National Congress. For example, in the third annual session of the Congress in 1887, out of 607 participants in the session, 15 were Indian Christians, and among those who addressed the assembly was Madhu Sudhan Das (1848-1934, popularly known as 'Utkal Gourab'), a well-known leader from the Christian community in Orissa. The number and influence of Indian Christians continued to be impressive in the subsequent sessions of the Congress. Kali Charan Banerjee (1847-1907), a Bengali Christian and a fine orator, regularly addressed the annual sessions of the Congress in moulding the policy of national movement. In the Congress session of 1889, among the ten women delegates, three were Christians: Pandita Ramabai Saraswati (1858-1922), Mrs. Triumbuck, Mrs. Nikambe.[179]

There are also records of active Christian participation in the *Swaraj* Movement (1905), the Non-Cooperation Movement (1920), the Civil Disobedience Movement (1930) and the Quit India Movement (1942). Since 1920s, many Christian institutions and organisations like the All India Conference of Indian Christians, the National Christian Council of India, Christian leaders and student groups related to United Theological College (Bangalore), Serampore College (Bengal), St. Paul's College, Calcutta (Bengal), Malabar Christian College, Calicut (Kerala), the Youth Christian Council of Action (Kerala), the Student Christian Movement of India, the Indian Christian Association of Bengal, a conference of Christians in Bombay, a meeting of Christians in Palayamcotta and Tinnavelly, etc., passed resolutions expressing complete solidarity with the freedom movement. Some of them even took part in massive demonstrations against the British colonial government.[180]

In 1973, the Tamil Nadu government published a list of freedom fighters of the state in three volumes under the title *Who is Who of Freedom Fighters, Tamil Nadu.* From these volumes D. Arthur Jayakumar has culled the names of 103 persons who have been positively identified as Christians.[181] Basing ourselves on Jayakumar's findings we mention below contribution of some of the outstanding Indian Christians who took part in the freedom struggle.

J.C. Kumarappa (original name John Jesudason Cornelius, 1892-1960) was a veteran Congress leader. He received degrees from Ohio Wesleyan University, Boston University and the Universities of Harvard and Columbia. He was Professor of Philosophy for some time at Lucknow University. On 9 May 1929 he met Mahatma Gandhi at Sabarmati Ashram and that resulted in their becoming close associates. He was a strong supporter of *Satyagraha*, and encouraged Christian participation in the national movement.[182]

Before Mahatma Gandhi set out for the Dandy March in 1931, he encouraged Kumarappa to write regularly for his weekly *Young India* and informed him that he would be its editor after his imprisonment. Thus, Kumarappa became the editor of *Young India* and his fiery writings gave him one-and-a-half years of rigorous imprisonment in 1931. But, fortunately, he was released after a couple of days, because of the Gandhi-Irwin Pact. He took up the editorship of *Young India* from Mahatma Gandhi in 1932, which again sent him to jail and was detained in Nasik Jail for two-and-a-half years. In 1942, he was under detention and trial for a year and a half in both Bombay and Nagpur. During the Quit India Movement, he had a hand in the underground activities in Bombay along with his Congress colleagues. These secret sabotage activities led to his arrest. He was sentenced to two-and-a-half years of rigorous imprisonment for three charges and sent to Jabalpur Central Jail until 1945. After his release from the prison, his health completely broke down by then, he took rest at the guesthouse of Leonard Theological College, Jabalpur.

In July 1947, he joined the delegation nominated by the Government of India to help India's economic interest in maritime transport at the meeting of shippers in London. Since he was also a prominent figure in Congress affairs, he was given a chance to be a member of the All India Congress Working Committee in place of Jay Prakash Narayan in 1947. But, he rejected the offer in spite of Gandhi's persuasion.[183]

Paul Ramasamy (b.1906) was another important Christian who took part in the freedom struggle. In 1930 he joined the freedom movement during the days of Salt *Satyagraha*. He picketed the Bishop Herber College, Thiruchirapalli. He was arrested and sentenced to six months of imprisonment and was kept at Thiruchirapalli and Alipuram jails.[184]

Venkal Chakkarai (b.1880) participated in the Civil Disobedience Movement started by Mahatma Gandhi.[185] In 1930 Kanakarayan Tiruselvam Paul (1876-1931) went to

England to participate in the first Round Table Conference. He decried the tendency among some Christians to keep aloof from the national movement.[186] There were many other prominent Christians who participated in the national movement either as part of the Congress or outside it.

Arthur Jayakumar says that when the Non-Cooperation Movement was started in 1920, there were many Indian Christians in the whole of India who took part in it.[187] The All India Conference of Indian Christians held at Lucknow from 27 to 30 December 1922 made a reference to some of the Indian Christians who had suffered imprisonment as a result of their involvement in the national movement.[188] N.H. Tubbs, the Principal of the Bishops College, Calcutta, wrote a confidential letter to his Mission on 23 February 1921 stating "a very significant feature of the last months has been the deep interest of Christian students in the national non-co-operation movement".[189] In 1930, the editor of *The Guardian* said that a number of Christian young men have joined the Civil Disobedience Movement.[190] Nirad Biswas, who later became the bishop of Assam of the Church of India Burma and Ceylon (CIBC), joined the national movement in making salt outside Calcutta in 1932.[191]

George Thomas notes that Barhmabandhab Upadhyaya (1861-1907), a 'Hindu Catholic' *sadhu* and theologian, played a leading role in the *Swadeshi* Movement. He was also one of the early leaders who enunciated the philosophy of Non-Cooperation Movement. He edited *Sandhya,* a national journal founded in 1904, and it had a decisive influence on the masses because it was the only vernacular paper in Bengali, which boldly advocated complete Indian nationalism. Again, a conference of leading Christians from all over India held at Ranchi in 1923 passed a resolution to give full support to the national movement. In 1930, among the 78 persons who accompanied Mahatma Gandhi during his Salt March from Sabarmati Ashram to Dandi, there was a Christian named Thevarthundiyil Titus, a young disciple of Gandhi and a member of a Christian family of Travancore. In the freedom and pro-democracy movement in Travancore in the 1930s and 1940s, prominent Christian leaders like T.M. Varghese, A.J. John, Anne Mascarenes and Akkamma Cherian were pioneering forces.[192] Philippose Elanjikkal John (1903-1955) was another prominent member of the Travencore State Congress.[193]

Joachim Alva (1907-1979)[194] was another outstanding personality in the history of the freedom struggle. He was profoundly influenced by Mahatma Gandhi's ideals. As a student leader, he was the pioneer of youth movement in India. He gave whole-hearted devotion to the national movement and gave up his lucrative job in order to dedicate himself for the freedom struggle. He was also a journalist of high calibre who vigorously advocated the concept of *swadeshi* and human brotherhood, especially through his *Forum* (1943), which was a 'fighting paper' from the beginning. His editorial 'Settling the Accounts with the British' resulted in his being prosecuted for sedition in 1943.[195] Mrs. Violet Alva (1908-1969) was another personality with abiding nationalist interest. About the involvement of the Alvas in the freedom movement it has been said: "The combination of Joachim Alva and Violet Alva to the Freedom Movement is significant [....] They risked their all, but they served [the country] to the full extent of their ability which they had in plenty."[196]

M.V. Kamath, an RSS ideologue and a regular columnist in the RSS weekly, the *Organiser,* is a person with little sympathy for Christians. Yet, in his autobiography, he acknowledges that several Christians took part in the freedom movement. He mentions the names of Cyprian Alvares, Joachim Alva, Marcel A.M. D'Souza as Christian freedom fighters.[197] He says: "It is necessary to state that many Roman Catholics I personally know of were very much in the freedom movement and national mainstream."[198]

Travancore received English education by foreign agencies as early as 1806. The new generation under the impact of

Western civilisation came to have a broad social and political outlook. The people became independent in spirit and critical in their attitude. They also became conscious of their rights and privileges.[199] For example, the popular agitation, which came to be known as the "Travancore Memorial" or the "Malayali Memorial" of 1861, drafted and presented to the Maharaja on 11 January 1891, a demand for the political rights for the people of Travancore. The Malayali Memorial was an important landmark in the political awakening of the people for mightier movements in later days. The submission of the demand by the Memorial marks the awakening for the first time, of the educated sections of the state of Kerala. It reflected the political aspirations of the leading communities like Nair, Ezhava, Nambudiri, Latin Christian, Syrian Christian and Anglo-Indian.[200]

Many Christians were associated with the Malayali Memorial and some of them presided over its public meetings. The political meetings held at North Parur, Kottayam and Trivandrum were presided over by Christians like Father Hilarion, Vicar of the Parur Church, Rt.Rev.Mar Athanasius, the Metropolitan of the Syrian Church and T.F. Lloyd, an Anglo-Indian. The conference held at Kottayam on 3 June 1891 to examine the contents of the Memorial was attended by prominent Christians like Varghese Mappila and Mani Kathanar, along with leaders of various other communities.[201]

George Joseph (1887-1938)[202] was another outstanding Christian who engaged in the freedom struggle. He was one of the three members of the Home Rule deputation sent to England in 1918 to present the Indian case before British people. It has been said that the landslide in the opinion of the Indian Christian community in favour of nationalism was very much ascribable to his dynamic leadership.[203]

Joseph represented a high type of culture. He studied at Madras Christian College then he passed out of the Middle Temple, England in 1909. He started legal practice at Madurai, his town of adoption, and was soon attracted to the Home Rule Movement and given training in political organisation by Mrs. Annie Besant. He was one of the first batch of barristers who sacrificed their comforts to engage themselves in national work and joined the Non-Cooperation Movement and boycott of foreign cloth shops. At the bidding of Pandit Motilal Nehru he discarded his fashionable dress for the coarser homespun and associated himself as editor of the Allahabad daily *The Independent*, which used to exercise a profound influence on its readers. In 1920 he courted arrest and was kept in Allahabad Jail. He was subsequently sentenced to rigorous imprisonment in the course of the Non-Cooperation Movement in 1921. Later, he became the editor of the *Young India* – Mahatma Gandhi's weekly.[204] In 1922, he was arrested for sedition and spent a year in the Lucknow district jail along with Jawaharlal Nehru, Mahadev Desai, Purushottamdas Tondon and Devdas Gandhi.[205] In 1924, after resigning his membership of the Indian National Congress, he went back to the bar, shifting his practice later to Madras. But, again, he became an active Congress worker. In 1937 George Joseph was elected to the Central Legislative Assembly.[206] He was also the editor of the *South Indian Mail*.[207]

Joseph was also invited to assume the leadership of the *Satyagraha* Movement. He led the Vaikam *Satyagraha* for which he was beaten and arrested and sentenced to jail. Mahatma Gandhi wrote to George Joseph on 6 April 1924 that the latter should let the Hindus do the job and not offer *Satyagraha* himself so far as the Nagpur resolution of the Congress had called on the Hindus to wipe out untouchability. However, before the letter reached, George Joseph had already joined the *Satyagraha*.[208]

Joseph expired on 6 March 1938. He was one of the Keralites who had projected themselves significantly on the national political plane before the independence of India. Jawaharlal Nehru makes a reference to him in his autobiography. Of him it is said that he did not pop his tail between the hind legs but if he sowed the wind he was equally ready to reap the whirlwind.[209] It has also been observed that the Indian Christian community was drawn into the vast arena of national politics by the dynamic personality of George Joseph. He roused national consciousness and a high sense of patriotism among the Christians.[210]

C. Samuel Aaron was another noteworthy Christian who participated in the national movement with great zeal. He was a great industrialist of North Malabar. The active participation of the Aarons in the national movement began with the Salt *Satyagraha* of 1930. As the Salt *Satyagrahis* of Kerala reached the village of Chombal on 16 April 1930, the local residents under the leadership of Samuel Aaron gave them a rousing reception.[211] On 21 April 1930 when the Salt *Satyagrahis* led by K. Kelappan reached the village of Pariyaram near Payyannur, Mrs Gracy Aaron led the women and showered flowers and rice on them.[212] The *Satyagraha* camp at Payyannur was located on the spacious premises of the large coconut farm belonging to Samuel Aaron.[213]

Samuel Aaron had given the Brighter Hotel buildings at Cannanore belonging to him for temporary use by the Congress *Satyagrahis* intent on breaking the salt law from 22 May to 1 June 1930. E.M. Gawne, Collector of Malabar, requested Samuel Aaron to evict the *Satyagrahis* on the threat of prosecution. Samuel Aaron replied that he was willing to face the prosecution though, he added, he could not guess what offence he had committed, for the Congress had not yet declared to be an unlawful organisation. He was charged under section 157 of IPC and sentenced to pay a fine of Rs 1,000 or undergo rigorous imprisonment for six weeks in default. Since Samuel Aaron refused to pay the fine, he was sent to the Central Jail at Cannanore. On 18 July the Payyannur Police went to the weaving factory owned by Samuel Aaron at Pazhayangadi with a warrant for claiming his movable property to realise the fine of Rs 1,000 imposed on him. They took car-loads of things found in the factory.[214] It has been observed that the participation of the Samuel Aaron in the national movement was of unique importance for the Christian community in South India.

Among the leading Christian women leaders, who took part in the freedom struggle, mention may be made of Mrs. George Joseph,[215] Mrs. Gracy Aaron,[216] Mrs Margaret Pavamani,[217] Miss Mary Thomas[218] and Miss Matilda Kalten.[219]

The rise of modern journalism in Kerala gave a great impetus to the growth of political consciousness. The press became an important medium through which the Western ideas of freedom and democracy began to permeate among the members of the middle class and gradually among the masses. Printing press had been introduced into Kerala by Christian missionaries at the end of the 16th century. Probably, *Rajya Samacharam* published by the Basel Mission at Tellicherry from June 1847 was the first journalistic publication in Malayalam and its virtual editor was the Christian missionary Herman Gundert. Next came *Paschimodayam*, a monthly, published by Basel Mission at Tellicherry from October 1847. It was followed by *Paschima Taraka* published from Cochin in 1862-63 and later from Trivandrum. *Satyanada Kahalam* was published first from Koonamavu and later from Varapuzha and Ernakulam. This was the predecessor of *Satyanadam*, which came to be published as a weekly, and a certain C. Varkey served as its editor for about 48 years.[220] In 1887, *Nazrani Deepika* appeared and in the course of time it became a daily with the title *Deepika*, published from Kottayam.[221] In 1888, *Malayala Manorama* was started at Kottayam by Varghese Mappilla Kandathil (1858-1904).[222] He was first the editor of *Kerala Mitram*, a weekly newspaper, and later of *Malayala Manorama* (1890 onwards).[223] All these journalistic writings, which contributed to political awakening and shaped public opinion and national consciousness, were run by Christians.

Considering the numerical insignificance of the Christians in India compared to the Hindus who form the majority population, the Christian contribution to freedom struggle is indeed commendable. In addition, we need to remember that the vast majority of the Christians of India belong to the lower castes and during the independence movement they were still struggling to emancipate themselves from the clutches of the upper castes of Hinduism. Again, Christianity moulded the minds of men, women, children and youth through their educational institutions so that they began to long for freedom from every form of oppression, including the colonial rule. This was also a form of participation of the Christians in the freedom struggle.

Thus patriotism is indeed a Christian virtue. The Indian Christians *truly identified themselves* with the Indian national movement and demonstrated their deepest concern for the cause. In fact, they were among the prominent persons who pioneered and shaped the goals of Indian nationalism. Therefore, as George Thomas rightly observes, the Indian Christian community *was not behind any other community* in their desire for national freedom and in their readiness to work and make sacrifices for it.[224]

But, contrary to the general belief, patriotism was not always a Hindu virtue. The narrow-minded Hindus and their organisations like the Hindu Mahasabha, RSS and others fought for the Hindu religion, Hindu culture, Hindu society and Hindu *rashtra*. *Their real enemies were not the British but the Muslims and the Christians, as is evident from their numerous subversive activities and aggressive pronouncements.* Prominent Hindu leaders like Swami Dayananda Saraswati, Swami Vivekananda, Bal Gangadhar Tilak, Keshav Baliram Hedgewar, V.D. Savarkar, B.S. Moonje, M.S. Golwalkar and others became ardent proponents of the Hindu *rashtra*. Theirs was, therefore, a negative nationalism. The Hindu Mahasabha and the RSS did not participate in the Congress-led independence movement. For most of them, reforming Hindu religion and Hindu society had priority over asking the British to quit India as was the case with Swami Dayananda Saraswati, Swami Vivekananda and Gopal Krishna Agarkar, a close associate of

Tilak. Nathuram Godse assassinated Gandhi because the independent India was not the Hindu *rashtra* he had dreamt and laboured for. *Whenever occasion demanded, several Hindu leaders tried their best to curry favour with the British with the secret hope that when the latter leaves India the country would be handed over to the Hindutva ideologues so that their pet dream of a Hindu rashtra could be realised.*

The Indian struggle for independence was a complex phenomenon with various streams and forces contributing to it. Among those who fought for the freedom of the country were great men like Mahatma Gandhi, Jawaharlal Nehru and other secularists. Most of them belonged to the Indian National Congress. There were also true patriots who did not belong to the Congress. However, *the one thing common to all of them was that they conceived a secular and culturally pluralistic India* – unlike the Hindutva ideologues – and among them were also, as we have seen, many Christians. Their vision of India went beyond the Hindu *rashtra*. Thus, they advocated positive nationalism. Hence, the question as to who really fought for the freedom of India can be very embarrassing for many Hindutva organisations and Hindutva ideologues like Golwalkar.

Christians are anti-Hindu

Golwalkar alleges that the Indian Christians are anti-Hindu. But this is again an allegation without foundation. First of all, it is to be noted that Golwalkar's treatment of Christianity seldom goes beyond the period of British imperialism. Thus, he reduces the history of 2,000 years of Christianity in India to 200 years of British rule, and for all practical purposes he equates Christianity with colonialism. But, in reality, Christianity is not synonymous with the British and other Western colonisers. Christianity in India is older than many forms of modern Hinduism. It is as old as Christianity itself. Benjamin Walker says: "Christianity is of greater antiquity in India than in any other country in the world except Palestine – it is older in India than in Rome itself."[225]

Christians are one of the most peaceful communities in India. Kerala with a sizeable Christian population, for example, has a history of 2,000 years of peaceful co-existence with people of different faiths.[226] The services of the Christians are open to all, irrespective of caste, colour, religion, ethnic origin and regional differences. None can deny the extent, variety and magnitude of their contribution to nation-building, especially through their outstanding educational institutions, health care and human developmental works, social reforms, contribution to the development of regional languages and indigenous cultures. In most cases the vast majority of the beneficiaries are Hindus. Hence, how can they be anti-Hindu?

If a Hindu feels that the Christian institutions are out to convert the Hindus, he is always free to go elsewhere. And yet paradoxically, some of the prominent leaders who are on the forefront of the attack on the Christians are persons who have benefited from their services. Golwalkar studied at Hislop College, which was a Christian institution.[227] Several prominent BJP leaders are products of Christian institutions – minus the universal values these institutions profess and propagate. The Hindutva hardliner L.K. Advani was a student of St. Patrick's School, Karachi; Arun Shourie who is obsessed with an anti-minority syndrome, is a product of St. Stephens', New Delhi, and Arun Jaitley, one of the leading strategists of the BJP, was a student of St. Xavier's, New Delhi – to name a few. If gratitude is a sign of civilisation, some of the Hindutva ideologues obviously lack it. Christianity is not in any sense anti-Hindu or anti-any other religion. Christianity stands for such universal values as justice, peace, love, tolerance, patriotism and service of one's neighbour.

Golwalkar did not fight for free India but for Hindu *rashtra*

If we carefully analyse the views of Golwalkar, it will become clear that he fought not for a free India which is culturally pluralistic, but for a monolithic Hindu *rashtra*. His real enemy was not the British colonisers but the Muslims and Christians. P. Kanungo says: "Golwalkar never participated in the anti-British struggle. Therefore, he could conveniently ignore whatever little anti-British legacy Hedgewar left behind."[228] In other words, Golwalkar could not conceive an independent India which is multi-religious, multi-ethnic and multi-cultural but a Hindu *rashtra* with one religion (Hindu) and one culture (Sanskrit) as its foundation. This is true also of the RSS organisation and members of the Sangh Parivar. Here lies the difference between the true freedom fighters of India and the pseudo-freedom fighters of the Hindutva fold.

Hence, Golwalkar as the leader of the RSS has no moral right to accuse the Indian Muslims or Christians or Communists or anyone else for that matter that they did not participate in the Indian national movement. The true freedom struggle was not undertaken along religious parameters but along secular lines in which Indians from all walks of life participated[229] – minus the Hindu *rashtravadis*.

Nathuram Godse, who assassinated Mahatma Gandhi, the father of the Indian nation, is the representative of those Hindus who fought only for a Hindu *rashtra*. Godse's ashes are still kept waiting for the day when India will become a Hindu *rashtra* to be immersed in the Ganges. Godse wrote in his last will: "My ashes may be sunk in the Holy Sindhu river when she will again flow freely under the aegis of the flag of Hindusthan. [....] It hardly matters even if it took a couple of generations for realising my wish. Preserve the ashes till then."[230]

Conclusion

From what we have seen, it is clear that Golwalkar was a narrow-minded Hindutva ideologue who lived for a Hindu *rashtra* and judiciously cultivated an anti-'other' attitude towards the religious minorities of India. He drew inspiration for his ideology from Adi Sankara, Swami Dayananda Saraswati, Swami Vivekananda, Bal Gangadhar Tilak, Keshav Baliram Hedgewar, Adolf Hitler and his Nazi ideology.

Sumit Sarkar, the noted historian, considers Golwalkar as more socially conservative than V.D. Savarkar. Golwalkar has no hesitation to state that in the Hindu nation people are characterised by *varnas* (castes) and *ashramas* (the four life stages of an orthodox Hindu) learning their duties at the feet of the eldest-born – the Brahmins.[231] Yechury says that Golwalkar rejected everything modern in human civilisation – liberty, equality, fraternity, secularism, democracy and parliamentary institution – as alien concepts.[232] His conservative views and narrow-minded vision took him backward by several centuries to medieval times. As a leading ideologue of Hindutva, he should have propagated his ideas not in the 20th century but in the middle ages. But, it is unfortunate for India that his backward looking ideology has many takers, particularly among the Hindu families and the Hindu organisations.[233]

Golwalkar's ethical relativism is characterised by his double talk, 'big lies', xenophobia, and obsession with the Nazi concept of pure Aryan race. Kushwant Singh says that every fascist regime needs communities and groups it can demonise in order to thrive. It starts with one group or two. But it never ends there. A movement built on hate can only sustain itself by continually creating fear and strife.[234] For Golwalkar, the Muslims, Christians and Communists provided the fodder for his demonising activities.

The 'will to Hindu *rashtra*' dominates Golwalkar's thought. It is his major obsession. His social order is dictated by the upper castes.[235] His patriotism does not surpass the Hindu *rashtra*. Unfortunately, as long as Golwalkar's ideas are in vogue, many Hindus will find it impossible to accept the fact of India's religious and cultural pluralism. In his political philosophy there is no space for tolerance, democracy and secularism. In his concept of Hindu *rashtra* only the Hindus will be the real citizens, and those who belong to other religious groups will be treated as guests, refugees, aliens, enemies, traitors and internal threats to the Hindu nation, who may live in India but at the mercy and good will of the Hindus.

Notes

1. The original surname was Golwalkar Padhye. See C.P. Bhishikar, *Shri Guruji,* 5.
2. See M.S. Golwalkar, *Spotlights*, vi-viii; R. Kohli, *Political Ideas of M.S. Golwalkar*, 1-9; P. Kanungo, *RSS's Tryst with Politics*, 64-65, note 78; "Shri Guruji: A Profile", xx-xxi. For a chronology of events in the life of Golwalkar see C.P. Bhishikar, *Shri Guruji,* 280-283.
3. Sitaram Yechury calls this work the RSS Bible and the basic primer in the indoctrination of the RSS volunteers. See S. Yechury, *What is this Hindu Rashtra?*, 3. For a similar idea see also P. Kanungo, *RSS's Tryst with Politics*, 111.
4. *We, Our nationhood Defined* was based on Ganesh Damodar Savarkar's *Rashtra Mimamsa* (in Marathi) which acknowledged the influence of European liberal nationalists like Giuseppe Mazzini (1805-1872), Johann Kaspar Bluntschli (1808-1881) and others. See K. Elst, *The Saffron Swastika*, vol. 1, 118-119. Golwalkar disclosed only in 1963 that *We, Our Nationhood Defined* was not his original work. See P. Kanungo, *RSS's Tryst with Politics*, 65, note 81.
5. This work is a collection of Golwalkar's views on various topics gathered from his many speeches, discussions and conversations extending over several years. See M.S. Golwalkar, *Bunch of Thoughts,* v (Preface to the third edition). It has been reported in the *Organiser* of 1 August 2004 that the RSS is getting ready to bring out a collection of Golwalkar's writings in 12 volumes. Initially it will be published in Hindi. See "Shri Guruji's *Complete Works* to be Ready Soon", 12.
6. See M.S. Golwalkar, *Bunch of Thoughts*, 177-201. Here he deals with Muslims, Christians and Communists in three different chapters with the title 'Internal Threats' in order to drive home his point.
7. See M.S. Golwalkar, *Bunch of Thoughts*, 60.
8. M.S. Golwalkar, *Bunch of Thoughts*, 125.
9. See M.S. Golwalkar, *Bunch of Thoughts*, 255.
10. Ibid., 34.
11. Ibid., 134.
12. M.S. Golwalkar, *Bunch of Thoughts*, 151-152.
13. See M.S. Golwalkar, *Bunch of Thoughts*, 226.
14. M.S. Golwalkar, *Bunch of Thoughts*, 156.
15. See M.S. Golwalkar, *Bunch of Thoughts,* 97, 138, 141.
16. Ibid., 127.

17. Ibid., 117. See also his *Spotlights*, 113-114.
18. See M.S. Golwalkar, *Bunch of Thoughts*, 72.
19. See M.S. Golwalkar, *We*, 14.
20. See M.S. Golwalkar, *Bunch of Thoughts*, 103.
21. Ibid., 159. See also his *Spotlights*, 131.
22. See M.S. Golwalkar, *Bunch of Thoughts*, 103.
23. Ibid., 177.
24. Ibid., 160.
25. See M.S. Golwalkar, *We*, 20.
26. See M.S. Golwalkar, *Bunch of Thoughts*, 183.
27. Ibid., 187.
28. Ibid., 177.
29. M.S. Golwalkar, *Bunch of Thoughts*, 178.
30. See M.S. Golwalkar, *Bunch of Thoughts*, 179.
31. Ibid., 184.
32. Ibid., 179.
33. Ibid., 303.
34. See M.S. Golwalkar, *Spotlights*, 43.
35. See M.S. Golwalkar, *Bunch of Thoughts*, 184-185.
36. M.S. Golwalkar, *Bunch of Thoughts*, 187.
37. M.S. Golwalkar, *Spotlights*, 65.
38. See M.S. Golwalkar, *Bunch of Thoughts*, 209.
39. Ibid., 142.
40. M.S. Golwalkar, *Bunch of Thoughts*, 152.
41. Ibid., 125.
42. Ibid., 216.
43. See M.S. Golwalkar, *Bunch of Thoughts*, 60.
44. Ibid., 186.
45. Ibid., 186. See also his *Spotlights*, 49. The idea that Muslims did not participate in the freedom struggle is widely propagated in the saffronised NCERT school textbooks published in 2002, and paint the Muslims in bad light and thus create many prejudices against them. For instance, in the NCERT school text book of Social Sciences for Class IX it is stated that Sir Syed Ahmed Khan was one who collaborated with the British, the Aligarh Movement was meant to make Muslims of India worthy and useful subjects of the British, the Muslim League is an organisation that did not collaborate with

the national movement, the Muslims are wedded to pan-Islamism, Indian Muslims were unhappy with the disintegration of the Ottoman empire, etc. See B.S. Parakh (ed.), *Contemporary India*, 26-28, 34.

46. See M.S. Golwalkar, *Bunch of Thoughts*, 146.
47. Ibid., 362.
48. Ibid., 103.
49. Ibid., 143.
50. Ibid., 86.
51. M.S. Golwalkar, *Bunch of Thoughts,* 86.
52. See M.S. Golwalkar, *Bunch of Thoughts,* 87. Here, Golwalkar exhibits his 'ignorance' of other religions. For example, in the Bible, Jesus Christ spoke in the first person and claimed himself to be God. He said: "The Father and I are one"; "He who has seen me has seen the Father"; "I am the way the truth and the life"; "I am the resurrection and the life"; "I tell you, someone greater than Solomon is here", etc.
53. See M.S. Golwalkar, *Bunch of Thoughts,* 144.
54. Ibid.
55. Ibid., 143
56. Ibid., 147.
57. Ibid., 86. It is doubtful whether Golwalkar ever studied Christianity seriously.
58. See M.S. Golwalkar, *Bunch of Thoughts,* 177-200.
59. Ibid., 193.
60. See M.S. Golwalkar, *Spotlights*, 85.
61. See M.S. Golwalkar, *Bunch of Thoughts,* 217. This simplified and erroneous view of Golwalkar about the Tamil culture is not supported by facts. The history of Tamil culture and Tamil language goes back to thousands of years. The early Tamil writing is referred to as *sangam* (literary academies) literature. The Tamil legends speak of three great *sangams* and they most probably flourished between the first and fifth centuries A.D. Thirteenth century A.D. is considered as the Golden Age of Tamil literature. See B. Walker, *Hindu World*, vol. 2, 479-480. Again, the distinction between *Aryavarta* and *Dravidanadu* (or *Tamizhakam* or *Dekshinpada*) is very ancient. The land from the Himalayas to the Vindhyas in the South was called *Aryavarta* and the area south of the Vindhyas was known as *Dravidanadu*. Aryans of the North looked upon the inhabitants of Dravidanadu as enemies and strangers, likewise the Dravidians

considered the Aryans as aggressors and foreigners. According to several authors, the *Ramayana* represents the conflict between the Aryans and the non-Aryans and the Aryan domination of the non-Aryans. But the Dravidians had already reached an advanced degree of civilisation when the Aryans broke down upon them. See A.D. Mattam, *Religions*, 52-53. Hence, the allegation of Golwalkar that movement for a separate Dravidanad in South India owes its origin to the scheming brain of a foreign missionary is without foundation.

62. See M.S. Golwalkar, *Bunch of Thoughts*, 369.
63. Ibid., 188. See also his *Spotlights*, 56.
64. See M.S. Golwalkar, *Bunch of Thoughts,* 189
65. Ibid., 193.
66. M.S. Golwalkar, *Bunch of Thoughts,* 193.
67. See M.S. Golwalkar, *Bunch of Thoughts*, 369
68. Ibid., 513.
69. The Niyogi Committee consisted of six members with Dr. M.B. Niyogi, and its Secretary, the only official representative of the Government, all others being non-officials. The only Christian member of the Committee was a man from Kerala who had many grievances against the foreign missionaries and had often attached them publicly in the press. Thus, the Committee gave the appearance of having a Christian representative among its members. Dr. Niyogi himself was a man deeply prejudiced against the foreign missionaries. See *The Niyogi Committee Report A Critical Appraisal*, 9, 13.
70. See M.S. Golwalkar, *Bunch of Thoughts,* 190-191.
71. For a critical response to the Niyogi Committee Report, see *The Niyogi Committee Report: A Critical Appraisal* (2000).
72. See V. Mangalwadi, *Missionary Conspiracy*, 297.
73. See M.S. Golwalkar, *Bunch of Thoughts,* 188.
74. Ibid., 170.
75. Ibid., 126.
76. Ibid., 369.
77. Ibid., 188.
78. Ibid., 128.
79. Ibid., 189.
80. Ibid., 193.
81. Ibid., 189

82. Ibid., 192.
83. Ibid., 194.
84. Ibid., 192.
85. M.S. Golwalkar, *Bunch of Thoughts,* 196.
86. See M.S. Golwalkar, *Bunch of Thoughts,* 191.
87. Ibid., 192.
88. M.S. Golwalkar, *Bunch of Thoughts,* 192. Nagaland received statehood on 15 December 1963.
89. See "Shri Guruji: A Profile", xxii. This is part of the armchair discourse of Golwalkar. He should have come to Northeast India and witnessed for himself the gross neglect of the region by the Indian government. Often rebellion is the last straw of the desperate humans. It is a language that needs to be de-coded by the political leaders and policy makers of India. But to blame the Christians for all the ailments of Northeast India is to make them a scapegoat by vested interests and organisations that are inimical to Christianity.
90. See M.S. Golwalkar, *Bunch of Thoughts,* 159.
91. Ibid., 136.
92. Ibid., 194.
93. Ibid., 193-194.
94. Ibid., 159-160.
95. Ibid., 210.
96. Ibid., 141.
97. Ibid., 190.
98. Ibid., 190.
99. Ibid., 141.
100. Ibid., 107.
101. Ibid., 194.
102. Ibid., 193.
103. M.S. Golwalkar, *Bunch of Thoughts,* 444.
104. Ibid., 70.
105. See M.S. Golwalkar, *We,* 10.
106. See M.S. Golwalkar, *Bunch of Thoughts,* 109.
107. Ibid., 70-71.
108. Ibid., 138.
109. Ibid., 141.
110. Ibid., 491.

111. Ibid., 107.
112. Ibid., 169.
113. Ibid., 171.
114. Ibid., 158.
115. M.S. Golwalkar, *We*, 44.
116. M.S. Golwalkar, *Bunch of Thoughts*, 127.
117. Ibid., 125
118. M.S. Golwalkar, *We*, 45-46.
119. See M.S. Golwalkar, *Bunch of Thoughts*, 127.
120. M.S. Golwalkar, *Bunch of Thoughts*, 127.
121. M.S. Golwalkar, *We*, 47.
122. Ibid., 47-48 (emphasis added).
123. See K.K. Gangadharan, *Sociology of Revivalism*, 99-102.
124. See Trimondi, V. and Trimondi, V., *Hitler, Buddha, Krishna*, 345.
125. Golwalkar's *We, Our Nationhood Defined* was withdrawn from circulation for a time because it contained many laudatory references to Hitler and his theory of racial superiority. See P. Kanungo, *RSS's Tryst with Politics*, 65, note 81.
126. See S. Mazumdar, "White Shirts and Khaki Shorts" as in K. Elst, *The Saffron Swastika*, vol. 1, 117. For similar ideas, see also "Fascist Lineage", 33.
127. See Trimondi, V. and Trimondi, V., *Hitler, Buddha, Krishna*, 93, 344.
128. M.S. Golwalkar, *We*, 35.
129. M.S. Golwalkar, *Bunch of Thoughts*, 155.
130. See S. Yechury, *What is this Hindu Rashtra?*, 6, 14-15.
131. According to the Jaina tradition, towards the end of his life Chandragupta became an ardent Jaina, abdicated his throne in favour of his son Bindusara and became an ascetic. He went to South India and there he ended his life by regulated slow starvation in the orthodox Jaina manner. See R. Thapar, *The Penguin History of Early India*, 178.
132. See M.S. Golwalkar, *We*, 8. P. Kanungo argues that the theory of indigenous origin of the Aryans serves a dual purpose: first, it refutes the claim of the Dravidians as the original inhabitants of India who were pushed beyond the Vindhyas by the Aryan aggressors; and second, it highlighted that Central Asian Muslim migrants alone were foreigners. See P. Kanungo, *RSS's Tryst with Politics*, 97.

133. Here, we are reminded by R. Prasannan: "Each culture has its own ideas of history. If every Chinese emperor believed that history began with him (so he burnt all the records of preceding reign), we Indians mythified everything and became the world's greatest myth-makers". P. Prsannan, "Truth behind the Myths", 21.
134. See R. Thapar, "The Tyranny of Labels", 10.
135. N. Smart, *The World's Religions,* 43.
136. See V.S. Naipaul, *India A Million Mutinies Now*, 416.
137. See M.S. Golwalkar, *Bunch of Thoughts,* 131.
138. Ibid., 160.
139. Ibid., 158.
140. Ibid., 321.
141. Ibid., 172.
142. See M.S. Golwalkar, *We*, 20.
143. See M.S. Golwalkar, *Bunch of Thoughts,* 165.
144. Ibid., 321.
145. Ibid., 37.
146. Ibid., 165.
147. Ibid., 106.
148. Ibid., 337.
149. Ibid., 165.
150. Ibid., 337.
151. M.S. Golwalkar, *Bunch of Thoughts*, 158.
152. Ibid., 125.
153. Ibid., 162.
154. Ibid., 125.
155. Ibid., 160.
156. See M.S. Golwalkar, *Bunch of Thoughts*, 490.
157. Ibid., 348.
158. M.S. Golwalkar, *Bunch of Thoughts*, 362.
159. See "Shri Guruji: A Profile", xxii.
160. M.S. Golwalkar, *Bunch of Thoughts,* 106.
161. See M.S. Golwalkar, *Bunch of Thoughts,* 106
162. See M.S. Golwalkar, *Spotlights*, 118-119.
163. See A. Shourie, *Missionaries*, 205-209.
164. See V. Mangalwadi, *Missionary Conspiracy*, 312.

165. See M.S. Aiyar, "Arun Shourie and His Acolytes", 10.
166. T. Menamparampil, as quoted in A. Shourie, *Missionaries,* 234 (emphasis original).
167. B.S. Parakh (ed.), *Contemporary India*, 6.
168. See V. Mangalwadi, *Missionary Conspiracy,* 11-13.
169. Ibid., 126.
170. Ibid., 127.
171. Ibid., 127, 161.
172. Ibid., 158.
173. Ibid., 167.
174. See S. Yechury, *What is this Hindu Rashtra?,* 7.
175. B.S. Moonje (P&J 5587), 1940, File 117/D-1, Hindu Mahasabha Copies of Resolution, etc, L/P&J/8/683, India Office, British Library, London, 1940. (Emphasis added).
176. See M.S. Golwalkar, *Bunch of Thoughts,* 190.
177. Ibid., 141.
178. See F. Wilfred, "Christians between Identity: Politics and Nationalism", 265, footnote 13.
179. See G. Thomas, "The Christians and the Freedom Movement", 63.
180. See G. Thomas, "The Christians and the Freedom Movement", 64-66. See also P.K.K. Menon, *The History of Freedom Movement*, vol. 2, 243, footnote 30.
181. See D.A. Jayakumar, *Christians and the National Movement,* 128.
182. Ibid., 129-131.
183. After the independence of India Kumarappa was not interested in power politics. He chose Gandhi Niketan Ashram at Kallupatti (Madurai) to be his headquarters. But his health further deteriorated and was finally admitted to the Government General Hospital in Madras. People of national importance like Rajendra Prasad, Jawaharlal Nehru, Rajaji, Kamaraj and C. Subramanyan frequently visited him. He died on 30 January 1960.
184. See D.A. Jayakumar, *Christians and the National Movement*, 131.
185. Ibid., 132.
186. Ibid., 134. See also, H.A. Popley, *Builders of Modern India K.T. Paul Christian Leader* (1938).
187. See D.A. Jayakumar, *Christians and the National Movement*, 121.
188. Ibid., 122.

189. Ibid., 123.
190. Ibid., 123.
191. Ibid., 124.
192. See G. Thomas, "The Christians and the Freedom Movement", 64-67.
193. Philippose was born in 1903 in a well-known Jacobite Syrian Christian family of Kerala. He did his higher studies in England. His meeting with Mahatma Gandhi was a significant point in his life. He was one of those sent to Wardha on delegation to meet Gandhi, and spent about three months with him. See "Philippose Elanjikkal John (1903-1955)", 169.
194. Joachim Alva was born on 21 January 1907 at Udipi, South India. He was educated at St.Aloysius College Bangalore. He studied for his B.A and L.L.B at the St. Xavier's College, Elphinstone College and Law College, Bombay. He served as Steering committee and the Executive Committee of the Bombay Congress Party. He was elected to the Lok Sabha from South Canara from 1952-1967. In 1969 he was a member of the Rajya Sabha. See "Alva Joachim (1907-)", 120-121.
195. "Alva Joachim (1907-)", 121.
196. Ibid.
197. See M.V. Kamath, *A Reporter at Large*, 15; 26-27, 106-107.
198. M.V. Kamath, *A Reporter at Large*, 27.
199. See P.K.K. Menon, *The History of Freedom Movement*, vol. 2, 1-2.
200. Ibid., vol. 2, 10.
201. Ibid., vol. 2, 12, footnote 21.
202. George Joseph was born on 5 June 1887 in a prosperous middle-class family belonging to the Syrian Christian community of Kerala. In 1931 he accepted Roman Catholicism. He was deeply rooted in his Christians principles and values. Among those who influenced his political philosophy mention may be made of Mrs. Annie Besant, Motilal Nehru, Mahatma Gandhi, C. Rajagopalachari, Dr. T.S.S. Rajan. See "Joseph George (1887-1938)", 250-252.
203. See P.K.K. Menon, *The History of Freedom Movement*, vol. 2, 91-92 footnote 9a.
204. Ibid., footnote 9a.
205. See D.A. Jayakumar, *Christians and the National Movement*, 128-129.
206. See P.K.K. Menon, *The History of Freedom Movement*, vol. 2, 91-92, footnote 9a.
207. Ibid., vol. 2, 91, 111, footnote 17.

208. Ibid., vol. 2, 146.
209. Ibid., vol. 2, 91-92, footnote 9a.
210. See "Joseph George (1887-1938)", 252.
211. See P.K.K. Menon, *The History of Freedom Movement*, vol. 2, 221, footnote 11.
212. Ibid., vol. 2, 223.
213. Ibid., vol. 2, 224.
214. Ibid., vol. 2, 239, footnote 23.
215. Ibid., vol. 2, 111, footnote 17.
216. Ibid., vol. 2, 223, 256, footnote 4, 261, 302, footnote 25.
217. Ibid., vol. 2, 263-266, 269, 273, 276 footnote 18, 277, footnote 20, 296.
218. Ibid., vol. 2, 276, footnote 19.
219. Ibid., vol. 2, 268.
220. Ibid., vol. 2, 580-581. However, a few scholars opine that *Gnananikshepam*, a newspaper published once a month from the C.M.S. Press Kottayam, was the first journal in Malayalam. Others hold that it was started only in 1848. See *Ibid.*, footnote 2.
221. See P.K.K. Menon, *The History of Freedom Movement*, vol. 2, 581.
222. Ibid., vol. 2, 581-582.
223. Varghese Mappila was born in a rich Jacobite Christian family of Tiruvalla, Kerala. After his early education he joined the Government College, Trivandrum. He acquired a sound knowledge of Malayalam and Sanskrit. See "Varghese Mappila Kandathil (1858-1904)", 245.
224. See G. Thomas, "The Christians and the Freedom Movement", 64-66.
225. B. Walker, *Hindu World*, vol. 1, 238.
226. Unfortunately, the Hindutva elements are bent on destroying the communal harmony that exists in Kerala. In fact, the recent growth of Hindutva forces and their violent activities in the State is astounding and alarming. For instance, on 13 January 2003, the American missionary Joseph William Cooper was attacked by some Hindu fundamentalist groups. See "An Emerging Threat", 41-42. On 22-23 January 2003 the Full Gospel Church at Cheengavallam, near Ambalawayal in Wayanad was burnt down. On 2 May 2003 at Marad, near Kozhikode, there was a serious communal clash between the Hindus and the Muslims. See N.P. Chakutty, "Massacre in Marad", 25-26. On 28 August 2004 Fr. Job Chittilapally (71) was found stabbed to death within the precincts of S. Varaprasadam Matha Church, near Chalakudy. A certain Raghu Kumar who is a BJP-RSS

loyalist is alleged to be the culprit. However, people believe that there is a conspiracy behind the dastardly act. See "Chandy's First Test", 24-26. On 25 September 2004 Sisters and Brothers of Mother Teresa's Missionaries of Charity were attacked twice, allegedly by BJP activists at a Dalit colony at Pantheerankave, Kozhikode, Kerala. The attackers shouted pro-BJP slogans. See "Attack on Sisters of Missionaries of Charity", 6. See also M.C. Menon, "Missionaries became Sitting Ducks", 30-32; R. Krishnakumar, "Targeting Missionaries", 39-40. On 29 September 2004 the altar in St. Thomas Mar Thoma Church at Pattorr in Thiruvananthapuram was burnt. See M.C. Menon, "Devil's in God's Land", 17. It is reported that members of the *Sangh Parivar*, especially the RSS and the BJP are responsible for most of these crimes. According to sources, the RSS circular directed its cadres to keep a vigil on Christian missionaries engaged in conversion and related activities. See *Ibid.*, 21.

227. See C.P. Bhishikar, *Shri Guruji*, 9.
228. P. Kanungo, *RSS's Tryst with Politics*, 52.
229. This idea is powerfully brought out in R. Dayal (ed.), *We Fought Together for Freedom* (1998).
230. N. Godse, *Why I Assassinated Mahatma Gandhi*, 186.
231. See S. Sarkar, *Beyond Nationalist Frames*, 251. Golwalkar rejected the view that caste was an evil institution. In his opinion, caste was a great institution, which served society and held it together when everything else seemed to collapse. He particularly highlighted the contribution of caste as a bulwark against Islam. See P. Kanungo, *RSS's Tryst with Politics*, 141-142.
232. See S. Yechury, *What is this Hindu Rashtra?*, 24.
233. In fact, in a three-day memorial lecture on Golwalkar held at Ahmedabad in March 2004 the Sangh Parivar declared Golwalkar as the biggest gift to the Hindu society in the 20th century. See *Organiser*, 4 April 2004, 8.
234. See K. Singh, *The End of India*, 72.
235. Kanungo states that for Golwalkar 'Hindu' appears as male, upper-caste and possibly north Indian as well. *Mlechhas* include Muslims, Christians and communists, insufficiently re-claimed untouchables and tribals, Kabirtpanthis, Satnamis, on occasion women and south Indians and north-eastern states of India and any other group that challenge the social laws of the Hindus. See P. Kanungo, *RSS's Tryst with Politics*, 115.

• VI •

Sita Ram Goel's Maligning of Jesus Christ and Christianity

Sita Ram Goel (1921-2003), the polemical writer and the Hindutva ideologue, was a controversial figure in modern Indian religio-political scenario. He was born on 16 October 1921 in Haryana and his highest formal qualification was a Master's degree in History from Delhi University. His background shows his association with Arya Samaj, a period of 'flirt' with Gandhism before he accepted Marxism, in 1941, as his framework for political analysis. However, in 1948, he was converted out of Communism by Ram Swarup and since then, for some years, Communism was his priority target of attack. In the meantime, political ambitions made him an ardent supporter of the Jana Sangh, the forerunner of the present right wing Bharatiya Janata Party. In 1956-57 he fought Lok Sabha elections from Madhya Pradesh as a Jana Sangh candidate and lost. He considered Ram Swarup – another Hindutva ideologue – as his mentor. Goel was a regular contributor to the *Organiser* – the RSS mouthpiece. In 1981, he started his own publishing house, the *Voice of India* – an anti-minority propaganda organisation based in New Delhi. As an author, his writings were practically boycotted by the media, both by reviewers and by journalists. Goel was one of the leading Hindu revivalists of modern India. His main targets of attack were Christianity, Islam and Communism. Goel passed away on 3 December 2003.[1]

Goel held a key position in the *Voice of India* and effectively used the print media to provide, what he called, the 'ideological defence' of Hinduism [Hindutva] against the minority religions and secular ideologies of India, especially Islam, Christianity, Communism and Nehruism. In the recent past, some of his main targets of attack have been Christianity and Islam, as is clear from his numerous controversial writings, such as: *Papacy: Its Doctrine and History* (1986); *Muslim Separatism, Crusades and Consequences* (1987); *Hindu Temples What Happened to Them* (2 vols., 1990-1993); *Hindu Society Under Siege* (1992); *Islam Vis-à-Vis Hindu Temples* (1993); *Heroic Hindu Resistance to Muslim Invaders* (1994); *Jesus Christ: An Artifice for Aggression* (1994); *The Story of Islamic Imperialism* (1994); *Catholic Ashrams: Sannyasins or Swindlers* (1994); *History of Hindu-Christian Encounters (AD 304-1996)* (1996); *Pseudo-Secularism, Christian Missions and Hindu Resistance* (1998) and so on.[2]

Unfortunately, most of Goel's writings cannot be qualified as scholarly and therefore they hardly merit a rebuttal or a rejoinder. In addition, an exercise of the sort will be useless against a prejudiced author like Goel. But, because of their innate capacity to poison the minds of uncritical readers and their tendency to legitimise and promote communal hatred between Hindus and Christians, Hindus and Muslims, Hindus and secular ideologists, a critique of his writings is called for. In this chapter we intend to concern ourselves with Goel's *Jesus Christ: An Artifice for Aggression* (1994).[3] However, whenever we judge it opportune, we will also be making references to Goel's other writings either to endorse or to supplement a point.

The 'truth' about Jesus Christ according to Goel

In this section I state only Goel's position without a critical evaluation.

The primary concern of Goel in writing *Jesus Christ: An Artifice for Aggression* is, as he claims, to expose the 'real' Jesus of Christianity. But, the book ultimately aims at *re-writing history*, both by erasing historical facts and by fabricating myths. Goel is convinced that the Hindus in India are ignorant of the 'truth' about the 'real' Jesus. Therefore, in order to lead his fellow religionists 'from darkness to light', he sets out to expose the 'truth about the 'real' Jesus. Here, we shall highlight only some of the dominant themes treated in his book with some critical observations.

Jesus of history is a myth

The central concern of Goel's *Jesus Christ: An Artifice for Aggression* is to project the Jesus of history as a myth. He informs his readers that for sometime he had been trying to have a *close look* at Jesus Christ, and in the process had become *very conversant* with the Christological research carried out in the modern West over the last two hundred years or so. But he adds that he had never imagined that Jesus was such a flimsy figure, historically as well as doctrinally.[4] He laments that unfortunately, in India, the search for the Jesus of history remains unknown even to the so-called educated elite. The search conducted so far has led to startling negative conclusions, and the endeavour, instead of propping up the case, has only led to its complete collapse. But, according to Goel, it was not the fault of history that the search for Jesus of history proved negative[5] but due to the fact that the so-called Jesus of history is in reality a 'Jesus of myth'.

Goel attempts to 'establish' his thesis by referring to some historians, both ancient and modern. Josephus Flavius (AD 36 or 37-99 or 100) completed two monumental works, namely, *The Jewish War* (77 AD) and *Antiquities of the Jews* (92 AD).

Goel argues that Josephus' first work has not a word about Jesus or his followers. However, in the latter, Christian apologists point to two passages, one long and the other very short, which mention Jesus as a wise man and also as Christ. But Goel states that scholars have proved quite convincingly that both the passages are either clumsy Christian interpretations or have been tampered with by Christian scribes[6] – an allegation which Goel will frequently employ in his book without substantiating it with documentary evidences. If history is a true narrative, documents and facts constitute its ultimate means of proof. Devoid of them the so-called history is mere fiction.

However, it may be mentioned that C.K. Barrett, a renowned biblical scholar, who carefully analysed the testimony of Josephus Flavius admits that some clauses in the text of Josephus could not have been written by him. But, when these are removed, there still remains valuable information about Jesus of Nazareth. Hence, it does not follow that the whole passage of Josephus is spurious.[7] Another biblical scholar, F.V. Filson also arrives at the same conclusion that there is no reason to doubt that Jesus lived a human life in Palestine. Roman, Jewish, and early Christian testimony unite to make that conclusion certain.[8]

Goel alleges that the vast rabbinical literature of the Jews, composed during the first two and a quarter centuries of the Christian era, contains only five authentic references to Jesus. Then, he goes on to state that they do not conclusively establish his historicity, as none of them is sufficiently early.[9] But it may be mentioned that, for those who are prejudiced against Jesus Christ, like Goel, even if five hundred authentic evidences exist, they may not be sufficient to prove anything conclusively! But, contrary to what Goel says, F.S. Filson notes: "[...]clearly authentic though not so favourable to Jesus, are the references in rabbinical sources [...] The rabbies are hostile witnesses [...] The rabbinical evidence shows a polemical spirit, but it confirms in some important respects the evidence of the Gospels."[10]

Goel further argues that the Talmud also betrays no knowledge of Jesus independent of the Christian tradition and it is conceded by most Christian scholars that it is useless as a source of information.[11] It is to be remembered that the Jews considered the Talmud as a kind of 'oral law' supplementing the written law (scriptures). In a text of such sacredness and dignity one should not expect eulogies about Jesus who was considered an enemy of the Jewish religion.

For Goel's discussion on the 'Jewish evidence' he is heavily dependent on G.A. Wells, Will Durant, Paul Johnson, Ian Wilson, Michael Arnheim and William Benjamin Smith.[12]

Goel then goes on to discuss the pagan evidence about Jesus of history. He notes that the Greeks and the Romans have left to posterity a vast historical and philosophical literature written in or referring to the time bracket when Jesus is supposed to have lived. But they are unaware of him. He conveniently downplays the testimony of pagan writers who *did refer* to Jesus like Pliny the Younger (60-114 AD), Tacitus (55-129 AD), Suetonius (70-120 AD) and Sulpicius Severus (d. 400 AD). He quotes Ian Wilson who says "in all this there is scarcely a crumb of information to compel a belief in Jesus' existence".[13] However, Filson notes that non-Christian sources clearly attest the historicity of Jesus, though they may not give us detailed information.[14] But Goel dismisses their testimony by using his common allegation that they are 'clever Christian fabrications'.[15] It is to be noted that, for the bulk of the information on the 'pagan evidence' Goel is greatly dependent on Ian Wilson, Paul Johnson, Georges Ory and Edward Gibbon.

Goel next discusses the evidence of the Gospels. He argues that the Gospels do not give us the date of birth of Jesus and that Bethlehem is not his place of birth. According to him, no responsible theologian or historian is now prepared to construct the life-story of Jesus from the materials provided in the Gospels.[16] Referring to Michael Arnheim, Goel states that the Christian claim to Bethlehem was a fraud from the beginning. Jesus came to be called Jesus of Nazareth because he may have belonged to a Jewish sect called Nazarene.[17] The conclusion of Goel is that the search for a Jesus of history in the Gospels has to be given up. Once again, Goel seeks endorsement for his views from Will Durant, Michael Arnheim and Ian Wilson. But, contrary to what Goel would have us believe, Raymond E. Brown, another renowned biblical scholar maintains that from the infancy narratives many facts concerning Jesus of history can be gathered.[18]

In the entire discussion on the so-called 'evidence of the Gospels', Goel is ignorant of the fact that Gospels are not textbooks of history but are spiritual writings which contain divine truths. Just as the *Bhagavadgita* or the *Mahabharata* are not historical books and from these one cannot arrive at the date or the place of birth of Krishna or Arjuna or Pandu or Dhritarashtra with accuracy, so also from the Gospels one cannot write an accurate account of Jesus of history – *though they no doubt contain many historical facts.*

Goel argues that many contemporary theologians regard the quest of the historical Jesus as both hopeless and religiously irrelevant. He bases himself on the views of some of the controversial scholars in the field, like Hermann Samuel Reimarus, Albert Schweitzer and Rudolf Bultmann. Reimarus subjected the Bible to a critical study. In his *The Aims of Jesus and His Disciples* (1778) he presented Jesus as a failed Jewish revolutionary whose dead body was stolen from his tomb by his disciples in order to spread the story of his resurrection.[19]

Schweitzer was the author of a work entitled *Von Reimarus zu Wrede* (Ger., 1906; Eng., *The Quest for the Historical Jesus,* 1910). Goel argues that Schweitzer's conclusion was that there is nothing more negative than the result of the critical study of the life of Jesus. Jesus of Nazareth never had any historical existence.[20] Goel quotes Schweitzer at length in order to impress upon the reader that since Jesus of history has no foundation, what is important is *Jesus of faith.* Thus, with Schweitzer – Goel claims – Christian theology managed to 'transcend' history and abandoned the quest for the historical Jesus.[21]

Geol also refers to Rudolf Bultmann who dismissed Jesus of history and advocated Christ of Kerygma. Bultmann condemned as useless any attempt to try to reconstruct the Jesus of history and invented a Jesus whom he named as the 'Christ of Kerygma'.[22] Thus, Bultmann became a radical sceptic of Jesus of history, and Goel found his thesis very useful for his purpose and with much delight he says: "It was quite a relief when critical history abolished him [Jesus], and emancipated his victims."[23]

Goel concludes with the tall claim that there is 'no dearth of scholars' who think that the Jesus of the Gospels never existed in history, that if he existed at all, nothing can be known about his person or teaching from all contemporary sources, that the historicity of Jesus is a big lie and that it is the die-hard Christian theologians who have invented the Jesus of history. Then with scorn he asks: "What has been your Jesus Christ except the Christ of faith, all these two thousand years?"[24]

Resurrection is a concocted tale

Resurrection of Jesus is the central belief of Christianity. But, according to Goel, it was a puerile invention.[25] He asks: "Have you ever cared to convince human reason or even common sense that the man who died on the cross rose on the third day?"[26] Resurrection, according to him, was a story concocted by a generation or more after the events supposed to have occurred. Besides, Goel alleges, the Jewish tradition confirms that Resurrection and Ascension were only stories invented and spread by the disciples.[27] Then, he goes on to make an overwhelming claim: "We are entitled to dismiss the gospel stories of Resurrection like the rest of Jesus' miracles. We are entitled not to treat it as history at all."[28]

A close reading of Goel reveals that he is dependent on many pseudo-scholars and writers of fiction for his material on the resurrection, and basing himself on them he arrives at the conclusion that resurrection of Jesus was a fraud. Some authors on whom Goel depends are: Friedrich Barhdt,[29] Karl Heinrich Venturini,[30] John Dominic Crossan,[31] D.H. Lawrence,[32] Ludwig Noack,[33] Ernest Renan,[34] Emile Lerou, a French lady who used the pseudonym Pierre Nahor,[35] Michael Arnheim,[36] and of course the Gospels, which Goel interprets with the competence and genius of an elementary school boy. Goel is totally unaware that without an adequate knowledge of biblical languages, biblical hermeneutics, biblical geography, biblical archaeology, methods of biblical criticism, and history of the early Church and Christology, it is impossible to make correct statements concerning Jesus of history or anything related to his life.

Raymond E. Brown and S.S. Donald are emphatic in stating that the resurrection of Jesus was the supreme intervention of God in human existence. The rationalistic or liberal criticisms of the last century discredited the resurrection stories as demonstrative either of apostolic fraud (stole the body) or apostolic crudelity and confusion (Jesus was not dead but was in coma). They remind us that some of the attacks were already current in the early first century and the New Testament writers had tried to answer them.[37] Besides, accounts of painstaking refutation of these attacks are also available in standard apologetic books.

However, it is also to be noted that, as John P. Meier has observed, the Jesus of history is by definition the Jesus who is open to empirical investigation by any and all observers. But the risen Jesus lies outside the scope of such investigation for he transcends time and space. But, this does not mean that the resurrection was not real.[38]

Jesus was born out of wedlock

Goel alleges that Jesus was born out of wedlock.[39] He further claims that Mary, his mother, was an unmarried woman, that the dogma of the virgin birth of Jesus and the permanent virginity of Mary are myths floated by Matthew, for she was mother of several children besides Jesus, and that it is only the Catholic Church which continues to stick to the dogma of the virgin birth of Jesus, and to the myth of Mary's permanent virginity.[40] According to Goel, the real reason for floating the myth of virgin birth seems to be that, there had always been a question mark hanging over Mary's sexual morality and that it was clearly a subject which caused the early Christians acute embarrassment. In fact, there has been a long-standing tradition among the Jews that Jesus was the fruit of an adulterous union between Mary and a Roman soldier named Panthera.[41] Referring to J.A.T. Robinson, Goel says that Jesus was conceived by Mary through some unknown male which Joseph subsequently condones.[42]

Basically, Goel is dependent on Will Durant, Michael Arnheim, Ian Stephen, Ian Wilson and Ludwig Noack, Paul de Regla's and J.A.T. Robinson for his discussion on the virgin birth and Mary's sexual morality.

Jesus was a homosexual and suffered from paranoia

Goel claims that Jesus was a homosexual and that he was suffering from paranoia.[43] Some leading psychologists in the West have seen in Jesus many unmistakable symptoms of mental sickness. In fact, some of them had rated him as stark mad.[44] Referring to Morton Smith Goel notes that Jesus was a hedonistic libertine and homosexual who thought himself above the constrains of the Jewish law and was able to do as he pleased.[45] Basing again on the writings of Morton Smith, Goel alleges that Jesus and Lazarus were homosexuals.[46] Hugh Montefiore also joins Smith in making the same allegation that Jesus was a homosexual.[47]

Referring to a number of writers of fiction, Goel states that Jesus of the Gospel was quick-tempered and egocentric, that he uttered threats against everyone who is established, powerful and rich, that he was sexually abnormal, and was a sorcerer who led people astray.[48] Goel also refers to writers who claim that Jesus was a guerrilla leader.[49] There is also an allegation that Jesus was married to Mary Magdaline.[50]

Goel is dependent on controversial writers like Nikos Kazantzakis, Albert Camus, D.H. Lawrence, C. Binet-Sangle, Wilhelm Lange-Eichbaum, Morton Smith, Herman H. Somers, Anita Mason – to name a few – who were (or are) novelists, story tellers, dramatists, psychologists who painted Jesus in strange colours and whose literary productions were mostly international best sellers due to their uninhibited, provocative and liberal style and content. Undoubtedly, for the purpose of maligning Jesus, the literary garbage of the West has served Goel well.

Adolf Hitler was the reincarnation of Jesus Christ

Goel in his hatred for Jesus Christ alleges that there are striking parallels between Jesus Christ and Adolf Hitler. He does not hesitate to claim that Hitler was an incarnation of Jesus Christ and that the Holocaust in which millions of Jews were slaughtered was directly inspired by the Jesus of the Gospels.[51] Basing himself on this conviction, Goel argues that, by the middle of the 20th century, the Jesus of the Gospel had become a thoroughly discredited figure in the modern world and could hardly be presented as Christ of Faith.[52] He also alleges that the Nazi creed as laid down by Hitler did not sound much different from the Christian creed.[53]

Jesus is junk

Goel laments that Jesus Christ has been the stock-in-trade of Christian missions down the ages. According to him, the Christian missionary propaganda in general leaves the impression as if Jesus Christ was a mighty figure who took the world by storm as soon as he appeared on the scene.[54] But, the 'real' Jesus was more and more brought down to earth in a manner that proved pretty painful, even alarming to the believing Christians.[55] The entire paraphernalia with which Jesus is equipped – virgin birth, baptism by water, miracles, parables, anointing, twelve apostles, trial, last supper, betrayal, passion, execution, resurrection, ascension, etc. – can be traced back to magic rites, mystery cults, mythologies, religions, and philosophies prevailing in the ancient world since long before Jesus is supposed to have been born.[56]

Goel also accuses the Hindus for having acknowledged Jesus as a spiritual leader, thus assisting in the invention of Jesus of Christianity. He says: "We [Hindus] have invented a 'real' Jesus and a 'true' Christianity [...] The missionary and the mullah smiles at our inventions but goes ahead and makes good use of our soft headedness. That is why, we have failed to solve the 'communal problem' all these years."[57]

After having analysed the 'truth' about Jesus, Goel concludes that *Jesus is junk*,[58] that he is a 'synthetic product'[59] and that the true Jesus is 'Jesus of fiction'.[60] Therefore, he demands that Jesus be rejected. He says: "It is high time for Hindus to learn that Jesus Christ symbolises no spiritual power, or moral uprightness. [...] Jesus means nothing but mischief for their country and culture. The West where he flourished for long, has discarded him as junk. [...] He is the type of junk that cannot be re-cycled. He can only poison the environment."[61]

Goel deliberately defames and denigrates, without any qualms of conscience, Jesus Christ whom millions consider as God and Saviour. Reading his book may even lead one to suspect the sanity of the author.

Gospels are a collection of lies

After declaring Jesus as junk, Goel turns to examine the nature of the Gospels. He notes that all languages, which have been influenced by Christianity, contain the expression 'gospel truth'. But he says that truth is exactly what we find missing from the Gospels when it comes to the life and teachings of Jesus.[62] The Gospels do not reflect the time and clime in which Jesus is supposed to have lived and functioned. What they represent are the beliefs held by certain Christian communities in the middle of the 3rd century A.D. Besides, the Gospels have undergone considerable editing and manipulation by Christian scribes.[63] In addition, the Gospels contradict and cancel each another when it comes to the salient features in the story of Jesus such as the date and the place of his birth, his ancestry and parentage, ministry, trial, death and resurrection.[64] Goel further claims that the evangelists who wrote the Gospels were fictitious characters. The names, Matthew, Mark, Luke and John are mere attributions and not necessarily those of their real authors.[65]

Therefore, according to Goel, no responsible theologian or historian is now prepared to construct the life-story of Jesus from material provided by the Gospels. He quotes Will Durant who says: "In summary, it is clear that there are many contradictions between one gospel and another, many dubious statements of history, many suspicious resemblances to the legend told of pagan gods, many incidents apparently designed to prove the fulfilment of Old Testament prophecies, many passages possibly aiming to establish a historical basis for some later doctrine or ritual of the Church."[66] Basing himself on Paul Johnson, Goel argues that the existing codices of the Gospels do not take us further back than the days of Jerome and Augustine, still leaving a huge 300 year gap.[67] The Gospels are therefore a collection of lies.

Gospels are the first Nazi manifesto

Goel alleges that the Gospels are the first Nazi manifesto[68] and the source of the poison is the Jesus of the Gospels.[69] Elsewhere also, he states that the Gospels are now regarded as the first Nazi manifesto by knowledgeable historians, sociologists, and psychologists and Christianity itself is a Big Lie.[70] Goel maintains that if Jesus was the only Son of God, who was sent down to earth for the purpose of washing the sins of mankind with his blood by mounting the cross, knowingly and willingly, the Jews should have been glorified for helping the divine plan. But, the gospel writers are guilty of committing one of the greatest crimes against humanity – the Nazi Holocaust.[71]

It is to be emphasised that if one turns to the Gospels with a prejudiced mind which conceives 'Jesus as junk', the 'Gospel as a collection of lies' and as the 'first Nazi manifesto' – as Goel does – it is impossible to discover anything good in it. Prejudice and objectivity cannot go together.

Christianity is a big lie

After having discussed the 'truth' about Jesus and the nature of the Gospels, Goel arrives at the conclusion that 'Christianity is a big lie' and that the missionaries are its traders.[72] Elsewhere, he states that Christianity has never been a religion in its long history.[73]

It is to be reiterated that if Goel's premises are from the accounts of atheists, agnostics, apostates, writers of fictitious lives of Jesus, rationalists, ultra liberals, scientific humanists, anti-Christians and the like, the conclusion that Christianity is a lie is the only logical one possible to arrive at.

An expose of Goel and his hidden agenda

So far we have been analysing the 'truth' about Jesus according to Goel. Although he had assured his readership that he would tell them the truth about the 'real' Jesus of history, all that he attempted to do was to create a 'Jesus of myth' by *hiding acknowledged historical facts* – which is part of the dubious Hindutva 'art' of re-writing history. Thus, the entire ink-spilling of Goel, under the guise of telling his countrymen the 'truth' about the 'real Jesus', has turned out to be an exercise in indoctrination, dissemination of falsehood and a semantic manipulation of 'history'. Hence, any one who reads Goel's book uncritically will be in serious danger of being misinformed, to say the least. This being the case, it is important that we examine the truth about Goel and his hidden agenda.

Second rate writings as primary sources

One of the major criticisms against Goel is that his primary sources are of dubious quality. The writers on whom Goel depends are either ultra-liberal or controversial who pose themselves as biblical scholars and Christian theologians. Hence, it is best to classify them as second-rate biblical scholars and third-rate theologians. In addition, many of them are prejudiced against Christianity and some are even pronounced anti-Christians. Some of the 'pseudo-scholars' on whom Goel depends are: Edward Gibbon, G.A. Wells, Ian Wilson, Michael Arnheim, Koenraad Elst, Will Durant, Paul Johnson, Georges Ory, William Benjamin Smith, Paul Winter, James P. Mackey and Michael Baigent. Let us take a brief look at the 'scholarly' credentials of some of the prominent ones among them.

Edward Gibbon was a British historian who blamed the Christians for the fall of the Roman Empire. Despite being reconverted to Protestantism, he actually lost faith in Christianity as he read more and more on philosophy, foreign cultures, and religious controversies through the years. In his writings Gibbon expresses the strongest opposition to Christianity and the Byzantine Empire, since he considered both the institutions to be in exact opposition to those of Republican Rome.[74] Gibbon's controversial work *The Decline and Fall of the Roman Empire* is an important source of information for Goel.

G.A. Wells is a retired Professor of German who became a self-styled scholar of the 'un-historical Jesus'. According to Gregory S. Neal, the problem with Wells' work on the 'un-historical Jesus' is not so much the author's lack of standing as a scholar in the field of New Testament Biblical Criticism as it is his utter failure to apply the standard tools and controls of the Historical-Critical field.[75] Goel profitably utilises Wells' *Did Jesus Exist?* (1986) for writing about Jesus of history.

Michael Arnheim is a professor of classical civilisation. J.P. Holding, who reviewed Arnheim's book entitled *Is Christianity*

True? (1984) – which is also among Goel's primary sources – comments that the book is "not as big a deal as the title pretends". Then speaking of its bibliography he notes that it is mildly impressive and internal footnotes number less than half a dozen, which is – very odd for a professor of classical civilisation. It is also equally odd that anyone could think of determining the truth of Christianity in a scant 150 pages coupled with about 50 more pages of complaining about Christian 'intolerance'. Holding says that he was disappointed about the book. Where he was hoping to find new challenges, he only discovered the same old stuff from the sceptics.[76]

Will Durant is generally known as the 'gentle philosopher' and the famous author of *The Story of Civilization* which he took five decades to complete. He is also rated among the most gifted prose stylists of the 20th century. But, his personal background ranged from being a candidate to Catholic priesthood, a young man dizzy with socialism, atheism, involved in radical circles and finally maintaining a vital conception of the world.[77] However, how competent is he in discussing biblical and Christological matters is very much open to question. Will Durant's *The Story of Civilisation*, vol. 3, *Caesar and Christ* (1944) is an important source of information for Goel.

Paul Johnson, though he is considered as a historian today, his background is that of a journalist. He was assistant editor of Paris-based *Realities* (1952-1955) and then the weekly *New Statesman* (1955-1970) and the last six years its editor. As a historian, he is sometimes described a 'raving left winger', 'provocative writer' and 'one who celebrates liberty'.[78] Thus, he too may not qualify himself to write authoritatively on Jesus of history. Yet, in Goel, one notices a high degree of dependence on Johnson's *A History of Christianity* (1978).

Ian Wilson is another British writer of little significance as far as biblical, theological and historical scholarship is concerned. Wilson's background is that of a dramatist, journalist, novelist and producer of television programmes. His

Jesus: The Evidence (1985), an international best seller to which Goel frequently refers, was the subject of a controversial television series.

Koenraad Elst is a noted pro-Hindutva 'scholar' from Belgium. Though he was born in a Catholic family, he does not accept any of the basic beliefs of Christianity. He says: "We know that Jesus was not God's only begotten son, that he did not save humanity from eternal sin, and that our happiness is this world or the next does not depend on believing these or any other dogmas."[79] Elst was also active for some years in the New Age movement. For all practical purposes he can be considered as an 'apostate'. But, Goel gathers much of his information about Western Christianity and Jesus from Elst's controversial *Psychology of Prophetism,* which is a summarised version of a controversial psychological analysis of Jesus by Herman H. Sommers, an ex-Jesuit, who abandoned the Christian faith.[80]

From the above analysis, it is clear that, from a scholarly point of view, one does not need any further reason to consider Goel's book as a collection of opinion of second and third rate authors, who are at best rationalists and sceptical biblical 'scholars'. Secondly, the themes he discusses lack objectivity and depth of treatment.

Selectiveness and one-sidedness of the sources

Another problem with Goel's *Jesus Christ: An Artifice for Aggression* is that his sources are noted for their selectiveness and one-sidedness. It may be remembered that most of the critical works on Jesus and the Bible, which appeared since the 17th, 18th and the 19th centuries, were influenced by immanentism, humanism, rationalism, empiricism and deism. *Immanentism* believed that reality can be explained by the principles of nature itself. *Humanism* exalted the human intellect and the senses, and claimed that knowledge of reality is attainable by intellectual and sense data alone. *Rationalism* and *empiricism* also exalted human knowledge which glorified reason, and rationalists ended up in complete rejection of the supernatural and in extreme empiricism, which terminated in subjectivism and scepticism.[81]

Deism was the most significant consequence of rationalism. Deists emphasised natural religion, denied revelation and rejected the supernatural. They questioned the integrity of the Bible, the personality of the central figure of Christianity and its dogmas.[82] Hermann Samuel Reimarus, Albert Schweitzer and Rudolf Bultmann from whom Goel draws generously to 'demolish' the Jesus of history were scholars who were influenced by the above pattern of thinking – either directly or indirectly.

Hermann Samuel Reimiarus (1694-1798) was a key but a controversial figure in the discussion on Jesus of history. He was prejudiced by rationalism's rejection of the supernatural and was a believer in deism. He made a distinction between the historical Jesus (a revolutionary Jew who failed in an attempt to establish an earthly messianic kingdom) and the Christ (a deception created by the disciples who stole his body from the tomb and invented the doctrine of the resurrection and the parousia).[83]

Albert Schweitzer (1875-1965) made an exhaustive survey of the life of Jesus from Reimarus to William Wrede. Goel maintains that there is nothing more negative than the result of the critical study of the life of Jesus by Schweitzer. The Jesus of Nazareth, who came forward publicly as the Messiah, who preached the ethic of the Kingdom of God, who founded the Kingdom of Heaven upon earth, and died to give his work its final consecration, never had any existence.[84] However, eminent biblical scholars like Kselman and Witherup maintain that today few would accept Schweitzer's reconstruction of the historical Jesus.[85] Stephen Neil, after making a careful study of Schweitzer's views, observes that Jesus is not after all so mysterious as Schweitzer will have us believe and that his solution is inadequate and weak for we can never separate 'the teaching of Jesus, from 'Jesus of history'.[86]

Rudolf Bultmann (1884-1976) was the theologian, who proposed the thesis of Jesus of Kerygma instead of Jesus of history. Hence, Goel says that the last nail in the coffin which carried the Jesus of history was hammered home by Bultmann.[87] However, it is to be noted that Bultmann's thesis was rejected outright by numerous scholars after him. For example, the German scholars like K. Barth, O. Cullmann, W. Pannenberg, the British scholarship spearheaded by E. Hoskyns, Vincent Taylor, R.H. Lightfoot, C.H. Dodd, and many of Bultmann's own disciples - the post-Bultmannians - such as E. Kasemann, E. Fuchs, G. Bornkamm, H. Conzelmann, J.M. Robertson, G. Ebling and so on.[88]

It is to be noted that Goel is *totally silent* about all the above scholars, who through their painstaking research had 'demolished' Bultmann's thesis. But he does not forget to refer to authors like Pastor J. Kahl, W. Trilling and G.A. Wells who endorse Bultmann's position.[89] As is obvious, Goel is highly one-sided and selective in his choice of his sources. It is also to be stated that, although Goel comments on theses of Reimarus and Bultmann with authoritativeness, *not even once* in his book he refers to them in the original. All his knowledge of them is limited to the reports of his select authors.

Dependence on fictitious writings

There is a third category of sources which Goel uses in his attempt to 'demolish' the Jesus of history, namely, fictitious writings. At the end of the 18th century and the beginning of the 19th century, based on the fictitious life of Jesus, there began to appear many studies on Jesus portraying him in a crude and fantastic manner. Most of such writings were extraordinarily provocative, revolutionary and original, often causing considerable scandal. Such literature was mainly in the form of stories, novels, dramas, liberal psychological studies, sensational journalistic accounts and manuscripts for television serials. Some of the authors referred to by Goel in his book are: Friedrich Barhdt, Karl Heinrich Venturini, Emile Lerou, G.L.

Loostan, C. Binet-Sangle, D. H. Lawrence, Wilhelm Lange-Eichbaum, Robert Graves, Nikos Kazantzakis, Albert Camus, Hugh Montefiore, W.E. Phipps, Carlyle Slaughter, J.A.T. Robinson, Morton Smith, Mariana Warner, Anita Mason, Michael Arnheim, Ian Wilson, Herman H. Somers, James P. Mackey, to name a few.[90]

Goel does not care to make a distinction between history, myth, novel, drama, private opinion and anti-Christian writings. He draws indiscriminately from all these materials which can serve his purpose of maligning Jesus Christ and Christianity and helpful in his attempt to erase evidences in favour of Jesus of history.

However, what is most surprising is that in spite of his dependence on fictitious writings and on controversial authors, Goel claims that he has made a *deep study* of Jesus Christ. He says: "I have been trying to have a *close look at Jesus Christ*, [...] and in the process have become *conversant* with the Christological research undertaken in the modern West over the last more than two hundred years".[91] "Hindus like me [...] have *studied him* [Jesus Christ] *first-hand* and in the context of the history he has created all through these two thousand years."[92]

Goel's claim that he had made a *deep* and *first-hand study* of Jesus is far from true. What he has done is to *collect and compile* the anti-Christian writings and provocative materials on Jesus available in the literary sewers of the Western world.

Use of language without refinement

In *Jesus Christ: An Artifice for Aggression* Goel uses a *language that lacks refinement*. He is an 'angry Hindu communalist' who shouts, yells, barks, thunders and spits venom and fury against Jesus Christ and Christianity. A cursory glance at some of his blasphemies will verify this fact. We shall quote Goel himself at some length:

> "Jesus of the gospels was quite an obnoxious character."[93]

> "He (Jesus) was intolerant, short-tempered, and foul-mouthed, and went about cursing everyone who did not applaud his tall talk."[94]

> "The ethics he preached was either sanctimonious humbug (Sermon on the Mount) which worked to the advantage of the bully and the robber and the spendthrift."[95]

> "Adolf Hitler reincarnated Jesus Christ."[96]

> "Leading psychologists in the West had seen in this Jesus many unmistakable symptoms of mental sickness; in fact, some of them had nailed him as stark mad."[97]

> "The salesmen of Jesus Christ should have thrown their discredited totem into the dustbin and gone in for something more worthwhile."[98]

> " His [Jesus'] advocacy of missions for bringing the whole world into his fold, was a mandate for gangsterism and predatory imperialism."[99]

> "All that you have always come up with is a broth of paper and ink, eulogised as the Word of God, and backed it up with brute force, military or financial or both."[100]

In Goel's other writings too we come across a style of language which is crude and uncouth. He says:

> "The biggest share in Christian crimes down the centuries can safely be allotted to the Roman Catholic Church, its head, its hierarchy, its theologians, its religious books and its missionaries."[101]

> "The Roman Catholic Church in India has remained true to the tradition. The literature it has produced during the last five centuries is full of lies of the filthiest sort, not only about Hindu religion and culture but also about its own 'religion' and role. And this garbage heap is topped by the hoax about the co-called St. Thomas."[102]

"Men like Francis Xavier stand out in this record as hardened criminals masquerading as religious priests."[103]

"Break a person's bones and then come back with bandage and some gruel – this is the logic. Mother Teresa happens to be the foremost in this dirty and despicable Christian game."[104]

"We [Hindus] were here long before Jesus Christ was born and hurled at an unsuspecting Pagan world. And I assure you we will be here long after the Bible starts selling as waste paper on pavements around the world."[105]

"Jesus Christ would have continued to stink in Hindu nostrils but for another historical process which was simultaneously at work in this country."[106]

As is evident, Goel's language is undignified, aggressive and crude. His statements are repugnant to any civilised person since they often degenerate into abuse. When someone warned Goel about the lack of refinement in his language his reply was the following: "So long as Christianity refuses to revise its theology and withdraw its missions, there was no language which was strong enough for it and its hirelings."[107] When an arrogant person advances in age, he can become incredibly incorrigible.[108]

Goel's words of disrespect, hatred, threat and intimidation of Christians make us think of the much touted myth of Hindu tolerance which the proponents of Hindutva proclaim, and reveals the advanced state of decay of the Hindutva culture.

Narrow minded and opposed to dialogue

Goel is amazingly narrow minded and opposed to dialogue. He says: "We object to Christian missions, but refuse to discuss Christianity and its God, Jesus."[109] "Hindus have nothing to learn from Christianity but a lot to teach."[110] Elsewhere, in his writings, he clearly states that what he advocates is not dialogue but a *battle* between Hinduism and Christianity. He says: "Hindus are committing a grave mistake in regarding the encounter between Hinduism and Christianity as a dialogue between two religions. [...] The encounter, therefore, should be viewed as a *battle between two totally opposed and mutually exclusive ways of thought and behaviour* [...] it is a *war* between *daivi* (divine) and *asuri* (demonic) *sampadas* (propensities)."[111]

Though Goel says that Hindus have nothing to learn from Christianity but a lot to teach, we are convinced that there is much good in every religion and that every religion can learn from others. For example, Goel forgets that since the 18th century, basically it was Christianity that led Hinduism to self-criticism and social reform than any other religion or ideology. Even a cursory reading of the writings of Raja Ram Mohan Roy, Mahatma Phule, Lokmanya Tilak, Gopal Krishna Gokhale and Mahatma Gandhi will convince anyone of this fact.[112] Even today, in the 21st century, it is Christianity which challenges India to improve its record in the areas of human rights, social reform, justice, gender equality, empowerment of women and the weaker sections of society, solidarity with the poor, eradication of caste system, illiteracy, alleviation of poverty and the like, than any other religion or ideology in the country.

Goel also claims that no stalwarts of the Indian Renaissance ever recognised Jesus as the Christ.[113] This shows his absolute ignorance of modern Indian history. Everyone conversant with the facts concerning Indian Renaissance knows that there were many learned and intelligent Hindus, besides numerous ordinary people, who not only admired Jesus Christ but even accepted him as their saviour. For example, the great personalities of modern India like Keshab Chandra Sen, Brahmabandhab Upadhyaya, Pratap Chandra Mozoomdar, Manilal C. Parekh, Narayan Vaman Tilak, Pandita Ramabai, Gandhi are among eminent personalities who found Jesus as a great teacher, a divine person, and saviour, and the Gospels, as a treasury of eternal truths.[114] Let us briefly examine some of these.

Keshab Chandra Sen (1838-1884) spent twenty years in an intense study of the Christian religion. The result was that he came to believe in Jesus Christ. In 1879, he said the following about Jesus Christ: "My Christ, my sweet Christ, the brightest jewel of my heart, the necklace of my soul – for twenty years I have cherished him in my heart [...] I have found joy and sweetness unutterable in my master Jesus. [...] and I fell at his feet saying: Blessed Child of God, when shall others see the light that is in thee?"[115]

Pratap Chandra Mozoomdar (1840-1905), who was a friend and disciple of Keshab Chandra Sen, was also a person deeply committed to Christ. He said: "I was mysteriously led to feel a personal affinity to the spirit of Christ. The whole subject of the life and death of Christ had for me a marvellous sweetness and fascination. [...] The response of my nature was unhesitating and immediate. Jesus, from that day, to me became a reality whereon I might lean."[116]

Brahmabandhab Upadhyaya (1861-1907), who became a 'Catholic Hindu' and a 'Christian Sanyasi' said: "One may believe or not believe that Christ is the Son of God, but there is not the least shadow of doubt that Christ claimed to be the Son of God."[117] Once he was fully convinced that Christ was the Son of God, he felt that he could not ignore the command of Christ to be baptised. On 1 September 1891, during a short stay in Karachi, he was received into the Catholic Church.[118]

Narayan Vaman Tilak (1861-1919) said: "At least to those who know me, here is an irrefutable miracle. Am I not a Christian? Have I not full faith in my Lord Christ? Only two years ago, was I not the sworn enemy of this Christ and his followers? With this hand, now so eager in his service, how many papers have I scribbled off in the heat of my scorn for Him? This tongue, which today is always ready to witness to the great mercy of Christ, has here-to-fore poured what unrestrained contempt on that Holy Name?"[119]

However, it appears that according to Goel's reckoning, the only stalwarts of Indian Renaissance worthy of the epithet are Swami Dayananda Saraswati, Swami Vivekananda, Bankim Chandra Chatterjee, Aurobindo, V.D. Savarkar, M.S. Golwalkar, Nathuram Godse, B.S. Moonje and S.P. Mookerjee, who were more noted for their Hindu cultural nationalism, narrow-minded vision and hardliner identity than for true patriotism.

Misrepresentation of Western Christianity

Goel spreads misinformation about Christianity in the West. According to him, Christianity has collapsed in the West and is trying desperately to secure a firm foothold in the East. He says: "Traditional religion has collapsed in Christendom, which is no more Christian."[120] "Christians as a religious body do not exist today in the Western world in a meaningful way."[121] Goel's information about Christianity in the West seems to have come from his two trips to Europe and America in 1979 and 1989 respectively[122] – probably on a tourist visa – and from Koenraad Elst[123] whose dubious credentials as a Christian we have already seen above, and who is convinced that the fundamental reason for the decline of Christianity is *intrinsic to the nature of the Christian faith.*[124]

What Goel describes as collapse of Christianity in the West is in reality a change of civilisation. Sooner or later the same forces will also strike India, and it is sure to alter the face of Hinduism in a formidable way. Hinduism has not yet seriously confronted the full impact of industrialisation, scientific and technological progress, rationalism, liberalism, humanism, gender equality, economic progress and consumerism.

In some areas of the West the Churches may be quite empty, for various reasons, beginning with the drastic reduction of population, and the disinterest of many in taking part in *formal* religious activities or due to the disagreement with certain teachings of the Church. This does not mean that they have abandoned Christianity. The majority of the Christians in the West have neither rejected Jesus Christ nor

Christianity. It is enough to recall the millions of people who gather for God-experience in such typically Christian centres of pilgrimage as Lourdes, Fatima, Medjugorje, Taize, Rome, the response of the young people to such world events as the International Day of Youth, the innumerable Western Christian organisations of solidarity that operate in every continent and the like. So, Christianity has not crumbled in the West, as Goel alleges.

Every reasonable person knows that practising Christianity does not imply in Church attendance or participation in some formal rituals alone. The values by which one lives are the primary determinants of one's religiosity. The Hindu temples in India may be full and the Hindu centres of pilgrimage may attract millions – *Kumabhamela* is a typical example. But, the very same so-called religious people perpetuate the inhuman caste system, Brahmanical domination in every sector of Indian life, enslavement of women, secret endorsement of *sati* (widow burning), child marriage, untouchability, temple prostitution, use of religion for political gain, acts of religious intolerance, and other forms of serious violation of human rights against adherents of minority religions. One wonders which is better, the values lived by the so-called 'de-Christianised' West or the 'highly religious' Hindu India?

Goel, while criticising Christianity, hides the truth of what Hindus themselves have done to Hindus during its long history. If the India of today is still largely underdeveloped, economically backward, caste ridden, blatantly corrupt, shockingly illiterate, blindly intolerant to minorities, Dalits and tribals, and women are treated as second-rate citizens, and justify these by appealing to some Hindu scriptures or to the theories of *karma* and rebirth, Hinduism should take the major share of the blame. No wonder then why Karl Marx said that Hinduism is the ideology of an oppressive and outworn society.[125] Thus, in reality, it is not the minority religions and secular ideologies of India that are obstacles to the progress of the nation but the religion of the majority, namely, Hinduism.

An attempt to re-write history

The central concern in Goel's book is to re-write history. Of course, tampering with history is part of the strategy of the contemporary Hindutva ideologues to whose camp Goel belongs. Through their silences and erasures, the accepted facts of the past are being re-written by the Hindutva historians. In this sense, Goel's *Jesus Christ: An Artifice for Aggression* is an epitome of the onslaught of Hindutva on established historiography. But, Romila Thapar reminds us that the fallacious idea that the past can be changed through destroying the surviving heritage from the past is a blatant attack on history: for the axiom of history is that the past cannot be changed.[126]

Today, Goel and those who share his ideology insist that Indus Valley civilisation is pre-Aryan is a myth, the Aryan invasion of India is a myth, Jesus of history is a myth, coming of St. Thomas the apostle to India is a myth, India's cultural pluralism is a myth, secular India is a myth and Hindutva ideology is communal is a myth. These claims are clear cases of distortion of historical facts. Their fixation with myth is a sign of their insecurity to face the truth, and their attack on history reveals their dread for the past. Hence, when Goel says that "Jesus of history is a myth", what he manifests is his insecurity and fear of truth.

History is a discipline based on evidence. Evidences are numerous to substantiate the truth of Jesus of history. It is not our purpose here to pursue this matter. However, suffice it to say that there are eloquent arguments from modern biblical scholarship to establish the truth about Jesus of history. The great breakthroughs in Christological studies over the past decades endorse Jesus of history. A corpus of archaeological and historical evidences that have profoundly influenced contemporary biblical studies also provide ample evidence of Jesus of history.[127] But Goel's thesis that 'Jesus is a myth' stands devoid of any convincing evidence. What drives his writings are prejudices, fears and enmity than scholarship.

A handbook for Hindu communalists

The content, intent and style of Goel's *Jesus Christ: An Artifice for Aggression* reveal that it is a well-designed handbook for Hindu communalists. He envisages an epic battle between the Hindus and the non-Hindus. Some of the statements of Goel in the book have a sinister power to indoctrinate. They can transform and misguide moderate Hindus to be militants, first-rate thugs, terrorists and street fighters. For example, he says: "Christianity has become a danger and a threat to the safety, security and freedom of India."[128] "The quantum of crimes committed by Muhammad's Islam was only slightly smaller than that of the crimes committed by the Christianity of Jesus Christ."[129] "...there is nothing common between Sanatana Dharma and the sinister cult of the Only Saviour"[130] preached by Christianity.

Elsewhere in his writings also Goel exhibits a similar attitude of intolerance towards Christianity. He states:

> "Jesus is only an artifice for mounting aggression against non-Christian societies and cultures, and no more an object of worship."[131]

> "I want Hindus to view Christianity as a wicked ideology like Communism and Nazism, and not as a system of spiritual seeking like their own schools of Sanatana Dharma."[132]

> "Hindus should know that Jesus means nothing but mischief for their country and culture, and stop showing any weakness for him."[133]

> "We believe that India is the homeland of Hindus and that the voice of Hindus is the voice of India."[134]

> "In the normal course, the Hindus who had such a glorious history should have come into their own after 1947 and resumed their career of newer cultural creations."[135]

He also does not hesitate to make statements of intimidation and threat to the Christian community. He says:

> "...the sooner the Christian missions close their shop in this country the better for them and their masters abroad."[136]

> "The better course for you [Christians] is to take the hint and stop selling your merchandise [Jesus Christ] under false labels."[137]

As is evident from the above statements, the purpose of Goel's book is to impress and indoctrinate Hindus against Christians. Therefore, the book is sure to have a great attraction among the protagonists of contemporary Hindutva, as it can stir up communal hatred.

In 1995, Winand Callewaert of the Department of Asian Studies (Belgium), after reading Goel's *Jesus Christ: An Artifice for Aggression,* made the following insightful observation:

"I can agree with much of the analysis you make about Christianity (or Islam), but where does it take one?

— The Christian believer will be antagonised and turn against you. Result: feelings of *hatred*.
— The non-believer will say: of course religion exploits people for its own end, you see. Result: he will turn against the believing Christian. *Hatred*.
— And the non-Christians in India and elsewhere will only be too happy to find arguments in your book to say: of course this intelligent man has given proof that Christianity is meant to exploit us. Let us suppress or throw out (if possible) the Christians in India. Result: *hatred*.
— I do not understand, Sita Bhai, how this can be your project.
What do you want to achieve?."[138]

Goel is an arch enemy of communal harmony and a symbol of the religious bigotry of the Hindutva ideologues.

Conclusion: An author to be sidelined and a book to be rejected

The overwhelming concern of Sita Ram Goel in his *Jesus Christ: An Artifice for Aggression* is to destroy the 'Jesus of history' and to sell a 'Jesus of myth' instead. Basically, Goel is asking Christians to surrender their affirmation of the historical Jesus so that Christ becomes a mere idea. But, as E. Kasemann has rightly pointed out, every verse of the Gospels tells us that the origin of Christianity is not the kerygma, not the resurrection experience of the disciples, not the Christ an idea but a historical event, the appearance of the Man Jesus of Nazareth and his Message.[139]

It follows then that, if anyone takes Goel's book as a source of information about Jesus Christ and Christianity, he is surely being duped. The book is simply an overview of the rationalist, agnostic, atheistic, sceptical and liberal biblical 'scholarship' available in the West. As we have already seen, most of Goel's informers about Jesus Christ are just cardboard figures that juggle around in the arena of biblical and Christological studies. They avoid the complexities of the questions they discuss, and flourish on ambiguities, fictional notions and fabricated fantasies of novelists, dramatists, journalists, pseudo-scholars and anti-Christian writers. Thus, from the point of view of scholarship, the book is of no significance. Consequently, Goel's much publicised presentation of the so-called truth about Jesus of history is reduced to a mere shell even though his claims are tall and staggering. His book is also a typical example of how history can be re-written along Hindutva lines.

Goel has imported to India a quantity of garbage gathered from the dustbins of the Western liberal and anti-Christian writings. The aim of the author, as evident, is to stir up and let lose the Hindutva brigade against the peace-loving and service-minded Christians of India.

If Goel wanted to be a historian of Jesus Christ, he should have engaged in serious scholarship and looked at Jesus Christ and Christianity with scientific temperament. It should be a study that ascertains, verifies and cross-checks statements and opinions of writers with professionalism, accountability, openness and exacting standards of objectivity. Unfortunately, this is not the case with Goel. In the preface to his book, Goel states that he long deliberated writing an essay entitled "The Advantage of Being an Ass".[140] This desire seems to have been fulfilled when he authored the book we have examined, which amounts to several such essays.

Thus, Goel is a pseudo-historian who writes about Jesus of history on the 'highest authority' of fictitious writings, opinion of second-rate scholars, outdated sources and shady works of anti-Christians, atheists and apostates. Due to the fatal attraction which his pseudo-scholarship can have for the uncritical and naive Hindu readership, the work deserved to be considered as a handbook for communalists, as it can be profitably be utilised to train the cadres of the RSS, VHP, BJP, Shiv Sena, Bajrang Dal, the whole Sangh Parivar, to wield *lathis, trishuls*, torches, guns and grenades, and engage in villainy and terrorism.

Goel, as we have seen, is also adept in the use of language without refinement. He disseminates falsehood and misinformation, and endorses communal hatred. Considering these factors – and fitting to his character as a fanatic Hindutva ideologue – the book deserves to be given the epithet of Goel's *magnum opus*.

However, the thesis propounded by Goel in the book concerning Jesus Christ and Christianity is absolutely unacceptable to Christians. It hurts their sentiments profoundly. But, the book contains the stuff necessary to buttress all the more the Hindutva offensive against Christianity in India. The assumptions that underlie his irrational arguments, the questions that are posed, and the manner in which they are stated are part of a wider sinister design to cleanse India of Christians and Christianity.

Again, the book is also deliberately political with decisive hegemonic objectives. It spurns the intellectual objective of searching for truth. It is communal in essence and structure, and the intention of the author is to make Christians hate-objects of Hindus in India. The book also identifies patriotic fervour with revenge, and sanctions violence against Christians. The author is certainly most familiar with the strategy of the Fascists and the ideology of the Nazis. In this sense, the only writing that can in some degree match Goel's *Jesus Christ: An Artifice for Aggression* is Adolf Hitler's *Mein Kämpf.* And it is tragic and alarming. This being the case, the book of Goel needs to be *rejected as seditious literature*, and its *author sidelined* by all true scholars worth their name and by every true patriotic Indian.

Notes

1. See K. Elst, *Decolonising the Hindu Mind*, 208-215; ID., "India's only Communalist", 7, 13; "The Sagely Activist", 52-55; *Organiser*, 14 December 2003, 7; *Organiser*, 4 January 2004, 13.
2. Perhaps, Sita Ram Goel may find a 'worthy' counterpart in Max Amann who was the director of the Nazi Publishing department, and who effectively used the printed word in order to propagate the ideology of Adolf Hitler. See M. Domarus, *Hitler Reden*, vol. 1, 340-341.
3. It is published by Voice of India, New Delhi, 1994, reprint 2001.
4. See S.R. Goel, *Jesus Christ*, 99.
5. Ibid., 61.
6. Ibid., 3-4.
7. See C.K. Barrett, *The New Testament Background*, 198.
8. See F.V. Filson, *A New Testament History*, 65.
9. See S.R. Goel, *Jesus Christ*, 4.
10. F.V. Filson, *A New Testament History,* 68.
11. See S.R. Goel, *Jesus Christ*, 4.

12. Ibid., 4-5. We will be examining the 'scholarly' credentials of some of these figures.
13. I. Wilson, *Jesus: The Evidence*, 51 as cited in S.R. Goel, *Jesus Christ*, 5.
14. See F.V. Filson, *A New Testament History*, 87.
15. See S.R. Goel, *Jesus Christ*, 5.
16. Ibid., 6-9.
17. See M. Arnheim, *Is Christianity True?*, 9, as cited in S.R. Goel, *Jesus Christ*, 9.
18. See R.E. Brown, *Birth of the Messiah*, 25-41.
19. See S.R. Goel, *Jesus Christ*, 36.
20. Ibid., 31.
21. Ibid., 66.
22. Ibid., 71.
23. S.R. Goel, *Jesus Christ*, 59.
24. Ibid., 60.
25. See S.R. Goel, *Jesus Christ*, 19.
26. S.R. Goel, *Jesus Christ*, 60.
27. See S.R. Goel, *Jesus Christ*, 24.
28. S.R. Goel, *Jesus Christ*, 19.
29. See S.R. Goel, *Jesus Christ*, 36.
30. Ibid., 37.
31. Ibid., 51.
32. Ibid., 41.
33. Ibid., 38.
34. Ibid., 39.
35. Ibid., 39.
36. Ibid., 20, 23-24.
37. See R.E. Brown, J.R. Donahue *et al*, "Aspects of New Testament Thought", 1373-1374.
38. See J.P. Meier, "Jesus", 1328.
39. See S.R. Goel, *Jesus Christ*, 38-39.
40. Ibid., 11.
41. Ibid., 12.
42. Ibid., 46.
43. Ibid., 27, 40.
44. Ibid., 66.

45. Ibid., 47.
46. Ibid., 27, 47.
47. Ibid., 43.
48. Ibid., 41-42.
49. Ibid., 41, 43.
50. Ibid., 46, 49.
51. Ibid., 70.
52. Ibid., 71.
53. Ibid., 68-69.
54. Ibid., 1.
55. Ibid., 40.
56. Ibid., 52.
57. S.R. Goel, *Jesus Christ*, vi.
58. See S.R. Goel, *Jesus Christ*, 85.
59. Ibid., 52.
60. Ibid., 80.
61. S.R. Goel, *Jesus Christ*, 85.
62. See S.R. Goel, *Jesus Christ*, 6.
63. Ibid., 26-27.
64. Ibid., 25.
65. Ibid., 25-26.
66. W. Durant *The Story of Civilization*, III, 556-557 as cited in S.R. Goel, *Jesus Christ*, 29.
67. See P. Johnson, *A History of Christianity*, 26, as cited in S.R. Goel, *Jesus Christ*, 26.
68. See S.R. Goel, *Jesus Christ*, 70.
69. Ibid., v.
70. See S.R. Goel, *History of Hindu Christian Encounters*, 438-439.
71. See S.R. Goel, *Jesus Christ*, 16.
72. Ibid., 76, 79.
73. See S.R. Goel, *Pseudo-Secularism, Christian Missions and Hindu Resistance*, 2.
74. E.Y.C. Ho, Edward Gibbon, Historian of the Roman Empire, Part I: The Man and His Book, www.his.com/z/gibho1.html.
75. G.S. Neal. "Who is G.A Wells?" www.errantskeptics.org/G_A_Wells.html.

76. J.P. Holding, "Is This Anything New? A review of Michael Arnheim's *Is Christianity True?*" www.tektonics.org/MAICT_0879752629.html.
77. www.willdurant.com.bio.html.
78. www.dailyobjectivist.com/Heroes/PaulJohnson.asp; www.libertyhaven.com/thinkers/pauljohnson/historipaul/html.
79. K. Elst, *Psychology of Prophetism*, viii.
80. See S.R. Goel, *Jesus Christ*, 51.
81. See A. Suelzer and J.S. Ksleman, "Modern Old Testament Criticism", 1114.
82. Ibid., 1114.
83. See J.S. Kselman and R.D. Witherup, "Modern New Testament Criticism", 1132.
84. See S.R. Goel, *Jesus Christ*, 31.
85. See J.S. Kselman and R.D. Witherup, "Modern New Testament Criticism", 1136.
86. See S. Neil, *The Interpretation of the New Testament 1861-1961*, 200.
87. See S.R. Goel, *Jesus Christ*, 32.
88. See J.S. Kselman and R.D. Witherup, "Modern New Testament Criticism", 1139-1142.
89. See S.R. Goel, *Jesus Christ*, 33.
90. Ibid., 36-59.
91. S.R. Goel, *Jesus Christ*, 99 (emphasis added).
92. Ibid., 102 (emphasis added).
93. Ibid., 66.
94. Ibid., 66-67.
95. See S.R. Goel, *Jesus Christ*, 66.
96. S.R. Goel, *Jesus Christ*, 70.
97. Ibid., 66.
98. Ibid., 61.
99. Ibid., 67.
100. Ibid., 61.
101. S.R. Goel, *History of Hindu Christian Encounters*, 420.
102. Ibid., 420
103. Ibid., 466.
104. Ibid., 411, footnote 7.
105. Ibid., 452.

106. Ibid., 435.
107. Ibid., 439.
108. The Indian Penal Code has stringent laws against deliberate use of words intended to wound the religious sentiments of people or to promote enmity between different groups of people, Nos. 153-A, 153-B, 295, 298, 505 deal specifically with this topic. See "IPC and Hate Speech", 16.
109. S.R. Goel, *Jesus Christ*, vi.
110. Ibid., 84.
111. S.R. Goel, *Pseudo-Secularism*, 2 (emphasis added).
112. See H. Staffner, *The Significance of Jesus Christ in Asia*, xii, xvii, 3-26.
113. See S.R. Goel, *Jesus Christ*, 84.
114. See H. Staffner, *The Significance of Jesus Christ in Asia*, 29-168.
115. D.C. Scott, *Keshab Chandra Sen Speeches and Writings*, 1979, 217 as cited in H. Staffner, *Jesus Christ and Hindu Community*, 7.
116. P.C. Mozoomdar, *The Oriental Christ*, Boston 1883, 8-12, as cited in H. Staffner, *The Significance of Jesus Christ in Asia*, 73-74.
117. See B. Animananda, *The Blade, Life and Work of Brahmabandhab Upadhyaya*, 1947, 40, as cited in H. Staffner, *Jesus Christ and Hindu Community*, 23-24).
118. See H. Staffner, *Jesus Christ and Hindu Community*, 24.
119. L. Tilak, *I Follow After*, 1950, 123, as cited in H. Staffner, *The Significance of Jesus Christ in Asia*, 125.
120. S.R. Goel, *Jesus Christ*, 90.
121. Ibid., 90.
122. See S.R. Goel, *Jesus Christ*, 81.
123. Ibid., 80-83.
124. See K. Elst, *Psychology of Prophetism*, 1.
125. See T. Bottomore, *Dictionary of Marxist Thought*, 203.
126. See R. Thapar, "In Defence of History", 67.
127. One may profitably read the following writings which discuss the question of the historicity of Jesus: J.P. Meier, "Jesus", 1316-1328; F.V. Filson, *A New Testament History*, 65-87; E. Kasemann, *New Testament Questions Today*, 23-65; C.K. Barrett, *The New Testament Background*. The latest in this field is the 'third quest' for the historical Jesus by G. Barbaglio in his *Gesù ebreo di Galilea indagine storica* (2002).
128. S.R. Goel, *Jesus Christ*, 93.

129. Ibid., 68.
130. Ibid., 84.
131. S.R. Goel, *History of Hindu Christian Encounters*, 439.
132. Ibid., 446-447.
133. Ibid., 439.
134. Ibid., 462.
135. S.R. Goel, *Hindu Society Under Siege*, 5.
136. S.R. Goel, *Jesus Christ*, 84.
137. See S.R. Goel, *History of Hindu Christian Encounters*, 463.
138. S.R. Goel, *History of Hindu Christian Encounters*, 444 (emphasis added).
139. See E. Kasemann, *New Testament Questions Today*, 25.
140. See S.R. Goel, *Jesus Christ*, vi (emphasis added).

Conclusion

Our study of the worldviews of the six Hindu nationalists of modern India has been designed to expose their real identity which has often been kept concealed owing to ideological and political reasons. There is hardly anyone among them who deserves being considered as a moderate. Each in his own way was a champion of aggressiveness towards non-Hindus, some to the extent of being avowedly militant and xenophobic.

One of the things common to all the six Hindu nationalists is that they were persons anxious to preserve the Hindu culture and Hindu religion at any cost. They freely engaged in manipulating the symbols of Hindu identity which often had anti-minority connotations. In the process, they became icons of a narrow-minded vision and Hindu cultural chauvinism. All of them developed a *modus operandi* which involved stigmatising the religious minorities and secularists of India. In one form or another they subjectively perceived Christianity and Islam as the greatest threats to Hindu culture and *their* Hindu nation.

Reforming the Hindu society was never their primary agenda. Even when they concerned themselves with social question, they did so not for its own sake but to counteract the imaginary threat posed by certain groups and organisations that were on the vanguard of social reforms, especially Christianity and the British colonial government. Thus social reform became a tactic to be used to counteract the influence of non-Hindus on the Hindu society. Such a ploy, in reality, was an expression of the inferiority complex and the internal vulnerability of Hinduism.

The Hindu nationalists we have examined have displayed blatant opposition to secularism and the pluralistic ethos of India. The ideological framework with which they operated was that India is a Hindu *rashtra*. Thus, they challenged the concept of India as culturally, religiously and ethnically plural. Some of them went to the extent of invoking fascist and militant models of operation in order to realise their dream of building a Hindu *rashtra* in India. Hence, they isolated and waged war against the enemies of their Hindu *rashtra*, namely, the Indian Muslims, Christians, Communists and all Secularists.

All the six Hindu nationalists epitomise the constant tension that exists between non-violence and violence in India in modern times. It was as if they had to choose between Gandhi and Godse; and they preferred the latter. Hence, Rajmohan Gandhi is right when he states that violence versus non-violence was a major question during India's freedom struggle.[1] What Ashis Nandy says gives us further insight into this general trend among the Hindu nationalists towards ethics of violence. He says: "Godse's hand was forced by the real killers of Gandhi: the anxiety-ridden, insecure, traditional elite concentrated in the urbanised, educated, partly westernised, tertiary sector whose meaning of life Gandhian politics [of non-violence] was taking away."[2] In 2003, a feature article in *India Today* dealing with the topic "56 Events that Changed India" we are told about the predicament of Gandhi and his concept of non-violence: "Gandhi has taken refuge in textbooks, not certainly the passion that assassinated him [....] the idea that killed Gandhi is alive – and thriving."[3]

Hindu religion was at the heart of the entire ideology of the six Hindu nationalists. They blurred the boundary between the secular and the religious and freely made communal appeals in order to propagate their ideology. Due to their writings, speeches and tireless propaganda, it struck roots in many Hindu minds. Some of their writings are clearly meant to awaken the Leviathan in the Hindus against the religious minorities in India and several of them succeeded in massive mobilisation of Hindus. In their hands communalism turned into an obsessively anti-Muslim, anti-Christian and anti-Communist affair. In this sense, the roots of Hindu communalism clearly go back to the 19th century A.D. Here, we are reminded of Jawaharlal Nehru who said: "The Hindu communal organisations are definitely aggressive and they can play on the religious or other feelings of the majority community."[4]

All the six Hindu nationalists we have examined in this book have, in varying degrees, used politics for the promotion of Hindu religion and vice versa. They maintained that non-Hindus are not part of the Hindu nation and that they are either descendants of migrants or converts from Hinduism. Their highest expression of tolerance consists in conceding a subordinate position to non-Hindus devoid of any rights and privileges. But Nehru, who was an uncompromising secularist, was one of the few who perceived the danger involved in the Hindu nationalists mixing religion and politics. He said: "...the so-called religion in India today encroaches on every department of life – political, social, economic, cultural – and I have taken strong exception to this and have expressed a wish that it should not be permitted to make this encroachment."[5]

The concept of nationalism of the six personalities was distorted by yet another factor. It was an elite ideology centred around the hegemony of the upper castes of Hinduism. Swami Dayananda Saraswati was a Brahmin and so was Swami Vivekananda; Tilak and Savarkar shared the same identity of being Chitpavan Brahmins; Golwalkar was also a Brahmin; and Sita Ram Goel belonged to the upper caste Agarwal. This reminds us once again that Hindu nationalism is essentially an ethno-religious movement of the upper caste Hindus.

Another common factor we notice among the six Hindu nationalists is that they followed the path of ethical relativism, aggressiveness, fanaticism, violence, extremism and hatred of persons belonging to other faiths and communities so that they were thoroughly unscrupulous in the means they employed in order to achieve their ends. Some of them founded or assumed leadership of communal organisations, political parties and institutions. Others promoted mass movements of Hindus in order to spread their ideology. We may recall here the Arya Samaj founded by Swami Dayananda Saraswati, the Ram Krishna Mission of Swami Vivekananda, the Ganapati festivals, Shivaji festivals and Gymnastic Society of Tilak, the Mitra Mela, Abhinav Bharat and the Hindu Mahasabha of Savarkar, the Rashtriya Swayamsevak Sangh of Golwalkar, and the 'Voice of India' of Sita Ram Goel.

The six Hindu nationalists were wedded to a negative concept of nationalism and patriotism. Their spirit of violence expressed in their speeches, writings and activities would intimidate any right-thinking person. When objectively considered, they were not agents of peace and toleration but of disharmony and hatred of the other. For them, punishing the Indian Muslims and Christians[6] was more important than freeing India from the British colonial rule. Thus 'threatening others' was at the foundation of their ideology and methodology of action. A number of them were responsible for arousing in many Hindus the primal instincts and animosity by openly promoting militancy, extremism and terrorism in the name of Hindu religion and Hindu nation.

Freedom of religion is a presupposition of civilised life. Unfortunately, none of the six Hindu nationalists, at any time in their life, cared to endorse it. Yet it was Nehru who said that by a secular state we do not mean a state where religion as such is discouraged. It means freedom of religion and conscience, including freedom for those who may have no religion.[7] He argued: "Our Constitution is based on this secular conception and gives freedom to all religions, even freedom to proselytise."[8] Writing about religious intolerance he added: "There must be perfect toleration of other faiths and beliefs and religious practices, and every man or woman must have full liberty to hold and practice and give expression to his faith. There must be no persecution for the holding of any opinions on matters of religion."[9] What India has inherited from the six Hindu nationalists goes squarely against this conviction.

Speaking about the nature of Indian nationalism, Nehru said that in a country like India, which has many faiths and religions, no real nationalism can be built up except on the basis of secularism. Any narrower approach must necessarily exclude a section of the population, and then nationalism itself will have a much more restricted meaning than it should possess. In India we would have then to consider Hindu nationalism, Muslim nationalism, Sikh nationalism, Christian nationalism and so on and not Indian nationalism.[10] Hence he said: "We talk about a secular state in India [....] Some people think that it means something opposed to religion. That obviously is not correct. What it means is that it is a state which honours all faiths equally and gives them equal opportunities."[11]

Often, the Indian masses are victims of the manipulative tactics of privileged, powerful Hindu nationalist elite groups. Our study of the six major Hindu nationalists is meant to create an awareness among the Indians as to who they really were and what they stood for. Unfortunately, an average Indian can be too naive. He seldom studies personalities and ideologies with a critical mind. Hence, he can be easily influenced and indoctrinated. Only deserving heroes should be given the honour of being patriots. Some of the so-called patriots of India were led by subjective ethics and principles of expediency; some were cowards who surrendered their dignity for selfish or communal gains; some were pygmies in the national scene but pretended to be titans; some have feet of clay in the history of India's freedom struggle; and some of them had only a limited and a narrow vision of India that did not go beyond the concept of Hindu *rashtra* founded on Hindu cultural nationalism.

We need to be critical of the six Hindu nationalists as those who have nothing to offer to build a nation which is culturally, ethnically and religiously plural, secular and democratic. To equate Indian culture with Hinduism is preposterous. Hence, we should go beyond a nationalism founded on Hindu religion and Hindu culture. As Felix Wilfred has rightly observed, religion and nation are not and cannot be linked. Nationalism based on religion is not tenable.[12] We need a civilisational approach to the whole concept of India as a nation where the contribution of such cultures as the Hindu Buddhist, Christian, Islamic, Sikh, Jain, Jewish and even materialistic and atheistic are considered important and significant. Recognition of such a plurality requires a vision of nationalism which transcends all religions. This calls for a clear distinction between religion and nation. Hence, nationalism based on religion has to be dismissed as a relic of the past and as one which represents a backward looking and outdated worldview.

Today, India experiences the devastating consequences of the negative ideology of personalities likes the ones we have examined in this study. Unfortunately, even now, there are not a few who take them to be their ideological mascots, ignorant of the dubious aspects of their worldviews. Rajmohan Gandhi says that behind the present-day tribulations of India's minorities lies an insecurity pumped into the Hindu majority by a pre-meditated five-decade campaign that portrayed Muslims and Christians as disloyal, anti-nationals or criminals.[13] However, we argue that the history of hatred of the majority group towards the minority will go beyond five decades of history to at least fifteen decades, as is evident from our present analysis.

Ashis Nandy says that Hindutva is one of those pathologies that periodically afflict a religion.[14] All the six Hindu nationalists we have examined have wasted much of their energy in pursuing goals that are unworthy of India, because Hindu religious fanaticism, fundamentalism, cultural nationalism, militancy and hatred of other communities are the foundations of their ideology. Today, many Indians are slaves of their narrow-minded and aggressive worldview, especially many middle and upper class Hindus. Consequently, we witness a bankruptcy of good sense, tolerance, secularism, democracy and cultural pluralism. Hindu nationalists and fundamentalists like Swami Dayananda Saraswati, Swami Vivekananda, B.G. Tilak, V.D. Savarkar, M.S. Golwalkar and Sita Ram Goel have a fair share of responsibility in creating such a state of affairs.

In contemporary India, passion and prejudice are displacing sanity and reason and its agents are organisations like the RSS, BJP, VHP, Bajrang Dal, Shiv Sena and other affiliates of the Sangh Parivar. Nehru, after the assassination of Mahatma Gandhi, said: "[that] there are people in this country who have adopted this method [of violence] to gain political ends is of the gravest import. Perhaps we have been too lenient in dealing with these various elements in the country."[15] That leniency is responsible for the steady growth and spread of Hindu cultural nationalism which has become a notorious nation-wide movement, and consequently we are in the midst of a great crisis. T.N. Seshan, former Election Commissioner of India, gives us a clue as to what could possibly be the outcome of this crisis. He said: "It is a crisis of civilisation. India will survive – of that I have no doubt. But what kind of India will it be? Will it be an India enfeebled by wars within"?[16] If India follows the ideology of Hind cultural nationalism, Seshan's nightmare might come true. Therefore, it is the duty of every true patriot to prevent such a catastrophe. For this, the first step is to promote secularism uncompromisingly,[17] and perhaps the best example of it is Jawaharlal Nehru – the first Prime Minister of India.

Hindu cultural nationalism is a sign of not only a decaying civilisation, but also a larger crisis and a movement towards the disintegration of India. The Indian Catholic theologians, after their 23rd Annual Meeting in Bangalore in April 2000, seem to have made a correct assessment of Hindutva. They said: "Hindutva is a dangerous ideology. It is a falsification and distortion of Hinduism that should be resisted and rejected by all true Hindus of our country. We call upon all the peoples of India to be united and face this challenge, and expose its dangers, distortions and fallacies".[18] Our study reiterates and endorses the same, and call upon all men and women of good will to join hands in defeating this vicious ideology so that India may become truly secular and democratic and live by its pluralistic cultural ethos, respecting the fundamental rights and freedom of conscience of every individual.[19]

Notes

1. See R. Gandhi, *Revenge and Reconciliation*, 1.
2. A. Nandy, *Bonfire of Creeds,* 81.
3. *India Today*, 18 August 2003, 13.
4. S. Gopal and U. Iyengar (eds.), *The Essential Writings*, vol. 1, 190.
5. Ibid., 140.
6. P. Kanungo observes that Christians have always remained one of the enemies of the Hindu *rashtra*. While Muslims have been perceived as 'Enemy Number One', the Christians have occupied the status of 'Enemy Number Two'. See P. Kanungo, *RSS's Tryst with Politics*, 243.
7. See S. Gopal and U. Iyengar (eds.), *The Essential Writings*, vol. 1, 192.
8. Ibid., 193.
9. Ibid., 138.
10. Ibid., 194.
11. Ibid., 194.
12. See F. Wilfred, "Christians between Identity-Politics and Nationalism", 268.
13. See R. Gandhi, "Christianity in India", 31.

14. See A. Nandy, *Bonfire of Creeds,* 129.
15. S. Gopal and U. Iyengar (eds.), *The Essential Writings*, vol. 1, 168.
16. T.N. Seshan, *The Regeneration of India,* x.
17. The Congress Party has been frequently criticised for its 'soft-Hindutva' stand, and there seems to be much truth in it. Arundhati Roy says: "In India, there is a difference between an overtly fascist party (the BJP) and a party that slyly pits one community against another (Congress), and sows the seeds of communalism that are then so ably harvested by the BJP." A. Roy, "Public Power in the Age of Empire", 8.
18. "Concluding Statement", 322.
19. It is to be stated that besides the six Hindu nationalists we have analysed in this study, there are also other personalities like Bankim Chandra Chatterjee (1838-1898), Ramesh Chandra Dutt (1848-1909), Swami Shraddhananda (1856-1926), Bipin Chandra Pal (1858-1932), Lala Lajpat Rai (1865-1928), Aurobindo Ghose (1872-1950), Kesav Baliram Hedgewar (1889-1940), Syama Prakash Mookherjee (1901-1953) and so on, who also deserve to be studied in order to understand better the narrow-minded vision they had of India, epitomised in their concept of Hindu *rashtra* (nation).

Glossary

Abhinav Bharat	Young India, Modern India. The association founded by V.D. Savarkar on the model of Giuseppe Mazzini's 'Young Italy'
Advaita	Non dualism, monism
Advaita Vedanta	A school of Hindu theology of non-dualism
Agnihotra	Vedic sacrifice
Ahimsa	Non-violence
Akhand Bharat	Undivided India
Antyodaya	Rise of the lowest or the last
Anushilan Samiti	Disciplinary Organisation
Arjuna	One of the five Pandava brothers who was known for his martial skill, and who is Krishna's interlocutor in the *Bhagavadgita*
Arya	Noble
Aryans	A family of people belonging to the Indo-European linguistic group
Arya Samaj	Noble Society. A crusading reform movement founded in 1875 by Swami Dayananda Saraswati
Aryavarta	The land of the Aryans
Ashram	Hindu stages of life; hermitage
Avatar	Descent of God

Ayurveda	Divine knowledge of life, ancient Indian science of health
Bajrang Dal	The Force of Strong-bodied Hanuman or the Army of Hanuman; the VHP youth wing
Bharata Dharma Mahamandala	All India Religious Association
Bharat Mata	Mother India
Bharat Ratna	Jewel of India
Bhakti	Loving devotion to God
Brahman	A concept which designates the Ultimate Reality in the Hindu thought
Brahma Samaj	A religious reform movement founded in 1838 by Raja Ram Mohan Roy
Brahmin	One who belongs to the priestly class of the Hindu society
Buddha	'The Enlightened One'. The term is generally used for Gautama Buddha, the founder of Buddhism
Carvaca	Indian school of materialism
Caste	A hereditary stratification of society defining status, occupation and inter-group ranking in Hindu tradition, namely, *Brahmins* (priests), *Kshatriyas* (warriors), *Vaisyas* (merchants, cultivators) and *Sudras* (labourers). Those who are outside these four classes form a fifth caste called the untouchables
Dalit	Oppressed, downtrodden
Dharma	Traditional Indian term for religion, code of conduct, duty, cosmic order and virtuous action
Dharam Sansad	Parliament of Hindu religion
Diaspora	Dispersion. The member of a religion scattered outside its main homeland: for example, the Jews outside Israel
Dravidian	A linguistic group believed to have been the original inhabitants of India, and whose early

	civilisation reaching its apogee in the Indus Valley or Harappan culture in third millennium B.C
Durga Vahini	Brigade of the Tiger-Goddess
Ekal Vidyalaya	One-teacher school
Ekatmata yatra	Chariot procession for national unity
Fascism	A hyper-nationalist, totalitarian ideology. An ideology that advocates extreme right-wing views under one party or leader For example, the ideology of Mussolini, and Adolf Hitler's Nazism
Ganesh	Elephant-headed son of Shiva and Parvati
Gharvapasi	Home coming, re-conversion to Hinduism
Gita	Short form for *Bhagavadgita* ('The Song of the Lord'), which is one of the most famous Hindu scriptures
Gitarahasya	The Secret of the *Gita*. A celebrated commentary on the *Gita* by B.G. Tilak
Guru	'The weighty one', spiritual teacher
Hanuman	The monkey-god who assisted Ram in his struggle against Ravana
Harijan	God's people, untouchables
Hindu *rashtra*	Hindu nation
Hindutva	A modern term for 'Hindu-ness'. As an ideology it stands for Hindu fundamentalism and Hindu cultural nationalism
Janmabhoomi	Birth place
Jihad	'Effort', the struggle for Islam, interpreted either as righteous war against 'infidels' or as a spiritual striving
Kali	Ultimate Reality conceived as a female deity in Hinduism
Karma	'Action' or 'deed'; the law governing human lives from birth to death
Karma Yoga	Way of action
Kar seva	Rendering physical service as a sign of devotion to God

Kar sevaks	Volunteers for physical service
Kauravas	The opponents of the Pandavas in the fratricidal war for the throne of Hastinapura, which is the central theme of the *Mahabharata*
Kirpan	Weapon
Kshatriya	The warrior caste of Hindu society
Krishna	The incarnation of Vishnu
Kumbhamela	'Pot-fete', the largest of the Indian religious gatherings celebrated in special places situated on river banks
Kurukshetra	The site of one of the most renowned battles of ancient Hindu history between Pandavas and Kauravas, which is the central theme of *Mahabharata*
Lathi	Stick, rod
Lok Sabha	People's Assembly, the Lower House of Indian Parliament
Machiavellianism	The art of government based on the principles enunciated by Niccolo Machiavelli which justifies the use of force and any form of repression in order to safeguard one's rule
Madrassa	Muslim school
Mahabharata	An abbreviated form of *Mahabharata-yudha* ('The Great Battle of the Bharatas'). One of the great Indian epics
Manu	The author of the *Manusmriti* or system of Hindu Law
Manusmriti	'The Law of Manu'
Masjid	Mosque
Math/mutt	Monastery
Mein Kampf	'My Struggle'. Adolf Hitler's biography and ideological tract, which contains the essence of Nazism
Mela	Festival, fair
Mitra	Friend

Mleccha	Barbarian, impure. A term applied derisively by Vedic Aryans to non-Aryans who did not speak Sanskrit or perform Vedic rituals or abide by caste system
Nazism	The exaggerated nationalist ideology as propounded by Adolf Hitler racist German-first ideology
Om	An important auspicious and sacred syllable in Hindu, Buddhist and Jain traditions
OBC	Other Backward Classes
Pandavas	The rivals of the Kauravas and the rightful heirs to the throne of Hastinapura. The struggle between the Pandavas and the Kauravas constitutes the central theme of the *Mahabharata*
Parivar	Family
Pitrubbu	Fatherland
Pracharaks	Full-time volunteers
Punyabhu	Holy land
Rajya Sabha	The Upper House of Indian Parliament
Rama	Incarnation of Vishnu, hero of the *Ramayana*
Ramayana	One of the great Indian epics
Ram Rajya	Ram's kingdom
Rashtra	Nation
Rath yatra	Chariot procession
Rigveda/Rig Veda	The main collection of the Vedic hymns in ancient India
Sadhu	Monk
Saffronisation	Reference to the colour 'saffron'. Imposition of Hindu cultural nationalist ideology on aspects of Indian life
Sammelan	Conference, convention
Samiti	Committee
Samskara	Ritual. A rite by which a person is sanctified and raised to a special state

Sanatana Dharma	Eternal religion, Eternal Law
Sangh	Community, association
Sanghatan	Organisation
Sangh Parivar	Affiliates of the RSS family
Sanyasin	Hindu monk
Sarsanghchalak	Supreme chief of the RSS
Sati	The practice of burning of widows on their husbands funeral pyre
Satyagraha	'Holding on to truth'. In the Gandhian sense it means relying on the truth and justice of a cause rather than force to achieve one's goal
Sena	Army
Sevika	Woman volunteer
Shakha	Branch
Shilayana	Ceremony of laying foundation
Shiv Sena	Army of Shivaji. A militant political Hindutva organisation set up in Mumbai in the 1960s by Bal Thackeray
Shuddhi	Purification; re-conversion ceremony
Sinn Fein	An Irish nationalist movement which began in 1902
Swadeshi	'One's own country'. An ideology which favours indigenous means of production of goods or knowledge over those imported from abroad
Swaraj	Self-rule
Swastika	A Sanskrit symbol signifying prosperity, auspiciousness and wellbeing. Nazis in Germany used it as their party's emblem because of its Sanskrit-Aryan connection
Swayamsevak	An RSS volunteer
Trishul	trident
Upanishads	A major philosophical section of the Vedic revelation
Vanavasi	Forest-dweller

Vande Mataram	A hymn which celebrates India as Divine Mother
Vastusastra	Ancient science of Indian of architecture
Veda	Knowledge. The corpus of revealed texts that belonged to the Aryans, namely, the Sahmita, Brahmana, Aranyaka and Upanisad.
Vedanta	End of the Veda or the Upanishads
Veerata	Bravery
Yajna	Sacrifice
Yoga	System of physical and mental discipline, one of the six orthodox schools of Hindu philosophy
Yudha	Warfare
Xenophobia	A pathological dislike for 'outsiders'

Bibliography

"Against the Law", *Communalism Combat*, May 2003, 6-10.

Aiyar, M.S., "Arun Shourie and His Acolytes", *Sunday* 25 April-1 May, 1999, 8-10.

"Aiyarspeak", *Indian Currents*, 12 September 2004, 23-25.

"Alva Joachim (1907-)" in N.K. Singh (ed.), *Encyclopaedia of the Indian Biography*, vol. 1, New Delhi, 2000, 120-121.

Anand, S., "The Emergence of Hindutva" in J. Mattam and P. Arockiadoss (eds.), *Hindutva: An Indian Christian Response*, Bangalore, 2002, 103-222.

Andersen, W.K. and Damle, S.D., *The Brotherhood in Saffron*, New Delhi, 1987.

Athalye, D.V., *Swami Vivekananda*, New Delhi, 1979.

"At Last they Got Him", *Communalism Combat*, August 2004, 29-31.

"Attack on Sisters of Missionaries of Charity", *The Hindu*, 26 September 2004, 6.

Aurobindo, *India's Rebirth*, Mysore, 2000.

Banerjee, N.N., *The Golden Jubilee* (1966).

Barbaglio, G., *Gesù ebreo di Galilea indagine storica*, Bologna, 2002.

Barrett, C.K., *The New Testament Background*, New York, 1961.

Basham, A.L., "Hinduism" in R.C. Zaehner (ed.), *The Concise Encyclopaedia of Living Faiths*, London, 253.

Baxter, C., *The Jana Sangh: A Biography of an Indian Political Party*, Philadelphia, 1969.

Ramakrishnan, V., "BJP's Failing Tactics", *Frontline*, 8 October 2004, 4-8.

Bhishikar, C.P., *Shri Guruji Pioneer of a New Era*, English translation Sudhakar Raje, Bangalore, 1999.

Bidwai, P., "Caught in Historical Cliches", *Frontline*, 24 September 2004, 101-103.

—, "For Justice in Gujarat", *Frontline*, 13 February 2004, 121-122.

Bottomore, T., *Dictionary of Marxist Thought*, Bombay, 1983.

Brown, R.E., *Birth of the Messiah*, New York, 1977.

Brown, R.E. and Donahue, J.R. *et al*, "Aspects of New Testament Thought" in R.E. Brown, J.A. Fitzmyer and R.E. Murphy (eds.), *The New Jerome Biblical Commentary*, Bangalore, 1995, 1354-1381.

B.S. Moonje (P&J 5587), 1940, File 117/D-1, Hindu Mahasabha Copies of Resolution, etc, L/P&J/8/683, India Office, British Library, London.

Brüdigam, H., *Das Jahr 1933 Terrorismus an der Macht*, Frankfurt am Main, 1978.

Burke, M.L., *Swami Vivekananda in the West: New Discoveries*, vol. 1, Calcutta, 1992.

—, *Swami Vivekananda in the West: New Discoveries*, vol. 3, Calcutta, 1985.

—, *Swami Vivekananda in the West: New Discoveries*, vol. 5, Calcutta, 1998[4].

Chakutty, N.P., "Massacre in Marad", *Communalism Combat*, May 2003, 25-26.

Chamupati, "The Arya Samaja" in H. Bhattacharya (ed.), *The Cultural Heritage of India*, vol. 4, Calcutta, 1969, 634-639.

Chandrasekhar, S., "Sanskrit Varsity in Kerala", *Organiser*, 10 August 2003, 4.

"Chandy's First Test", *Indian Currents*, 19 September 2004, 24-26.

Chitkara, M.G., *Hindutva*, New Delhi, 1997.

Clarke, N.G., *Hitler's Priestess. Savitri Devi, the Hindu-Aryan Myth, and Neo-Nazism*, New Delhi: 2000.

The Collected Works of Mahatma Gandhi, vol. 8, Ahmedabad, 1962.

The Collected Works of Mahatma Gandhi, vol. 15, Ahmedabad, 1965.

The Collected Works of Mahatma Gandhi, vol. 17, Ahmedabad, 1965.

The Collected Works of Mahatma Gandhi, vol. 20, Ahmedabad, 1966.

The Collected Works of Mahatma Gandhi, vol. 22, Ahmedabad, 1966.

The Collected Works of Mahatma Gandhi, vol. 24, Ahmedabad, 1967.
The Collected Works of Mahatma Gandhi, vol. 32, Ahmedabad, 1969.
The Collected Works of Mahatma Gandhi, vol. 37, Ahmedabad, 1970.
The Collected Works of Mahatma Gandhi, vol. 70, Ahmedabad, 1968.
The Collected Works of Mahatma Gandhi, vol. 73, Ahmedabad, 1978.
The Collected Works of Mahatma Gandhi, vol. 76, Ahmedabad, 1979.
The Collected Works of Mahatma Gandhi, vol. 82, Ahmedabad, 1980.
The Collected Works of Mahatma Gandhi, vol. 88, Ahmedabad, 1983.
The Complete Works of Swami Vivekananda, vol. 1, Calcutta, 2000.
The Complete Works of Swami Vivekananda, vol. 2, Calcutta, 1999.
The Complete Works of Swami Vivekananda, vol. 3, Calcutta, 1997.
The Complete Works of Swami Vivekananda, vol. 4, Calcutta, 1998.
The Complete Works of Swami Vivekananda, vol. 5, Calcutta, 1997.
The Complete Works of Swami Vivekananda, vol. 6, Calcutta, 1995.
The Complete Works of Swami Vivekananda, vol. 8, Calcutta, 1999.
The Complete Works of Swami Vivekananda, vol. 9, Calcutta, 1997.

"Concluding Statement The Challenge of Hindutva: An Indian Christian Response" in J. Mattam and P. Arockiadoss (eds.), *Hindutva: An Indian Christian Response*, Bangalore, 2002, 303-323.

Coward, H., "Dayananda's Approach to Other Religions" in G.R. Garg, *World Perspectives on Swami Dayananda Saraswati*, New Delhi, 1984, 264-275.

Daniel, P.S., *Hindu Response to Religious Pluralism*, New Delhi, 2000.

Dayal, R. (ed.), *We Fought Together for Freedom*, Delhi, 1998.

Deshpande, V.G., *Hindu Socialism Explained*, Presidential Address, at the 45th Annual Seminar of the All-India Hindu Mahasabha, Shimoga, 29 May 1960, New Delhi, 1960.

Devaraja, N.K., *Hinduism and Modern Age*, New Delhi, 1975.

Domarus, M., *Hitler Reden und Proklamationen 1932-1945*, vol. 1, Triumph 1932-1934, Leonberg, 1987.

Durrani, F.K., *Swami Dayananda: A Critical Study of His Life and Teachings*, Lahore, 1929.

Edgarton, F., *The Bhagavad Gita*, London, 1972.

Elst, K., *Decolonising the Hindu Mind*, New Delhi, 2001.

—, "India's only Communalist", *Organiser*, 14 December 2003, 7,13.

—, *Psychology of Prophetism A Secular Look at the Bible*, New Delhi, 1993.

—, *The Saffron Swastika*, 2 vols., New Delhi, 2001.

"An Emerging Threat", *Frontline*, 28 February, 2003, 41-42.

Farquhar, F.N., *Modern Religious Movements in India*, New Delhi, 1967.

"Fascist Lineage", *Communalism Combat*, August 2004, 32-33.

File 50 Hindu Mahasabha Resolutions passed at the 18th session, held at Lahore (17 December 1936-7 January 1937), Resolution No. 13, p.8, L/P&J/71186, India Office, British Library, London.

File 359 Savarkar Case; Cases, Counter Cases and Replies, etc. (15 December 1910-10 March 1911), L/P&J/6/1060, India Office, British Library, London.

File 778 Savarkar Case, trial and conviction, question of extradition in the case of failure at the Hague (9 December 1910-23 February 1911), L/P&J/6/1069, India Office, British Library, London.

File 847 V.D. Savarkar; arrest and extradition, escape and recapture at Marseilles (18 March–7 October 1910), L/P&J/6/994, India Office, British Library, London.

File 1131 Savarkar Case; Proceedings at the Hague (including result) (28 January–21 April 1911), L/P&J/6/1077, India Office, British Library, London.

File 2286, Report on V.D. Savarkar imprisoned for importing weapons to India; treatment of prison in the Andamans (12 June 1914-24 September 1914) L/P&J/6/1314, India Office, British Library, London.

Filson, F.V., *A New Testament History*, London, 1965.

Frawley, D., *How I became a Hindu, My Discovery of Vedic Dharma*, New Delhi, 2000.

Frontline, 7 April, 1995.

Frontline, 1 December, 1995.

Gandhi, R., "Christianity in India: Today Fear is the Key" in *Christianity in India Yesterday and Today*, Varanasi, 2000, 30-35.

—, *Revenge and Reconciliation*, New Delhi, 1999.

Gangadharan, K.K., *Sociology of Revivalism: A Study of Indianisation, Sanskritisation and Golwalkarism,* Delhi, 1970.

George, T.J.S., *The Enquire Dictionary*, New Delhi, 1998.

Ghosh, T., *The Gandhi Murder Trial*, New Delhi, 1961.

Godbole, S., "Congress Loves to Hate Savarkar", *Organiser*, 12 September 2004, 15.

Godse, N., *Why I Assassinated Mahatma Gandhi*, Delhi, 2003.

Goebbels Reden 1932-1939, Band 1, München, 1971.

Goel, S.R., *Hindu Society Under Siege*, New Delhi, 1992.

—, *History of Hindu-Christian Encounters (AD 304-1996)*, New Delhi, 1996.

—, *Jesus Christ: An Artifice for Aggression*, New Delhi, 1994.

—, *Pseudo-Secularism Christian Mission and Hindu Resistance*, New Delhi, 1998.

Golwalkar, M.S., *Bunch of Thoughts*, Bangalore (1966), 1996.

—, *Spotlights*, Bangalore, 1975.

—, *We or Our Nationhood Defined*, New Delhi, 1939.

"Gopal Godse" 'Nathuram did not Leave the RSS'", *Communalism Combat*, August 2004, 27-28.

Gopal, S. and Iyengar, U. (eds.), *The Essential Writings of Jawaharlal Nehru*, vol. 1, New Delhi, 2003.

Goyal, S.R., *The Kautilya Arthasastra*, Jodhpur, 2000.

Griswold, H.D., "Arya Samaja" in J. Hastings (ed.), *Encyclopaedia of Religion and Ethics*, vol. 2, New York, 1981, 57-62.

Gupta, C., "Life of Barrister Savarkar" in V. Grover (ed.), *V.D. Savarkar (Political Thinkers of Modern India –14)*, New Delhi, 1993, 191-304.

Gupta, S.C.S., *Swami Vivekananda and Indian Nationalism*, Calcutta, 2001.

Hohli, R., *Political Ideas of M.S. Golwalkar*, New Delhi, 1993.

Indian Currents, 15 September 2004.

India Today, 18 August 2003.

"IPC and Hate Speech", *Communalism Combat*, May 2003, 16.

Jaffrelot, C., *The Hindu Nationalist Movement and Indian Politics*, New Delhi, 1996.

Jagtiani, G.M., *Militant Hinduism ("Third Eye" of the Hindu)*, Bombay, 1993.

Jayakumar, D.A., *Christians and the National Movement: The Memoranda of 1919 and the National Movement with Special Reference to Protestant Christians in Tamil Nadu: 1919-1939*, Calcutta, 1999.

Joglekar, J.D., "Veer Savarkar: Profile of a Prophet" in V. Grover (ed.), *V.D. Savarkar (Political Thinkers of Modern India –14)*, New Delhi, 1993, 305-341.

Jones, K.W., *Arya Dharma: Hindu Consciousness in the 19th Century*, New Delhi, 1976.

—, "The Arya Samaj in British India" in R.D. Baird (ed.), *Religion in Modern India*, New Delhi, 1981, 33-52.

—, "Swami Dayananda Saraswati's Vision of the Past, Present, and Future" in G.R. Garg (ed.), *World Perspectives on Swami Dayananda Saraswati*, New Delhi, 1984, 283.

Jordens, J.T.F., *Dayananda Sarasvati: His Life and Ideas*, Bombay, 1978.

"Joseph George (1887-1938)" in N.K. Singh (ed.), *Encyclopaedia of the Indian Biography*, vol. 1, New Delhi, 2000, 250-252.

"Kalam Unveils Savarkar Portrait", *The Hindu*, 27 February 2003, 1.

Kamath, M.V., *A Reporter at Large*, Mumbai, 2002.

Kanungo, P., *RSS's Tryst with Politics: From Hedgewar to Sudarshan*, New Delhi, 2002.

Käsemann, E., *New Testament Questions Today*, London, 1969.

Katakam, A., "A Tomb as Target", *Frontline*, 8 October 2004, 11-13.

Keer, D., *Lokamanya Tilak Father of the Indian Freedom Struggle*, Bombay, 1969.

—, *Veer Savarkar*, Bombay, 1950.

Kelkar, B.K., "Savarkar: A Three-Dimensional View" in V. Grover (ed.), *V.D. Savarkar (Political Thinkers of Modern India – 14)*, New Delhi, 1993, 342-366.

Khare, N.B., *Presidential Address, Akhil Bharat Hindu Mahasabha*, Special Session, Jaipur, 28 April 1951.

Krishnakumar, R., "Targeting Missionaries", *Frontline*, 22 October 2004, 39-40.

Kselman, J.S. and Witherup, R.D., "Modern New Testament Criticism" in R.E. Brown, J.A. Fitzmyer and R.E. Murphy (eds.), *The New Jerome Biblical Commentary*, Bangalore, 1995, 1130-1148.

Kumar, K. "Hindu Revivalism and Education in North-Central India", 545 in Martin E. Marty and R. Scott Appleby (eds.), *Fundamentalisms and Society*, Chicago, 1993, 536-557.

Mainstream, 25 September 2004, 14-15.

Majumdar, R.C., *The History and Culture of the Indian People: Struggle for Freedom*, Bombay, 1988.

—, *Penal Settlement in Andamans*, New Delhi, 1975.

—, *Swami Vivekananda: A Historical Review*, Calcutta, 1965.

Malik, Y.K. and Singh, V.B., *Hindu Nationalists in India: The Rise of the Bharatiya Janata Party*, New Delhi, 1994.

Mangalwadi, V., *Missionary Conspiracy Letters to a Postmodern Hindu*, Mussoorie, 1996[2].

Mattam, A.D., *Religions and Religious Freedom in India*, New Delhi, 2004.

Meier, J.P., "Jesus" in R.E. Brown, J.A. Fitzmyer and R.E. Murphy (eds.), *The New Jerome Biblical Commentary,* Bangalore, 1995, 1316-1328.

Menon, M.C., "Devil's in god's Land", *Indian Currents*, 10 October 2004, 17-21.

—, "Missionaries became Sitting Ducks", *Indian Currents*, 3 October 2004, 30-32.

Menon, P.K.K., *The History of Freedom Movement in Kerala,* vol. 2, (1885-1938), Trivandrum, 2001.

Naipaul, V.S., *India A Million Mutinies Now*, London, 1998.

—, *India: A Wounded Civilisation*, New Delhi, 1977.

Nair, P., "RSS' Godse Shrine", *Indian Currents*, 19 September 2004, 47.

Nanda, M., "Postmodernism, Hindu Nationalism and 'Vedic Science'" Part I, *Frontline*, 2 January 2004, 78-82.

Nandy, A., *Bonfire of Creeds,* New Delhi, 2004.

The Niyogi Committee Report: A Critical Appraisal, Varanasi, 2000.

Nehru, J., *An Autobiography*, London, 1936.

—, *Glimpses of World History*, New Delhi, 1982.

—, *The Discovery of India* (1946), New Delhi, 2004.

—, *Selected Writings of Jawaharlal Nehru*, Second Series, vol. 7, New Delhi, 1988.

Neil, S., *The Interpretation of the New Testament 1861-1961*, London, 1964.

Noorani. A.G., "The Collaborators", *Frontline*, 1 December, 1995.

—, "Savarkar and Gandhi", *Frontline*, 28 March 2003, 34-36.

Organiser, 5 January 2003, 17.

Organiser, 14 December 2003, 7.

Organiser, 4 January 2004, 13.

Organiser, 4 April 2004, 8.

Panikkar, K.M., "Hindu Revival in the 20th Century", K.M. Panikkar Papers, Serial No. 1288, National Archives of India, New Delhi, circa 1960 (manuscript).

—, "Impact of Europe on Asia in the Twentieth Century", K.M. Panikkar Papers, Serial No. 1291, National Archives of India, New Delhi, n.d. circa 1960, 1-24 (manuscript).

—, "A Primer of India", K.M. Panikkar Papers, Serial No. 1292, National Archives of India, New Delhi, n.d. circa 1960, 1-52 (manuscript).

Parakh, B.S. (ed.), *Contemporary India Textbook in Social Sciences for class IX*, New Delhi, NCERT, 2002.

Pattanaik, D.D., *Hindu Nationalism*, vol. 2, New Delhi, 1998.

"Philippose Elanjikkal John (1903-1955)" in N.K. Singh (ed.), *Encyclopaedia of the Indian Biography*, vol. 6, New Delhi, 2000, 169.

Pingle, M., "Bring Real History of the Country before People", *Organiser*, 16 February, 2003, 14.

"'Please don't Get Angry with your Shihsya' New Light on Godse-Savarkar Connection", *The Hindu*, 20 September 2004, 1.

Popley, H.A., *Builders of Modern India K.T. Paul Christian Leader*, Calcutta, 1938.

Prasannan, R., "Truth behind the Myths", *The Week*, 29 June 2003, 21-48.

Pupshparajan, A., "A Secular Critique of Hindutva" in J. Mattam and P. Arockiadoss (eds.), *Hindutva: An Indian Christian Response*, Bangalore, 2002, 223-258.

Radhakrishnan, S., *The Bhagavadgita with an Introductory Essay, Sanskrit Text, English Translation and Notes*, New Delhi (1948), 1993.

Rai, L.L., *The Arya Samaj*, New Delhi, 1991.

Ramachandran, R., "The Mastermind?", *Outlook*, 6 September 2004, 33-35.

Rath, D.K., "A Centre for Dialogue on Civilisations", *Organiser*, 7 March 2004, 17.

Rodrigues, V. (ed.), *The Essential Writings of B.R. Ambedkar*, New Delhi, 2002.

Rolland, R., *The Life of Vivekananda and the Universal Gospel*, Calcutta, 1934.

—, *The Prophets of the New India*, London, 1931.

Roy, A., "Gujarat, Fascism and Democracy" in C. Krishna (ed.), *Fascism in India: Faces, Fangs and Facts*, New Delhi, 2003, 29-44.

—, "Public Power in the Age of Empire", *Frontline*, 22 October 2004, 5-16.

"RSS Boss M. Sudarshan said on the 'Epic War'" in J. Dayal (ed.), *Gujarat 2002*, New Delhi, 2002, 1075-1077.

"The Sagely Activist", *Hinduism Today*, July-September 2004, 52-55.

Sahgal, P. and Walla, K., "Losing Control?", *Sunday* 2-8 August 1998, 16, 23.

Saraswati, D., *Autobiography of Swami Dyananda Saraswati*, K.C. Yadav (ed.), Delhi, 1976.

—, *Rigvedadi Bhasya Bhumika (Introduction to the Commentary on the Vedas)*, G. Ram (tr.), Uttar Pradesh, 1925.

—, *Rishi Dayananda Saraswati ke Patra aur Vijnapan (A Collection of Letters and Notes written by Dayananda Saraswati*, Y. Mimamshak (ed.), Amritsar, 1955[2].

—, *Satyartha Prakash*, Ganga Prasad Upadhyaya (tr.), *The Light of Truth*, Allahabad, 1956.

—, *The Ten Commandments of Dayananda*, Chamupati (tr), Lahore, n.d.

Sarkar, S., *Beyond Nationalist Frames Relocating Postmodernism, Hindutva, History*, New Delhi, 2002.

—, "Hindutva and the Question of Conversions" in K.N. Panikkar (ed.), *The Concerned Indian's Guide to Communalism*, New Delhi, 1999, 73-106.

Savarkar, V.D, "Facts Without Comment" in V. Grover (ed.), *V.D. Savarkar (Political Thinkers of Modern India-14)*, New Delhi, 1993, 179-184.

—, *Hindu Sanghatan: Its Ideology Immediate Programme*, Bombay, 1940.

—, *Hindutva: Who is a Hindu?*, (1923) New Delhi, 2003.

—, *Historic Statements*, Bombay, 1967.

—, "Nehru's Nightmare - Hindu Raj? Carpet Knights" in V. Grover (ed.), *V.D. Savarkar (Political Thinkers of Modern India-14)*, New Delhi, 1993, 170-173.

—, "Problems Before Hindudom After Bloodless(!) Vivisection" in V. Grover (ed.), *V.D. Savarkar (Political Thinkers of Modern India-14)*, New Delhi, 1993,174-178.

—, "Then Who is Who, Pray?" in V. Grover (ed.), *V.D. Savarkar (Political Thinkers of Modern India-14)*, New Delhi, 1993, 165-169.

Saxena, G.S., *Arya Samaj Movement in India 1875-1947*, New Delhi, 1990.

Seshadri, H.V (ed.), *Dr. Hedgewar: The Epoch-Maker*, Bangalore, 1981.

—, *Hindu Renaissance Under Way*, Bangalore, 1984.

—, "The Swatantrya-Veer: Epitome of 'Swatantrata' and 'Veerata'" in V. Grover (ed.), *V.D. Savarkar (Political Thinkers of Modern India-14)*, New Delhi, 1993, 367-375.

Seshan, T.N., *A Heart Full of Burden*, New Delhi, 1995.

—, *The Regeneration of India*, New Delhi, 1995.

Sharma, A., "Gandhi or Godse? Power, Force and Non-Violence" in N. Smart and S. Thakur (eds.), *Ethical and Political Dilemmas of Modern India*, New York, 1993, 15-29.

—, *Modern Hindu Thought: The Essential Texts*, New Delhi, 2002.

—, "Swami Dayananda Saraswati and Vedic Authority" in R.D. Baird (ed.), *Religion in Modern India*, New Delhi, 1981.

Shourie, A., *Missionaries In India*, New Delhi, 1994.

"Shri Guruji's *Complete Works* to be Ready soon", *Organiser*, 1 August 2004, 12.

"Shri Guruji: A Profile" in M.S. Golwalkar, *Bunch of Thoughts*, Bangalore, 1996, xx-xxii.

Singh, K., *The End of India*, New Delhi, 2003.

Smart, N., *The World's Religions*, Cambridge, 1989.

—, *World Philosophies*, London, 1999.

Smith, D., *Hinduism and Modernity*, Oxford, 2003.

"Some Eminent Freemasons", *Sunday*, 28 March–3 April, 1999, 53.

Speeches and Writings of Swami Vivekananda, 2 vols., Allahabad, 1988.

Staffner, H., *The Significance of Jesus Christ in Asia*, Anand, 1985.

—, *Jesus Christ and Hindu Community*, Anand, 1988.

Strenski, I., "Legitimacy, Mythology and Irrational Violence in Hindu India" in N. Smart and S, Thakur (eds.), *Ethical and Political Dilemmas of Modern India*, New York, 1993,1-14.

Suelzer, A., and Ksleman, J.S., "Modern Old Testament Criticism" in R.E. Brown, J.A. Fitzmyer and R.E. Murphy (eds.), *The New Jerome Biblical Commentary*, Bangalore, 1995, 1113-1129.

Swain, P.C., *Bharatiya Janata Party*, New Delhi, 2001.

Thomas, G., "The Christians and the Freedom Movement" in *Indian Christian Directory for the New Millennium*, Kottayam, 2000, 63-67.

Tilak, B.G., *The Arctic Home of the Vedas* (1903), Pune, 2001.

—, *The Orion or Researches into the Antiquity of the Vedas* (1893), Pune, 1999.

—, *Selected Documents of Lokamanya Bal Gangadhar Tilak (1880-1920)*, 4 vols., R. Kumar (ed.), Delhi, 1992.

—, *Srimad Bhagavadgita-Rahasya or Karma-Yoga-Sastra* (1915), A.S. Sukthankar (trs.) Poona, (1922), 2000.

"Tilak, Balgangadhar (1856-1920)" in N.K. Singh (ed.), *Encyclopaedia of the Indian Biography*, vol. 8, Delhi, 2000, 117-122.

Thapar, R., "In Defence of History", *Seminar* 521, January 2003, 65-72.

—, *The Penguin History of Early India*, New Delhi, 2002.

—, "The Tyranny of Labels" in K.N. Panikkar (ed.), *The Concerned Indian's Guide to Communalism*, New Delhi, 1999, 1-33.

Trehan, J., "Savarkarism" in V. Griver (ed.), *V.D. Savarkar (Political Thinkers of Modern India-14)*, New Delhi, 1993, 500-574.

Trimondi, V. and Trimondi, V., *Hitler, Buddha, Krishna: Eine unheilige Allianz vom Dritten Reich bis heute*, Wien, 2002.

"Varghese Mappila Kandathil (1858-1904)" in N.K. Singh (ed.), *Encyclopaedia of the Indian Biography*, vol.8, New Delhi 2000, 245.

Walker, B., *Hindu World. An Encyclopaedic Survey of Hinduism*, 2 vols., New Delhi, 1968.

Walport, S.A., *Tilak and Gokhale Revolution and Reform in the Making of Modern India*, Delhi, 1982.

Waradpande, N.R., *The Nemesis of Nehru-Worship*, Bangalore, 2001.

Wilfred, F., "Christians between Identity-Politics and Nationalism" in J. Mattam and P. Arockiadoss (eds.), *Hindutva: An Indian Christian Response*, Bangalore, 2002, 259-281.

Willims, G.M., *The Quest for Meaning of Swami Vivekananda*, Chicago, 1974.

Yechury, S., *What is this Hindu Rashtra? On Golwalkar's Fascistic Ideology and the Saffron Brigade's Practice*, Madras, 1993.

Zaehner, R.C., *The Bhagavad Gita*, London, 1969.

Internet Websites

HO, E.Y.C. *Edward Gibbon, Historian of the Roman Empire*, Part I: *The Man and His Book*, www.his.com/z/gibho1.html

Holding, J.P., "Is This Anything New? A review of Michael Arnheim's *Is Christianity True?*" www.tektonics.org/MAICT_0879752629.html

Neal, G.S., "Who is G.A. Wells?" www.errantskeptics.org/G_A_Wells.html

www.willdurant.com.bio.html

www.dailyobjectivist.com/Heroes/PaulJohnson.asp;www.libertyhaven.com/thinkers/pauljohnson/historipaul/html

Index